SKY

*altocumulus
clouds*

NATIONAL GEOGRAPHIC NATURE LIBRARY

SKY

NATIONAL GEOGRAPHIC NATURE LIBRARY

by Marfé Ferguson Delano

NATIONAL GEOGRAPHIC SOCIETY

Washington, D.C.

*Venus and the moon glow above
Africa's Ruwenzori Mountains.*

Table of Contents

astronaut

swamp trees

eagle

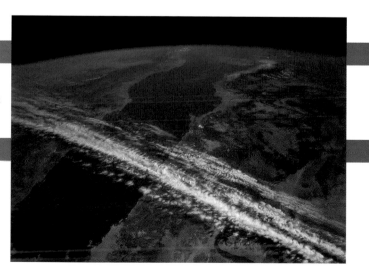

jet stream

sun dog

hurricane

comet Hale-Bopp

WHAT IS THE SKY?

If you're like most people, when you think of the sky you look up. It's true that the sky is above you, but it's also all around you. In fact, the sky begins where your feet meet the Earth, and it extends beyond the farthest stars you can see. The sky is the air surrounding the Earth as well as the vast, airless region called space—the realm of the sun, the moon, the planets, and countless billions of stars—that lies beyond our world.

These pages will take you on an armchair tour of the sky. As you prepare for your journey, keep these facts in mind:

- The AIR you breathe is part of the sky.
- The layer of air that surrounds the Earth is the ATMOSPHERE.
- WINDS, WEATHER, AND CLOUDS occur in the atmosphere.
- SPACE begins where Earth's atmosphere ends.
- The MOON, SUN, PLANETS, and STARS are located in space.

cumulus clouds

rain

6

aurora

planet

moon

star

comet

contrail

cumulonimbus
cloud

tornado

lightning

stratus clouds

rainbow

7

The Big Picture

An invisible blanket about 600 miles thick wraps all around Earth, much like the peel surrounds an orange. This special blanket, called the atmosphere, is made of air, which is a mixture of gases. Air is what we breathe, and run through, and fly kites in. A natural force called gravity, which pulls objects toward the center of a planet or other heavenly body, holds the atmosphere close to Earth.

AIR TO GO
Astronauts don't leave home without it—air, that is. There's not a bit of air in outer space. But there are plenty of harmful rays from the sun. That's why astronauts wear protective suits. The thin blue glow at Earth's edge in the background is the atmosphere.

A LONG SHOT
Seen from space, Earth looks blue, thanks to sunlight reflecting off the atmosphere and the oceans. The clouds swirling over the planet are in the lowest layer of the atmosphere, where they are blown by winds that carry weather systems around the world.

GIVE ME FIVE!

Earth's atmosphere has five different layers. We live in the lowest layer, the troposphere (TROHP-uh-sfear). Gravity's pull packs more than three-fourths of the total air in the atmosphere into this layer. Air gets thinner and more spread out in the higher layers of the atmosphere because gravity weakens as height increases. The lack of gravity in the highest layer, the exosphere (EK-soh-sfear), allows the atmosphere to dwindle away into outer space.

The exosphere extends up to about 600 miles from Earth. Many satellites orbit Earth in this layer.

The thermosphere (THUR-muh-sfear) is 50 to 300 miles from Earth. Meteorites burn up here, and the space shuttle flies here.

The mesosphere (MEZ-uh-sfear) is 30 to 50 miles from Earth. It is the coldest region of the atmosphere.

The stratosphere (STRAT-uh-sfear) is 10 to 30 miles above Earth's surface. Supersonic planes fly here.

The troposphere is about ten miles deep. Most of the world's weather, winds, and clouds occur here.

The Sky Nearby

Air is a mixture of mostly nitrogen and oxygen gases. Like all things, gases are made of tiny particles called molecules (MAHL-uh-kyools). Every time you breathe, your lungs fill with millions of these molecules. You can't see air, but it has weight, and it is constantly pressing against everything on Earth—including you! This force is called air pressure.

SNIFF, SNIFF
Blame the air the next time you catch a whiff of a skunk—or a rose. The movement of air as you breathe carries odors both good and bad to your nose.

AIR BRAKES
Air trapped in the parachute slows down a skydiver, letting him float gently to the ground.

Without a parachute, a skydiver would fall 30 feet in the time it takes to blink.

Earth's atmosphere weighs 5,000 trillion tons. Gravity keeps it from floating off into space.

OXYGEN, ANYONE?
Climbing a tall peak? Better pack an oxygen tank. Air thins out the higher up in the sky you go, which means there's less oxygen to breathe.

DAYTIME BLUES

Air itself has no color, but the sun's white light contains all the colors of the rainbow. When sunlight hits the air molecules in our atmosphere, the blue part of the light is split off, or scattered. So blue is the color we see in the sky on a sunny day.

THE SCOOP ON SOUND

Drumbeats and other sounds zip through air at about 740 miles per hour! The air carries sound waves to our ears.

11

Life Support

Today's atmosphere is perfect for life on Earth, but it wasn't always so friendly. Not until plants appeared on the planet did the air start to change into something we could breathe. Plants use sunlight to make food out of carbon dioxide and water. In the process, they release life-giving oxygen into the atmosphere.

THANKS FOR RECYCLING

The next time you breathe, thank a tree or other green plant. If they weren't here to recycle the air, we'd run out of oxygen.

About 4.6 billion years ago Earth formed from dust particles in a cloud of gas surrounding the sun.

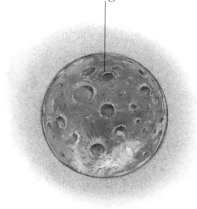

Volcanoes shot water vapor and carbon dioxide into the sky about 4 billion years ago.

About 3 billion years ago water vapor formed clouds. Rain fell for millions of years, and Earth's oceans were born.

Green plants appeared on Earth about 2 billion years ago. Oxygen-rich atmosphere gradually developed.

BLAST FROM THE PAST

It took billions of years for Earth's atmosphere to become just right for oxygen-breathing animals. Along the way, our planet underwent some radical changes.

BEARS GOTTA BREATHE

And so do all other animals. In the process, they use up oxygen and give off carbon dioxide.

The carbon dioxide exhaled by animals is used by plants.

13

Staying Alive

Earth's atmosphere is like a protective cocoon. It lets just the right amount of the sun's heat pass through it. Without the atmosphere to shield us, Earth would get way too warm for us to survive. In the stratosphere, a thin band of gas called the ozone layer blocks out most of the sun's harmful ultraviolet rays. The ozone layer is fragile, however, and can be damaged by the release of certain chemicals into the sky.

SEEING RED
The sky turns red, orange, or yellow at sunset or sunrise, when the sun is low in the sky. Dust particles in the air bounce those colors to our eyes. The dustier the air, the redder the sky.

BALANCING ACT
Only about 50 percent of the sun's energy makes it all the way through the atmosphere to Earth's surface, where it is absorbed by the ground and oceans. The atmosphere absorbs 20 percent of the solar energy and reflects 30 percent right back into space.

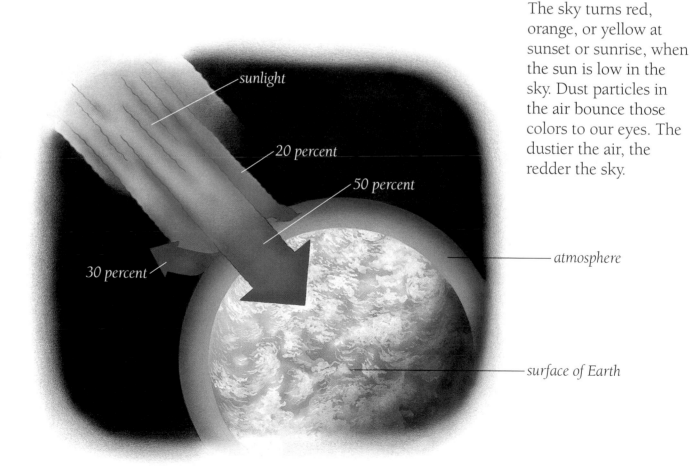

sunlight

20 percent

50 percent

30 percent

atmosphere

surface of Earth

14

NATURAL POLLUTION
Volcanoes spew dust and gases into the atmosphere when they erupt. Forest fires and dust storms can also make the air dirty.

HUMAN-MADE POLLUTION
Air pollution from industry and automobiles can upset the delicate balance of Earth's atmosphere.

Pass the sunscreen! Damage to the ozone layer means more of the sun's burning rays reach Earth.

15

2 Air in Motion

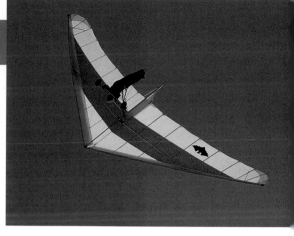

Do you know what happens when warm air and cool air trade places? Wind blows! When the Earth's surface is warmed by the sun's heat, it, in turn, warms the air above it. As air heats, it becomes lighter and rises. The gap it leaves is filled by cooler, heavier air that rushes in from another area of the sky. This rush of air creates wind. Eventually the rising air gets high enough to cool off. Then it sinks, and the cycle repeats.

AIR JOCKEYS
To stay high in the sky, hang gliders hitch a ride on thermals (THUR-muhls), invisible currents of warm air rising from the ground. Thermals often occur near the edges of cliffs or steep hills.

UP, UP, AND AWAY
Hot air is lighter than cold air. That's why a balloon pumped full of hot air floats. Once it's risen into the sky, a hot-air balloon can be carried thousands of miles by the wind.

Broad wings help eagles take advantage of rising air currents.

HIGH FLIER

Eagles soar to dizzying heights on thermals. Glider pilots sometimes look to eagles and other soaring birds, such as buzzards and gulls, for clues to where the rising columns of air might be found.

BLOWN OVER

In some parts of the world, the wind blows so strongly and steadily from one direction that the trees all grow with the wind.

Land warms up and cools down faster than water. On a sunny day the air above the land warms up quickly and rises. Air cooled by the sea flows in to take its place, creating a breeze. At night, the reverse happens.

Wind Power

The wind is a hard worker. It shapes the land by hauling sand and soil around and wearing away rocks. Strong winds carry dust, sand, and water around the globe. Seeds, pollen, and some small animals catch shorter rides on the breeze. People use wind to power sailboats and windmills.

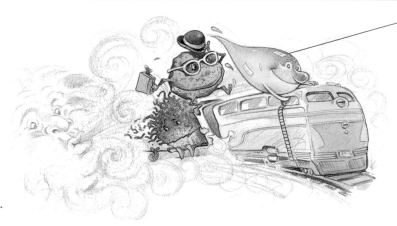

All aboard! Dust, sand, and moisture travel thousand of miles on the wind.

POWER TOWERS
Blown by the wind, the blades of a windmill turn gear wheels inside it. The gears move machinery that can grind grain, produce electricity, or, in the case of these windmills, lift water.

RIDERS IN THE SKY
The fluffy hairs around milkweed seeds help them snag a ride on the breeze. Milkweed is one of many plants that rely on the wind to spread their seeds.

Just-hatched spiders shoot threads into the wind and are whisked miles away to a new home.

These rocky toadstools perch in Utah's Goblin Valley.

RADICAL ROCKS
The wind gave these stones their fantastic form. For countless centuries, it blasted them with sand, gradually carving them into giant mushroom shapes.

DUST STORMS
Strong winds blowing over dry ground can stir up huge walls of moving dust. This dust storm is in Africa.

Going Global

Some winds blow in patterns across the surface of the Earth. Called prevailing winds, they are set in motion by the sun. Warm air over the Equator, where the sun's rays are strongest, rises. It travels toward the Poles, cools, sinks, and returns to the Equator, where it begins the trip again. This global air circulation creates prevailing winds, as well as high-altitude winds called jet streams.

HIGHEST WINDS
A ribbon of clouds marks the jet stream over Egypt. Jet streams blow high in the atmosphere above prevailing winds. Flowing from west to east, they form where warm air and cold air meet.

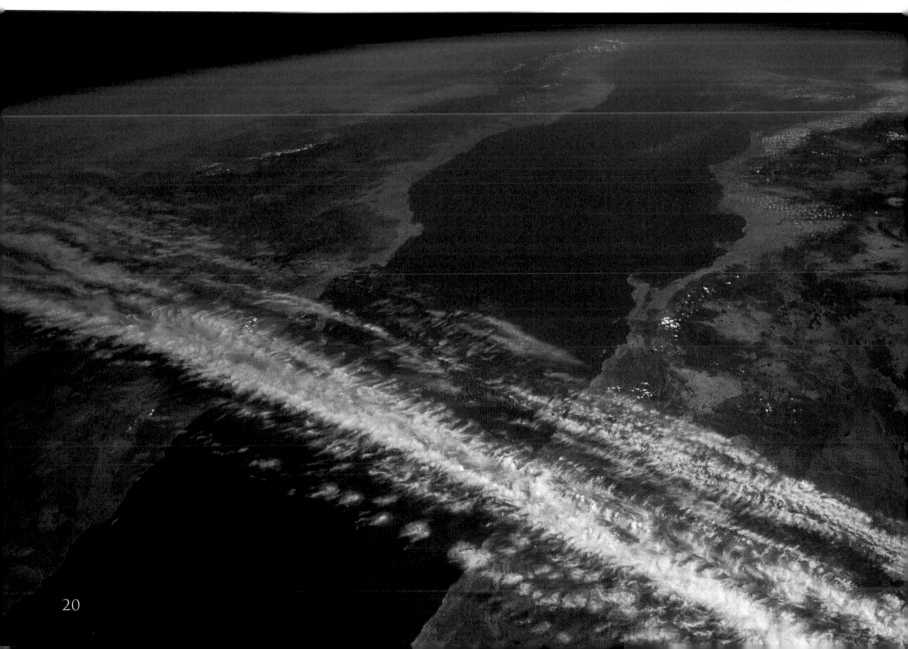

Trade winds blow from east to west. Christopher Columbus hoped these winds would carry him west around the world to China. The trade winds did, indeed, blow his ships west, but Columbus bumped into the New World!

PUTTING A SPIN ON THINGS

The rotation of the Earth curves winds to the right north of the Equator and to the left in the south. This is called the Coriolis effect, after the French engineer who discovered it.

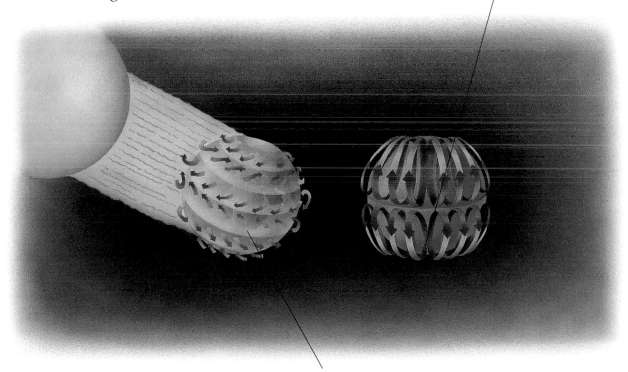

If the Earth did not spin, winds would follow a straight north and south pattern between the Equator and the Poles.

The Earth's rotation produces six loops, or cells, of prevailing winds, which blow in easterly and westerly directions in the troposphere. Depending on which way they blow, these winds are called trade winds, westerlies, or polar easterlies.

3 Weather

The changes we see and feel in the sky around us each day are what we call weather. All weather is powered by the sun's heating of the Earth. This sets global winds swirling over the face of the planet, carrying with them heat, cold, storms, rain, and snow. Weather changes from day to day, from season to season, and from place to place. The long-term weather pattern of an area is called its climate.

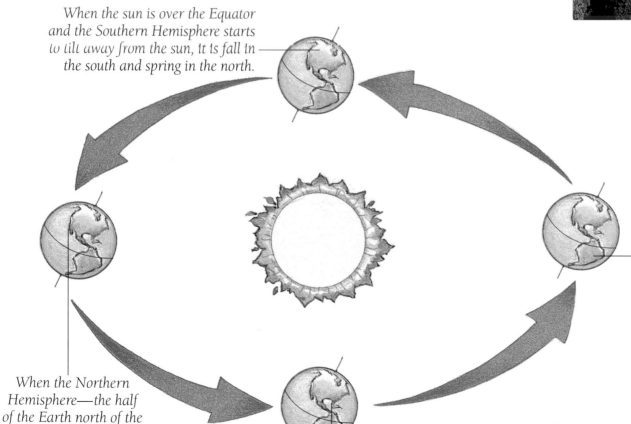

When the sun is over the Equator and the Southern Hemisphere starts to tilt away from the sun, it is fall in the south and spring in the north.

When the Northern Hemisphere—the half of the Earth north of the Equator—is tilted toward the sun, it is summer in the north and winter in the south.

When the sun is over the Equator and the Northern Hemisphere starts to tilt away from the sun, it is fall in the north and spring in the south.

When the Southern Hemisphere—the half of the Earth south of the Equator— is tilted toward the sun, it is summer in the south and winter in the north.

HOT AND STEAMY
Located close to the Equator where the sun shines most directly, tropical climates are warm all year. The high rainfall in these regions— often more than a hundred inches per year—gives rise lush tropical rain forests.

SEASON SENSE
Because Earth tilts as it orbits the sun, different parts of the planet get more or less sunlight at different times of the year. This causes regular weather changes, called seasons.

22

DRY AS A BONE

If a place receives an average of fewer than ten inches of rain a year, it's said to have a desert climate. The Namib Desert, right, is in southwest Africa.

CHILL OUT!

It doesn't get chillier than this! Centered on the South Pole, the Antarctic has the coldest climate on the planet, thanks mainly to its distance from the Equator. Average temperatures in Antarctica range from minus 67°F to minus 76°F.

4 Clouds

Clouds are made of millions of tiny water droplets or ice crystals that float together in the sky. Clouds often look white in daytime because the droplets reflect the sun's light. Thick clouds may look gray, because so little light can pass through them. Clouds give us the rain we need to survive. Like a blanket, they also help insulate the Earth. During the day, they block much of the sun's heat, keeping the Earth from getting too hot. At night, clouds hold in warmth.

High winds can make clouds change shape right before your eyes!

Warmed by the sun, moist air rises, then cools.

Water vapor in cooled air condenses and forms clouds.

Water falls from clouds as rain or snow.

Water returns to rivers and oceans, and the cycle begins again.

CLOUD CONNECTION
The air around us is filled with water, but we can't see it. That's because the moisture is in the form of an invisible gas called water vapor. The amount of water vapor air can hold depends on the air temperature. Warm air holds more water vapor than cold air. When the air can contain no more water vapor it is said to be saturated. The water vapor then changes from a gas into tiny water droplets, which form clouds. This process is called condensation (kahn-den-SAY-shun). The recirculation of water between the oceans, clouds, and land is called the water cycle.

COLOR IT BEAUTIFUL ▶
Clouds are not always white or gray. Light from the setting sun washed these clouds with a golden orange hue.

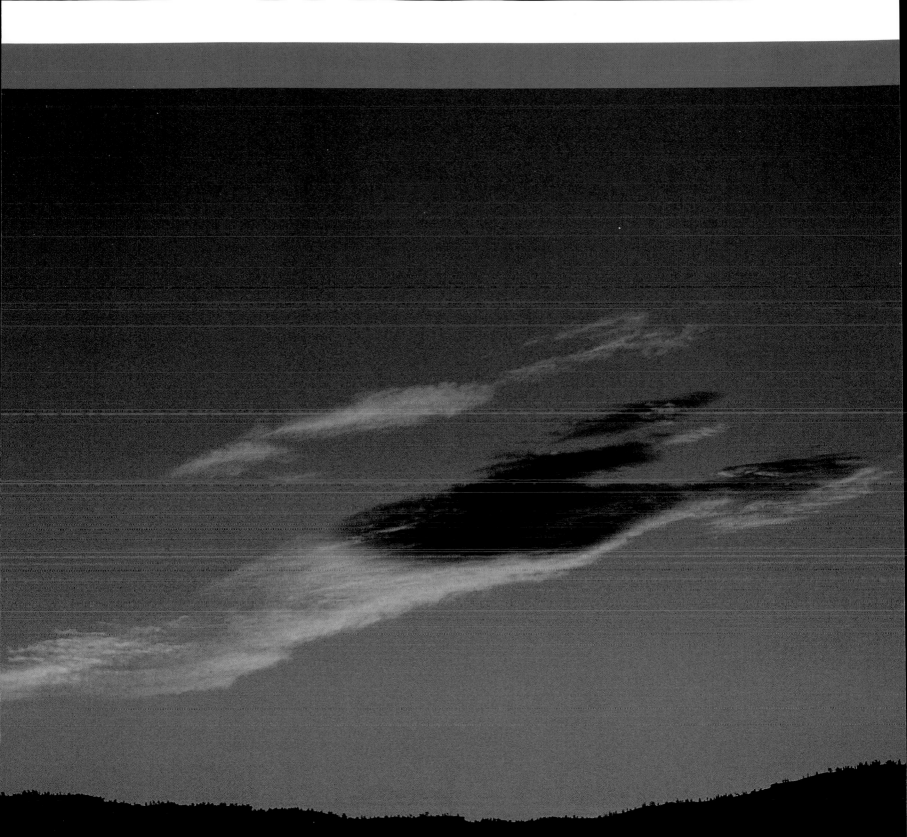

Cloud Collection

If you're a sky watcher, you've probably already noticed that clouds come in a wide variety of sizes and shapes. There are three basic types: cumulus (KYU-myuh-lus), stratus (STRAYT-us), and cirrus (SIR-us). Some days you can see two or three different kinds of clouds in the sky at the same time. Clouds with the word "nimbus" in their name produce rain.

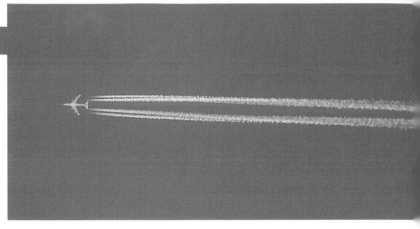

PLANE TALK

The condensation trail, or contrail, left behind by a high-flying aircraft is really a type of cirrus cloud. A contrail is formed when water vapor from a jet's exhaust freezes into ice crystals.

STRATUS CLOUDS

Stratus clouds form smooth, thick, dull gray layers that hang low in the sky, sometimes blanketing hilltops. They often produce drizzle or light rain.

CIRRUS CLOUDS

Often called mares' tails or painter's brush after their distinctive shape, these wispy, delicate clouds are made of tiny ice crystals. The highest clouds, they often occur when the weather is about to change.

cirrus

cirrostratus

cirrocumulus

altostratus

altocumulus

stratocumulus

cumulus

cumulonimbus

stratus

nimbostratus

CLOUD CROWD

The shape of a cloud depends on how high it is and the speed and direction of the air. Above are the ten most common clouds, arranged by their average height in the sky.

CUMULUS CLOUDS

Drifting across the blue sky, these fluffy, lumpy white clouds usually indicate fine weather. But look out if they start to grow larger. Then they may bring thunderstorms your way!

Fog, Frost, and Dew

Chances are, you've been in a cloud! Fog is a low-lying cloud that usually forms at night, when the sun has set and the ground has cooled, chilling the air above it. Water vapor in the cooled air condenses into tiny droplets, which hang together as fog. When this process occurs at ground level, beads of water called dew form on grass, leaves, and other surfaces.

GETTING FROSTED

When moist air near the ground cools to below freezing, the water vapor in it freezes and coats things, like these rose hips, with a layer of frost. When the air temperature falls below freezing, frost forms instead of dew. Frost is made of ice crystals, which you can see with a magnifying glass.

HOW DO YOU DEW? ▶

Dewdrops sparkle like diamonds on a spider web. In the morning, the sun's rays heat the air, and the dew turns back into water vapor, leaving the web high and dry.

WHICH WAY TO THE DOCK?

Sea fogs are created when warm, moist air moves over cool water and condenses into droplets. Fog droplets are about 1/200 of an inch in diameter. That's less than half the size of the period at the end of this sentence.

DOWN IN THE VALLEY

A wide band of fog cloaks a valley in Wyoming's Grand Teton Range. Fog usually evaporates, or turns back into water vapor, when morning sunshine heats the air. In winter, however, the sun's heat may evaporate only the edges of the fog, leaving a thick layer like this that can last for hours, or even days.

Moist, hot air rising from a tea kettle condenses into a cloud called steam as it cools.

The moisture in warm, exhaled breath condenses quickly in cold air, forming a little fog.

A cold drink in a glass cools the air around it, causing tiny drops to bead on the outside of the glass.

CONDENSATION ALL AROUND

Examples of condensation, the process that creates fog and clouds, are all around us.

29

 5 Precipitation

The water that falls from a cloud as rain, snow, sleet, or hail is called precipitation (pree-sip-i-TAY-shun). Precipitation is caused by the buildup of tiny water droplets or ice crystals as they are blown about by air currents inside a cloud. When the particles become too heavy to float in the cloud any more, they fall through the sky to Earth.

HOLY HAILSTONES!
Hailstones are pea-size—or larger—lumps of ice produced by some storm clouds. The largest hailstor on record was the size of a grapefruit and weighe 1.7 pounds.

APRIL SHOWERS
It takes about a million tiny cloud droplets to make just one raindrop. Raindrops, by the way, are shaped like pancakes, not teardrops.

Just a small change in the temperature can turn rain to snow or snow to rain.

RAP ON RAIN
As water droplets and ice crystals in clouds move about, they bump into each other, merge, and grow heavier. If they fall through warm air, they land as rain. Freezing air turns them into snow or sleet.

FLOODED OUT ▶
Broadscale floods, like the one that swamped this farm near the Missouri Rive in 1993, are caused by heavy rainfall over long period. Floods often cause property damage and loss of life.

31

Let It Snow!

The sky seems magical when it is filled with snowflakes—especially if the snow brings a day off from school! Snow begins as ice crystals in the cold upper levels of clouds. As the crystals fall through freezing air, they combine and form snowflakes.

Check out the flakes! On a snowy day, take a piece of black paper and a magnifying glass outside. Catch snowflakes on the paper and examine them. Try not to melt them with your breath. What shapes do you see?

WINTER WONDERLAND
A blizzard swirls around an elk in Yellowstone National Park. When heavy snowfall and strong winds make it impossible to see, the snowstorm is called a whiteout.

SNOW SIZE
The size of a snowflake depends on the temperature of the air. Very cold, dry air produces small, powdery snowflakes—just right for skiing. Warmer air, which contains more moisture, results in larger, wetter flakes that are great for making snowballs.

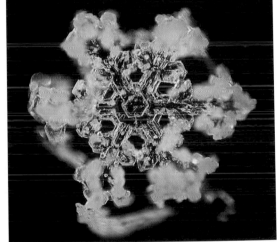

DRY ICE
Snowflakes are bigger than raindrops, but they contain a lot less water. In fact, you'd have to melt ten or more inches of snow to equal the amount of water in just one inch of rain.

SNOWFLAKES SHAPE UP
Snowflakes come in a vast variety of beautiful patterns, but most of them are hexagonal (hek-SAG-un-l), which means they are six-sided. A single snowflake can be made of 50 or more individual ice crystals loosely clustered together.

33

Rainbows

After a rainfall, you might spy a rainbow. The best time to see one is just as a storm has passed and the sun has come out. When sunlight strikes raindrops still in the air, the light is split into seven colors—red, orange, yellow, green, blue, indigo, and violet. Raindrops split the light into colors much as a prism does. The drops reflect the colors, and if you're in the right place you will see a beautiful rainbow glowing in the sky.

It's easy to make your own rainbow with a garden hose. Just stand with the sun behind you on a warm sunny day and spray a fine mist of water into the air in front of you. Presto, a rainbow!

MISTY MAGIC
A rainbow stretches across Victoria Falls in Zimbabwe. The multicolored marvel was formed by sunlight hitting the water droplets in the falls' spray. A rainbow depends on the position of the sun and the observer and the movement of the water droplets, so no two people ever see exactly the same rainbow.

HOT DOG, IT'S A SUN DOG

Sun dogs, also called mock suns, appear when the sun is low in the sky. They are formed when sunbeams are bent and reflected by ice crystals hanging in the air. This spectacular specimen was spotted in the skies above West Virginia.

RAINBOW REALITY

When sunlight enters a raindrop, it is bent and separated into colors, which are then reflected off the back of the raindrop. Millions of drops bending and reflecting light produce the distinct bands of color called a rainbow.

35

Every day about 40,000 thunderstorms flash and crash somewhere on Earth, unleashing drenching downpours, wild winds, lightning, and thunder. Thunderstorms are created by cumulonimbus (KYU-myuh-low-NIM-bus) clouds, also called thunderheads. These massive clouds can rise 11 miles or higher, jutting into the stratosphere.

KING OF CLOUDS ▶
Towering thunderheads can contain up to 110,000 tons of water, some of which may fall as hail. Radar helps airplane pilots pinpoint these storm machines and steer around them.

Powerful, rising air currents push the cloud higher to form a cumulonimbus.

Warm, moist air rises, cools, condenses, and forms a cumulus cloud.

The top of the cloud often fans out into an anvil shape in the stratosphere.

Water droplets and ice crystals in the top of the cloud begin to fall.

Falling precipitation creates falling air currents.

BIRTH OF A THUNDERSTORM
Thunderstorms are most likely to brew during the summer, when the air is hot and humid. Rising and falling air currents create violent winds inside a cumulonimbus cloud. Typical thunderstorms last one to two hours before the clouds break up.

36

37

Lightning and Thunder

The blazing lightning and booming thunder that thrill and chill us during thunderstorms are produced by a form of energy called electricity. Electricity builds up in a thunderhead as water droplets and ice crystals riding the rising and falling air currents in the cloud bump together. When enough electricity builds up, a giant spark jumps through the cloud. This spark is lightning.

People used to think that lightning was caused by an angry god hurling thunderbolts from his kingdom in the sky.

To estimate how far away a lightning bolt is, count the seconds between its flash and its thunder, then divide by five. The answer is the lightning's distance away in miles.

The temperature of a lightning bolt can exceed 30,000°F.

FLASH, CRASH, BOOM!

Lightning heats the air around it, causing it to expand. This makes sound waves, which we hear as thunder. Sound travels more slowly than light, so we always see lightning before we hear its accompanying thunder.

BOLTS WITH JOLTS

Lightning strikes Earth about a hundred times every second. One flash of lightning contains enough electricity to light a house for a year!

If you are swimming, leave the water right away.

Crouch down if you are caught in an open field.

Trees attract lightning. Don't stand under them.

Steer clear of metal fences and pipes; they carry electricity.

PLAYING IT SAFE

During a thunderstorm, it's best to stay inside, where you are protected against lightning. If you are caught outdoors in a storm, keep these safety tips in mind.

Clocking in at top speeds of more than 300 miles per hour, tornadoes are the swiftest and strongest winds on Earth. Produced by violent thunderstorms, these funnel-shaped columns of whirling air descend from storm clouds to the ground, where they demolish nearly everything they come across. The color of a tornado depends on the color of the dirt and debris it sucks up as it rages along.

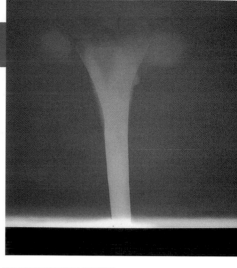

WATERSPOUT
A waterspout, like this one in the Gulf of Mexico, is a tornado that forms over a lake or the sea.

PATH OF DESTRUCTION
Like a giant vacuum cleaner hose, the funnel of a tornado sucks up trees, rooftops, cars, and anything else in its path. Most tornadoes, or twisters, last less than 15 minutes, but they can inflict deadly damage during that time.

NO PLACE TO HIDE
While a funnel of hot air called a dust devil whirls up from the dry plain, animals in Africa graze on.

TWISTER TERROR ▶
A dark gray tornado touches down in Kansas, in the heart of "Tornado Alley"—an area in the central United States where more than 700 tornadoes occur each year.

Hurricanes

Born over the warm waters of tropical seas, hurricanes are clusters of thunderstorms that spin together like a giant pinwheel. In the Northern Hemisphere, these huge storms rotate counterclockwise and tend to move west. They bring torrential rain and devastating winds that can exceed 150 miles per hour. Weather forecasters give hurricanes names, alternating girls' names with those of boys.

SKY-HIGH VIEW
Seen from the space shuttle, Hurricane Elena swirls like an enormous whirlpool. The storms known as hurricanes in the Atlantic Ocean are called typhoons (tie-FOONZ) or cyclones (SIE-klohnz) in the Pacific and Indian Oceans.

MONSTER WAVES
Whipped up by Hurricane Gloria, waves pound the New Jersey coast in 1985. Coastal regions are often flooded by a huge mound of water called a storm surge that sweeps inland with a hurricane.

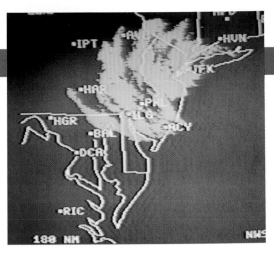

LANDFALL
A radar picture shows Hurricane Gloria moving inland over New Jersey. Hurricanes weaken once they strike land and are cut off from the sea, their source of moisture and energy.

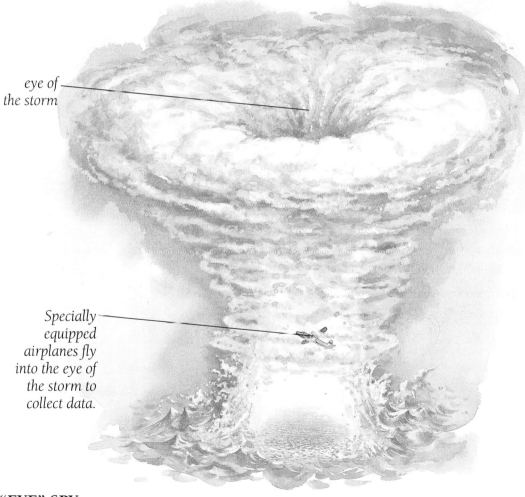

eye of the storm

Specially equipped airplanes fly into the eye of the storm to collect data.

WHEN THE WIND BLOWS
Palm trees bend before fierce gusts in Florida. To be classified as a hurricane, a storm's winds must exceed 74 miles per hour. The strongest winds in a hurricane are found just outside its center, but the storm can cause high winds and rain as far as 250 miles away.

"EYE" SPY
At the center of a hurricane, surrounded by a wall of clouds that can rise 10 to 16 miles above Earth, is a calm area called the eye. In the eye of the storm, there is no rain and little wind.

Watching the Weather

What will the weather bring tomorrow? In earlier times, clues to this question came from nature alone. Today, forecasters use computers, satellites, radar, and other devices that enable them to predict the weather more accurately than ever before and warn people when dangerous storms loom.

SIX-LEGGED THERMOMETER
Crickets chirp louder and louder as the temperature rises. If you count a cricket's chirps for 15 seconds and add 37, you'll find the Fahrenheit temperature.

PINECONE PREDICTION
Pinecones are reliable indicators of humidity (hyoo-MID-i-tee), or how much moisture is in the air. The scales on a pinecone close when the air is damp and open when it's dry.

THE WAY OF THE WIND
That's what a weather vane tells you. The head of the vane—here the bow, or front, of the sailboat—points in the direction from which the wind is blowing. This vane is pointing north.

Satellites take measurements of the atmosphere and send pictures of cloud formations back to Earth.

Aircraft fly into storms to measure temperature, humidity, air pressure, and wind speeds.

Balloons float high in the atmosphere to collect data.

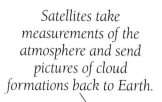

Ground-based weather stations around the world record local information. Anemometers (a-neh-MAH-muh-turz) measure wind speed.

Weather ships keep a watch on conditions at sea.

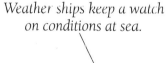

WEATHER WATCHERS
Instruments like these gather information, or data, that helps forecasters predict worldwide weather patterns, as well as conditions in your own neighborhood.

Meteorologists feed all this information into computers to prepare their weather forecasts.

⑧ Beyond the Atmosphere

here Earth's atmosphere ends, the rest of the universe begins. The universe includes everything that exists in space, all the sky we see, and beyond. Our closest neighbor in the universe is the moon. The moon is a satellite, a small body in space that orbits, or revolves around, a larger body. The moon travels around Earth about once a month.

The moon is 240,000 miles from Earth—close enough to have a lot of pull!

HIGH TIDE
Tides, the regular rise and fall of the ocean surface, are caused by the tug of the moon's gravity on the Earth's seas.

Hubble Space Telescope

LOOKING GOOD ▶
From the moon, Earth looks crystal clear. That is because the moon has no atmosphere to spoil the view! The moon also lacks water—and any sign of life.

telescope

binoculars

THROUGH THE LOOKING GLASS
With your eyes alone, you can see countless objects shining in the night sky. But Earth's atmosphere can distort your view. Sky-watching tools provide a sharper look at the universe.

mountaintop observatory telescope

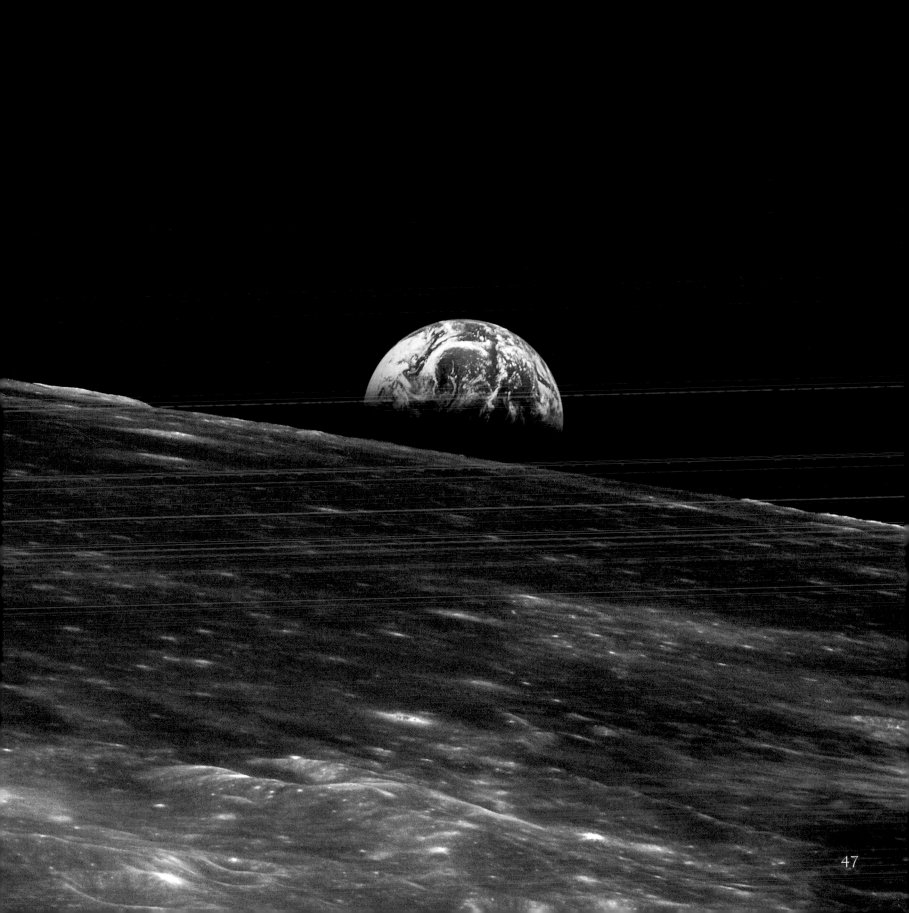

47

A Super Sun

Just as the moon orbits the Earth, Earth revolves around the sun. The sun is a star, which is a great ball of blazing hot gases. It is at the center of the group of planets and other objects in the sky that make up our solar system. The sun lights our sky and warms our world from a distance of 93 million miles. It is so big that more than a million Earths would fit inside it.

SUN BLOCK ▶
When one body in the sky passes in front of another body and hides part or all of it, the event is called an eclipse. An eclipse of the sun occurs when the moon moves between the sun and Earth. As shown here, only the corona (kuh-ROW-nuh), the sun's outer atmosphere, remains visible.

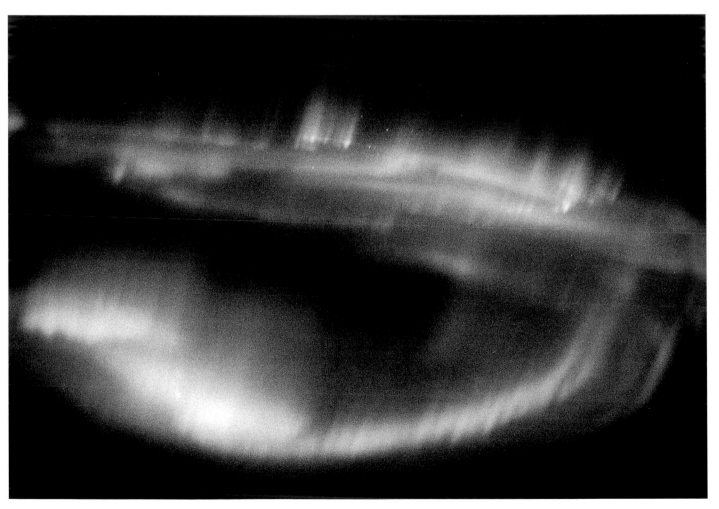

LOVELY LIGHTS
Shimmering sheets of color called auroras (uh-ROAR-uhz) appear in polar skies when tiny particles cast off by the sun enter Earth's atmosphere.

Never look directly at the sun. You could harm your eyes.

BUBBLE AND BOIL

The sun is never still. Boiling gases dance across its surface, and fiery eruptions called solar flares spew electrically-charged particles into space.

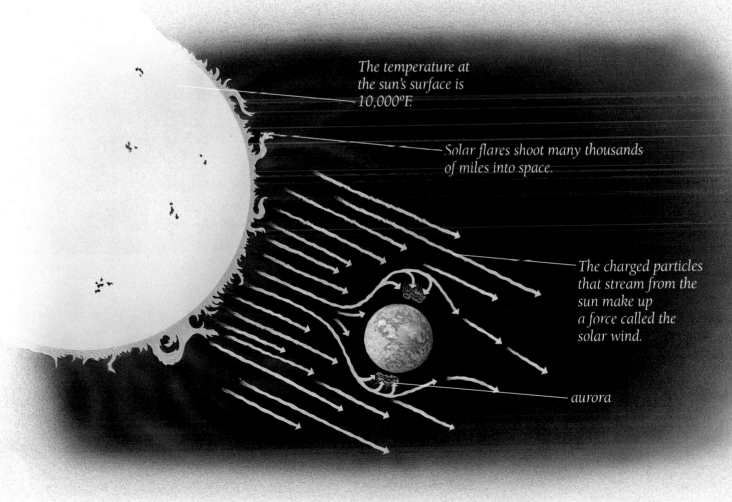

The temperature at the sun's surface is 10,000°F.

Solar flares shoot many thousands of miles into space.

The charged particles that stream from the sun make up a force called the solar wind.

aurora

49

Planet Power

Besides Earth, there are eight other known planets in our solar system. Like Earth, all the planets rotate, or spin, as they travel around the sun. They have atmospheres, although none of them appears to support life as we know it. Some of the planets have one or more moons.

MARS
A shot from a satellite reveals bluish cloud cover on Mars. Red dust in its atmosphere makes the planet look orange red when viewed from Earth.

JUPITER
With a telescope, you can see Jupiter's Great Red Spot, a storm cloud larger than Earth The largest planet, Jupiter looks like a bright, slow-moving star.

SATURN
From Earth, Saturn looks like a yellowish star. With a telescope you can see its rings, which are made of millions of icy rocks.

VENUS
Venus shines brighter than anything in the sky except for the sun and moon. Clouds made of acid float in its atmosphere, giving the planet a yellowish glow.

Mercury

Venus

Earth

Mars

Jupiter

Saturn

Uranus

Neptune

Pluto

THE SUN'S FAMILY
The sun's gravity keeps the planets in our solar
system traveling around it in paths called orbits.
Some planets, like Earth, have one or more moons
orbiting them. Together, the 9 planets in our solar
system have a total of more than 60 moons joining
them as they journey around the sun.

51

Visitors from Space

Sometimes other members of our solar system can be seen in our sky. Asteroids are chunks of rock that circle the sun like pint-size planets. Meteors are smaller objects made of asteroid fragments or comet dust. Comets are chunks of ice and dust from the outer limits of the solar system. Once in a while, these visitors from outer space land on Earth!

SPACE INVADER

Meteors usually burn up about 50 miles above the Earth. Those that make it through the atmosphere to hit the ground are called meteorites. The meteorite below, found in Russia, weighs about a pound and is almost four inches long. The largest known meteorite weighs 60 tons. It crashed to Earth during prehistoric times in present-day Africa.

WHAT A BLAST!

A meteorite the size of a railroad car smashed into the Arizona desert nearly 50,000 years ago and left a bowl-shaped hole, or crater. The crater is four-fifths of a mile wide. Lucky for us, meteorites this large rarely collide with Earth.

SHOOTING STARS

That's what meteors are often called, but they are not stars at all. They are really tiny rocks from space, most of them no bigger than a pebble, that burn up in a brilliant flash when they enter Earth's atmosphere. Your best chance to see a meteor is in a dark sky in the country, far away from city lights.

COMET CAPERS

Comet Hale-Bopp, which passed
Earth in 1997, was the brightest
visitor to our skies in more than
400 years. We see comets when
their orbit brings them near the sun.
The sun's heat melts the comet's ice,
giving it a cloudy head and a tail of
gas and dust millions of miles long.

*Asteroids come in many
shapes and sizes. The biggest is
600 miles across, but most are
just a few miles across.*

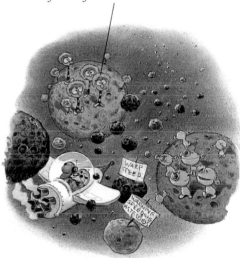

ASTEROID ALERT

In between Mars and Jupiter is
the asteroid belt, a region of
space chock-full of huge rocks
orbiting the sun. Most asteroids
are found here, but some have
orbits that occasionally take
them close to Earth.

Seeing Stars

All the stars we can see without telescopes, including our local star, the sun, are part of the Milky Way Galaxy. A galaxy is an enormous group of stars held together by gravity. There are billions of stars in galaxies, and there are billions of galaxies in the universe. The nearest star to our sun is over 25 trillion miles away from Earth—a small distance in the vast expanse that is the sky.

HOME SWEET GALAXY
From Earth, the Milky Way Galaxy looks like a creamy path across the sky. The Milky Way is made up of more than one hundred billion stars. Our solar system lies about two-thirds of the way between the Milky Way's center and its edge.

TWINKLE, TWINKLE
Stargazers of long ago grouped the stars into shapes called constellations (kahn-stuh-LAY-shunz) and gave them names. The stars above form Canis Major (KAY-nuhs MAY-juhr), or Great Dog. Stars seem to twinkle because of the air moving above us.

CONNECT THE DOTS
With a little imagination, stars become a dog! Canis Major has the brightest star in the entire sky. It is called Sirius (SEAR-ee-us), the Dog Star—what else?

54

HOT STUFF

The color of a star indicates how hot it is. Our sun is a yellow star.

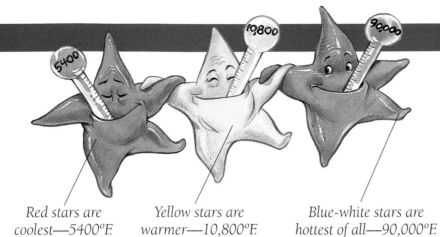

Red stars are coolest—5400°F.

Yellow stars are warmer—10,800°F.

Blue-white stars are hottest of all—90,000°F.

STAR TRAILS

Taken over many hours, this photograph captures the circular trail stars seem to follow. In fact, the stars stay in the same place. They seem to move because the Earth spins.

55

Did You Know...

1 **THAT** a ring, or halo, around the moon is a clue from nature that rain may soon be on the way? These glowing circles are caused by the bending of light rays as they pass through the ice crystals of cirrus clouds. Cirrus clouds often arrive ahead of rainy or snowy weather.

2 **THAT** it can rain salamanders or toads or fish? If a tornado happens to pass over a pond or lake, it can suck up some of the water, along with any critters unlucky enough to be in it. When the tornado weakens, the animals fall to the ground.

3 **THAT** according to Native American myth, thunder and lightning are caused by creatures called thunderbirds? The flashing eyes of the giant birds create lightning, and the beating of their enormous wings makes the sound of thunder.

4 **THAT** some people have mistaken this kind of cloud, called a lenticular cloud, for a flying saucer? These awesome clouds usually form in the rising and falling air currents near mountains. They often stay in one spot, hovering in the sky just like UFOs in movies!

5 **THAT** the light we see today from the North Star left there 680 years ago? That means we're seeing the star as it was in the past, not as it is now. Astronomers measure the vast distances of the universe in light years. A light year is the distance light travels in a year—about six trillion miles.

6 **THAT** scientists believe a small comet exploded over Tunguska (tun-GOO-skuh), a remote region of Russia, in 1908? Preceded by a brilliant light in the sky, the blast snapped trees as if they were toothpicks, leveling almost 800 square miles of forest.

Glossary

ANVIL A block of iron with a flat top used by blacksmiths. Thunderheads are often anvil shaped.

ATMOSPHERE The layer of gases surrounding a planet.

CARBON DIOXIDE A colorless, odorless gas made of carbon and oxygen, which we breathe out of our lungs.

CONDENSATION The process of water changing from a gas, or vapor, to a liquid.

CRATER A saucer-shaped hole made on a planet or moon by a meteorite.

CRYSTAL A particle with a number of flat surfaces.

EQUATOR An imaginary line around the Earth that lies halfway between the North and South Poles.

FLARE A bright blaze of light or flame.

GALAXY A huge cluster of billions of stars.

GRAVITY The natural force that holds planets and moons in orbit and holds you on the ground.

HEMISPHERE One half of the globe.

HUMIDITY The amount of water vapor, or moisture, in the air.

METEOROLOGIST A person who studies the weather.

MOLECULE The smallest particle that a substance can be broken down into and still remain that substance.

ORBIT The path followed by one object, such as the Moon, as it travels around another, such as Earth.

OZONE A kind of oxygen gas in the upper atmosphere that forms a layer that absorbs ultraviolet radiation.

PLANET A large object, such as Earth, that orbits a star, such as the sun.

POLAR EASTERLIES Global winds that blow toward the west, found near either Pole.

POLLUTION Wastes and poisons released into air, water, or land.

RADIATION Energy sent out in rays or waves, such as sunlight.

SATELLITE A natural or human-made object that orbits a planet.

SLEET Frozen raindrops.

TRADE WINDS Global winds that blow east to west.

ULTRAVIOLET RADIATION Invisible light from the sun that can cause sunburn and other damage to humans.

UNIVERSE Everything that exists in space: stars, planets, moons, galaxies, and dust.

WESTERLIES Global winds that blow west to east.

Index

Credits

rainbow

Published by

The National Geographic Society
Reg Murphy, *President
and Chief Executive Officer*
Gilbert M. Grosvenor,
Chairman of the Board
Nina D. Hoffman,
Senior Vice President
William R. Gray, *Vice President and Director, Book Division*

Staff for this Book

Barbara Lalicki, *Director of Children's Publishing*
Barbara Brownell, *Senior Editor and Project Manager*
Marianne R. Koszorus, *Senior Art Director and Project Manager*
Toni Eugene, *Editor*
Alexandra Littlehales, *Art Director*
Susan V. Kelly, *Illustrations Editor*
Marfé Ferguson Delano, *Researcher*
Jennifer Emmett, *Assistant Editor*
Meredith Wilcox, *Illustrations Assistant*
Dale-Marie Herring, *Administrative Assistant*
Elisabeth MacRae-Bobynskyj, *Indexer*
Mark A. Caraluzzi, *Marketing Manager*
Vincent P. Ryan, *Manufacturing Manager*
Lewis R. Bassford, *Production Project Manager*

Acknowledgments

We are grateful for the assistance of Tom Kierein, meteorologist for WRC-TV in Washington, D.C., *Scientific Consultant*. We also thank John Agnone and Rebecca Lescaze, National Geographic Book Division, for their guidance and suggestions.

Illustrations Credits

COVER: Thomas Ives
Interior photographs from Earth Scenes Division of Animals Animals Enterprises.
Front Matter: 1 John Lemker. 2-3 Bruce Davidson. 4 (top to bottom), NASA; Farrell Grehan; Johnny Johnson; Original NASA photograph printed from digital image © 1996 Corbis. 5 (top to bottom), Bates Littlehales; Original NASA photograph printed from digital image © 1996 Corbis; Jerry Schad/Photo Researchers. 6-7 (art), Carol Schwartz. 8 (both) NASA. 9 (art), Carol Schwartz. 10 (art), Robert Cremins. 10 (top to bottom), Richard Kolar; Zig Leszczynski; Mike Andrews. 11 (left), Francis Lepine; (right), Photosafari (PVT) Ltd.
Life Support: 12 (art), Robert Cremins. 12 Farrell Grehan. 13 Danny Lehman. 14 (art), Carol Schwartz. 14 David J. Boyle. 15 (art), Robert Cremins. 15 (left), Dieter & Mary Plage/ Survival/OSF; (right), Kim Westerskov/OSF.
Air in Motion: 16 (top), Michael Dick; (bottom), Ernest Wilkinson. 17 (art), Robert Cremins. 17 (top), Johnny Johnson; (bottom), Sam Abell, NGP. 18 (art, both), Robert Cremins. 18 (left), E.R. Degginger; (right) Lowell Georgia. 19 (upper), John Gerlach; (lower), Michael Fogden. 20 Original NASA photograph printed from digital image © 1996 Corbis. 21 (top art), Robert Cremins; (bottom art), Carol Schwartz.
Weather: 22 (art), Robert Cremins. 22 Bates Littlehales. 23 (top), Anthony Bannister; (bottom), James Brandt.
Clouds: 24 (top art), Robert Cremins; (bottom art), Carol Schwartz. 25 Bates Littlehales. 26 (upper), Harold E. Wilson; (lower), Bates Littlehales. 27 (art), Carol Schwartz. 27 (upper), John Lemker; (lower), Richard Kolar. 28 (left), Scott W. Smith; (upper right), Nancy Rotenberg; (lower right), Ray Richardson. 29 (art), Robert Cremins. 29 John Gerlach.
Precipitation: 30 (art), Robert Cremins. 30 (upper), Robert A. Lubeck; (lower), Carson Baldwin, Jr. 31 Charlie Palek. 32 (art), Robert Cremins. 32 J.H. Robinson. 33 (all), R.F. Sisson. 34 (art), Robert Cremins. 34 PhotoSafari (PVT) Ltd. 35 (art), Carol Schwartz. 35 Bates Littlehales.
Storm Machines: 36 (art), Carol Schwartz. 37 John Gerlach. 38 (art, both), Robert Cremins. 39 (art), Warren Cutler. 39 Michael Stoklos.
Severe Weather: 40 (art), Warren Cutler. 40 (top), E.R. Degginger; (bottom), Patti Murray. 41 E.R. Degginger. 42 Original NASA photograph printed from digital image © 1996 Corbis. 43 (art), Robert Cremins. 43 (left), Herb Segers; (both, right), E.R. Degginger. 44 (left), Patti Murray; (upper right), E.R. Degginger; (bottom right), John Pontier. 45 (art), Carol Schwartz.
Beyond the Atmosphere: 46 (art, all), Robert Cremins. 46 Joe McDonald. 47 Original NASA photograph printed from digital image © 1996 Corbis. 48 Original NASA photograph printed from digital image © 1996 Corbis. 49 (left art), Carol Schwartz; (right art), Robert Cremins. 49 C.C. Lockwood. 50 (left), NASA; (right, top to bottom), Dr. Philip James, University of Toledo/NASA; NASA; NASA. 51 (art), Carol Schwartz. 52 (left), Hansen Planetarium; (both right), Breck P. Kent. 53 (art), Robert Cremins. 53 Jerry Schad/Photo Researchers. 54 (art), Robert Cremins. 54 (upper), Akira Fujii; (lower), Victoria de Bettencourt. 55 (art), Robert Cremins. 55 John Lemker.
Back Matter: 56 (top art), Robert Cremins; (bottom art), Carol Schwartz. 56 Pekka Parvianen/Science Photo Library/Photo Researchers. 57 (art), Robert Cremins. 57 (top), Jean C. Neff/Houghton Mifflin; (bottom), Tass from Sovfoto. 60 C. Semner/National Center for Atmospheric Research.

COVER: During an August thunderstorm, a brilliant bolt of lightning zigzags groundward to strike Arizona's Tucson mountains.

Composition for this book by the National Geographic Society Book Division. Printed and bound by R.R. Donnelley & Sons Company, Willard, Ohio. Color separations by Graphic Arts Services, Nashville, Tennessee. Case cover printed by Inland Press, Menomonee Falls, Wisconsin.

Library of Congress CIP Data
Delano, Marfé Ferguson
    Sky / by Marfé Ferguson Delano
       p.   cm — (National Geographic nature library)
    Includes index.
    Summary: Examines various characteristics of the sky, including the atmosphere, weather, space, and the sun and stars.
    ISBN 0-7922-7047-9
    1. Meteorology—Juvenile literature.   2. Sky—Juvenile literature
3. Atmospheric physics—Juvenile literature.   [1. Sky. 2. Weather
3. Astronomy.] I. Title. II. Series.
    QC863.5.D45   1998
    551.5—dc21
                          97-28564
                            CIP

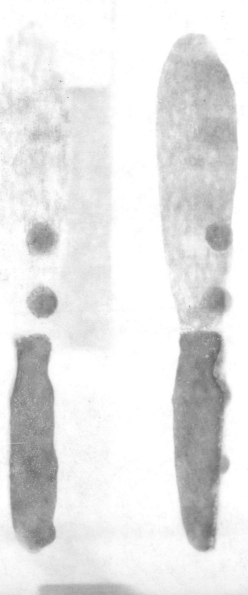

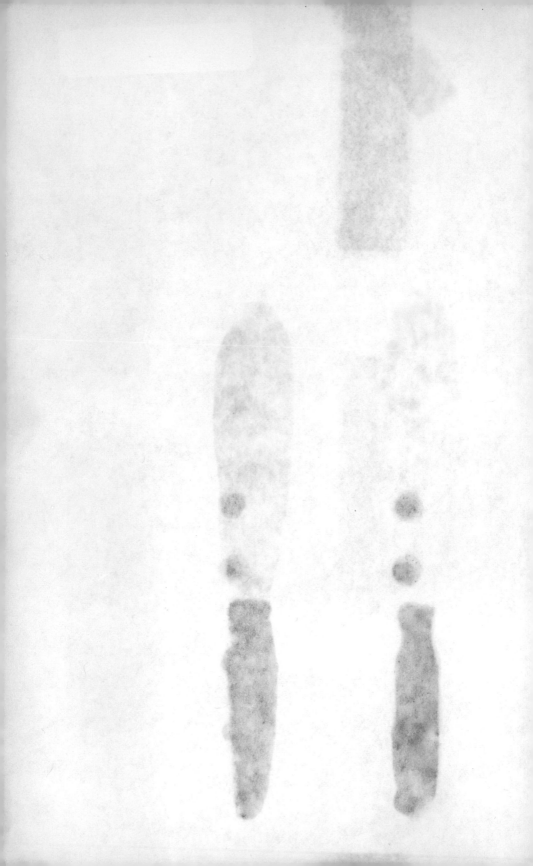

Monster
or Messiah?

Monster
or Messiah?

The COMPUTER'S
IMPACT on Society

EDITOR
Walter M. Mathews

UNIVERSITY PRESS OF MISSISSIPPI

Jackson

To Colleagiality

—That informal union which makes
the whole greater than the sum of its parts.

Copyright © 1980 by the
University Press of Mississippi
Manufactured in the United States of America
Designed by Larry E. Hirst and James J. Johnson

Library of Congress Cataloging in Publication Data

Main entry under title:
The Computer's impact on society.
   1. Computers and civilization. I. Mathews,
Walter M.
QA76.9.C66C654   301.24'3   79–16737
ISBN 0–87805–108–2

Grateful appreciation is due the following: *Dr. Shirley Hallblade* and *Kathleen Sullivan* who worked diligently with me to formulate and conduct the Computer Impact on Society Project. *Dr. Cora Norman*, Executive Director of the Mississippi Committee for the Humanities, who encouraged us from the beginning. *The Mississippi Committee for the Humanities* who supported the project from which these papers evolved. *Roy Cook* and *Debbie Barton* and the other graduate students at the University of Mississippi who helped along the way. *The University of Mississippi* who supported this volume; and of course *the scholars* published here who make this volume what it is.

Walter M. Mathews
University, MS
November 17, 1979

CONTENTS

INTRODUCTION

Since the coining of the phrase "post-industrial society" in 1962 by Harvard sociologist Daniel Bell, growing attention has been paid to the need for examining the direct and indirect effects of technological progress in the context of social and humanistic perspectives. A major characteristic of post-industrial civilization is the growing use of the most sophisticated tool humankind has yet created—the electronic computer. It is computer-based technology that is at the core of the fast-paced change which characterizes this second half of the twentieth century.

Despite only being commercially available since 1951, computers have come to affect the lives of virtually all citizens, making possible hundreds of services and products which contemporary society has learned to take for granted. The computer is an indispensable tool in the daily lives of a major portion of the population.

It is impossible to imagine our society without computers. The computer is here to stay; its very existence suggests that it must be dealt with. And yet, computer technology is not static. It is constantly changing, expanding, and permeating our lives more and more thoroughly. With each new technological advance in computer science come crucial questions and problems. For example, it has been predicted that by 1985 human behavior will be controllable through radio stimulation of the brain. If we *can* do this, *must* we? If we do use this technology, should its use be restricted? If so, to what extent and by whom?

ix

While this is a somewhat dramatic illustration, it points out that decisions about what is technologically feasible should be made in the context of the social and humanistic implications of the use of such technology. Failure to intelligently confront the problems and decisions of a developing technology may force a less open, less flexible society upon future generations. Intelligent decisions must be based on an adequate understanding of computer technology and its applications, and on a thorough study of the technology's implications for current and future generations.

The first consideration requires that people perceive the extent to which the computer and its accompanying technology have become a part of their daily lives, balanced with some understanding of what computers can and cannot do.

The second consideration for intelligent decisionmaking about the uses of computer technology calls for a thorough examination of individual and social values and, in light of these values, a consideration of technology's implications for the future. It is in this area that the perspective offered by the humanist becomes valuable. The concept of the "whole person" has long been a cherished ideal, but in an age of specialization and fragmentation, today's society may be farther than ever from realizing the humanistic ideal. Insights from the humanistic tradition can help us in our attempt to approach value decisions more intelligently. Perspectives from history, philosophy, religion, and other humanistic disciplines can provide guidance as citizens grapple with questions raised by concerns about life in a technological society.

Awareness of these needs for better understanding and of the roles which might be played by humanists led us to pursue a means by which these issues and questions could be addressed in community settings.

Support and funding for this effort was obtained through a grant from the Mississippi Committee for the Humanities, a state-based program of the National Endowment for the Humanities. The Mississippi Committee for the Humanities funds programs which involve scholars in the humanities in meaningful dialogue with the out-of-school adult public on matters of public policy which affect a broad spectrum of society.

The project consisted of ten day-long community seminars on the topic, "The Computer Impact on Society." The programs provided opportunities for citizens, humanists, and technologists to interact on questions such as:

1) How have computers affected society?
2) Should we intervene in regard to computer technology?
3) How can we prepare ourselves for the "post-industrial computer-age"?
4) How can we plan for the adaptation that future generations must make to live in such a world?

The collection of papers in this volume is an outgrowth of the project. Participating scholars from eight universities developed manuscripts from their unique perspectives. Following is a selection of those manuscripts. They provide insights from a variety of backgrounds with the combined result of focusing on vital questions and concerns about our technologically-oriented society. They help us examine the consideration of the computer as a monster or a messiah.

PART I

THE COMPUTER IN
HISTORICAL CONTEXT

Two hundred years ago almost everywhere human beings were comparatively few, poor and at the mercy of the forces of nature. Two hundred years from now we expect almost everywhere people will be numerous, rich and in control of the forces of nature. So goes Herman Kahn's general statement in *The Next 200 Years*. In the middle of this 400-year period we see the computer still in its infancy—having been born in our lifetime. While a relatively new technology, the computer is seen by some as having a major role in the reversal of humanity's fortunes as we project two centuries ahead. Yet we must first look backward to see forward with greater understanding.

In this section, two historians look at the computer in the context of the perspective of history. The idea of Progress is the concern of Fred Laurenzo (Chapter 1), who traces the concept from the eighteenth century philosophes whose beliefs were founded primarily on the achievements of science and technology. The achievements of the Industrial Revolution greatly strengthened the belief in Progress among all classes of society, but the first half of the twentieth century saw a decline of faith in Progress. Laurenzo argues that the computer has been the primary reason for the renewed faith in Progress in the past twenty years. This new technology has become a primary agent for creating a new society of greater wealth, comfort, and convenience. As such it has become the pri-

1

mary agent and symbol of Progress. Laurenzo also reports on the emergence of a school of "new philosophes," the futurists, who, like their eighteenth-century counterparts, show great faith in man, his future, and his technology—particularly the computer.

In Chapter 2, Michael Landon asserts that the professional historian is both a humanist and a social scientist—and therefore possesses a unique sensitivity to the computer's association with humankind. In his latter capacity he is inclined to welcome the advent of the computer as a useful new tool to aid in research work. As a humanist, however, the historian can also sympathize with the fears of those who worry about governments and other wielders of power using computers to find out and remember permanently in huge mechanical brains too much about the individual citizen. Because he is a historian he knows that mankind has always been trying to develop new and more powerful tools. He also knows that governments from time immemorial have sought to acquire as much quantitative information about their subjects as possible, and not always for bad reasons. The computer is a new tool, no more and no less, asserts Landon. It can be used or misused by governments and by individuals; but it should not be unduly feared or unduly revered. It should not always necessarily even be believed.

1

Computers and the Idea of Progress

FREDERICK E. LAURENZO

Not so very long ago the General Electric Company proclaimed to the world, "Progress is our most important product." The slogan expresses an idea which has been part of the thinking of the Western world for at least three centuries. It is no accident that one of the leading producers of technology should more successfully identify itself with the idea of Progress than any other contemporary organization. For the America of the 1970s the only organization which might more fittingly appropriate the slogan would be that other great producer of technology, International Business Machines Incorporated. The initials IBM are synonymous with the greatest technological achievement of our day, the computer. The computer has become the most important symbol and example of successful technology, and, as such, it has become in the minds of many both the symbol and the engine of Progress in the modern world. This association of technology with the concept of Progress is not new. The relationship has had a rather long history, and knowledge of that past can be of help in understanding present-day attitudes toward computers.

Historians trace the idea of Progress back to the seventeenth century.[1] This was the era dominated by Louis XIV of France and his glittering court. It was an age which saw great achievements in many areas of intellectual endeavor and great events in politics. The two dominating political facts of the age were that while France

3

was ruled by the greatest of absolute monarchs, England was establishing a constitutionally limited monarchy. These facts had an enormous effect on the shape of the modern world, but occurring simultaneously was a series of events of equal or greater importance. While kings and parliaments fought over the distribution of political power, others sought the keys to power in the natural world. They sought to reveal the laws of chemistry, physiology, botany, and physics, and their efforts produced a scientific revolution. Modern science was born in the seventeenth century and in an age of great minds and great achievements one figure emerged supreme—Isaac Newton. In 1687 Newton published his *Principia* which proclaimed the existence of a universe governed by natural laws that were absolute and unchanging. Moreover, he explained these laws with mathematical precision.

By the early eighteenth century, the news of the scientific revolution was being spread through all levels of literate society. The knowledge of scientific achievement strengthened a belief in Progress which had been growing since the middle of the seventeenth century. Starting as a belief that seventeenth-century literature was superior to the literature of all previous ages, the idea of Progress by the early eighteenth century was becoming an explanation for the alleged superiority in all respects of that age in comparison to previous ages. The belief was deepened and strengthened as the eighteenth century passed, the knowledge of science spread, and new technology was introduced.

The eighteenth-century group of intellectuals known as *philosophes* was comprised of literary men, social scientists, professional reformers, and popularizers of science. All were profoundly impressed with the recent achievements of Western society, and they were as convinced of their superiority over previous ages as they were that the next age would bring even greater achievements. Newton had taught them to look for laws governing the cosmos, and they eagerly sought to discover those laws not merely in the natural world but also in human society and in individual human behavior. The philosophes believed that their age was on the verge of unlocking the secrets of the universe and that the result would be an improvement in life in general and man in particular. In short they came to believe in the idea of Progress: that history was the record of the continual improvement of man and society and that such improvement would continue indefinitely into the future.

The identification of Progress with science, which was established by the philosophes in the eighteenth century, was broadened and strengthened by the Industrial Revolution. From the late eighteenth century through the nineteenth century, the Western world passed through changes which resulted in the creation of the Age of Machines. The new machines created a world of affluence and comfort which previous ages could not have imagined. At first, however, the new technology was not accepted. For some, at least, the new machines seemed to promise only dislocation, noise, filth, and unemployment. In England, workers, known as Luddites, responded to the changed conditions of life by going about smashing the machines which they feared, mistrusted, and blamed for their miseries.[2] Within about a generation this attitude toward machines had largely disappeared. By the middle of the nineteenth century, prosperity based on machines had become so widespread and obvious that technology was a matter of pride. England, the most highly industrialized nation at the time, expressed her pride and celebrated her technological superiority at the great Crystal Palace Exhibition of 1851. All classes shared in the celebration, and all classes equally shared the belief in Progress. Indeed England and the West were achieving so much, at least in a material sense, that people found it difficult not to believe in Progress; the idea seemed unshakable.[3]

Nevertheless, the calamities of the twentieth century succeeded in changing opinions. World War I created disillusionment in much of Western society. Technology had not prevented catastrophe but actually enhanced it. After the war, confidence in science, technology, and the future continued to wane. During the decade of the thirties, the gloom deepened as dreams of universal affluence were swallowed by worldwide depression. World War II seemed to contemporaries to be the end of all hope; it was in fact a new beginning. The pivotal point in the changing tide of opinion probably came with the explosion at Hiroshima in 1945. Science and technology had produced terrible destruction, but they had also produced victory.[4]

Since World War II there has been a continuing shift in attitudes. Although the despair of the pre-War generation did not immediately dissipate, there has emerged a new sense of confidence in the future—in effect a revival of the idea of Progress and a tendency to base that hope on technology. Victory in 1945, which owed so much to science and technology, set the stage. The successful exploration of space, while it produced a backlash, nevertheless contributed to the growing sense of confidence. In the past twenty years nothing has contributed more to this renewed belief in Progress than the "computer revolution."

It was only in the mid-fifties that computers were put on sale for uses other than pure science. Today these machines are invading virtually every sector of life. The early computers were far bulkier than today's models, and they calculated at speeds 10,000 times slower.[5] This rapid increase in the sophistication of computer technology, along with the explosion in the number of computer users, has been accompanied by a renewed sense of confidence in technology and in the future.

Certainly the acceptance of computers has been neither immediate nor uniform. As machines have done in the past, computers have engendered resentment, fear, and confusion. Indeed there has been an almost Luddite response on the part of many. Confronted with a charge account statement which demanded excessive interest or a payroll statement which recorded excessive deductions, many have been filled with a desire to destroy the machines which allegedly committed those errors. When the same outraged victims received form letters from the machines against which they complained, their fury was boundless. The first encounters with the computer produced a sense of outrage which became almost commonplace or even fashionable. Fears arose that the "machine was taking over" and that the individual was being reduced to helplessness and anonymity—a mere number. The uncontrolled development of large data banks of personal information further heightened fears—and with good reason! The new machine seemed to be threatening a society which no longer valued the individual or individual rights. There were also fears that this powerful new instrument of technology would directly replace many individuals— that it would render people unemployed and useless.

These fears are at present still with us in some measure, but the most remarkable aspect of the negative view of computers is that it is receding rapidly.[6] The Luddism is evaporating as people come into daily contact with computers. One symptom of changing attitudes is the present ambivalent use of the word *computerized*. Used in regard to an individual, it implies something undesirable or derogatory; however, the word as applied to society generally implies a desirable condition—progressive, efficient, etc. Eventually the language will catch up with rapidly changing attitudes, and the negative connotations of *computerized* will be dropped. The process is almost literally visible; every day we are offered new reasons for viewing computers as objects of pride. One automaker boasts of a computer which makes its car more efficient, and microwave ovens, we are told, are controlled by computers which are products of superior space-age technology. In a period of two or three years pocket calculators have become commonplace and are touted in advertising as "mini-computers" which are "pocket genies." The computer has become the munificent genie in Aladdin's magical lamp instead of a dehumanizing and troublesome machine.

If language and advertising reflect and encourage the growing acceptance of computers, even more persuasive is the daily contact which people have with computers. In the business world, secretaries are using automatic typewriters, and file clerks are using data control systems which depend on the latest computer technology. Virtually every large business in America is employing computers to control inventory. Warehouse workers, whose primary contact with technology ten years ago was the telephone and the fork-lift truck, now daily come in contact with the computer. In factories computers are being used increasingly to regulate more efficiently the assembly line and the consumption of power. Contact with computers scarcely ends at the close of the workday. The men who formerly cursed the machine which sent them form letters are now being seduced nightly on countless street corners by "sexy" little computers variously named Annie, Tillie, and Mimi, who click, whirr, and produce bank statements on command. The fear of a dehumanized, machine-controlled society fades literally at the touch of a button; the machine has been restored to its proper place as servant.

As computers have become more deeply embedded into the routine of daily living, they have become the symbol and the direct producers of material progress. The new machine is cutting costs of production and providing new goods and services. Automatic banking and the new computer-controlled charge account systems have greatly expanded credit and increased convenience and are at present on the verge of rendering money totally unnecessary. In short, computers are raising the material standard of living; they are making living and working easier, more comfortable. The average individual has inevitably begun to view the new machine as not merely a provider of new wealth but as the very symbol of Progress in the future. The fear and mistrust of the machine are being replaced by a sense of power and confidence. Certainly the secretary whose work output has increased, the warehouse worker who now maintains better control of inventory, and the file clerk who retrieves data more efficiently have all felt a greater sense of confidence; computers have enabled them to better control their work environments.

This impact which computers are having on contemporary living and thinking is very reminiscent of the impact railroads had in the nineteenth century. In England, which was the first nation to build an extensive rail system, people talked of the "railway revolution" and the "railway age" in much the same way that contemporary America talks of the "computer revolution."[8] A parallel can be made, however, which is more concrete than language or symbolism. The railroad was basic to the development of the industrial economy; it produced new wealth, directly and indirectly, and altered life styles by injecting a new mobility into society. The computer promises to fill a similar role in the "post-industrial" age

which has emerged. Computers are producing wealth and alter
life styles. They provide the key element in the technological advances of the present, and, like the nineteenth-century railways,
they have strengthened the belief in Progress.

The renewed faith in Progress and the strengthened confidence
in technology are more discernible among a group of people who
are directly involved with the solution of problems by computer
technology than they are in society at large. Social scientists,
professional policy planners, and some humanists manifest a new
sense of confidence and even arrogance due to their work with
computers. This group has traditionally been concerned with the
shape and direction of society. Now they have acquired a powerful
new instrument for analyzing old solutions and attacking new
problems. Even the writing of history, which aside from the typewriter seemed impervious to technological improvement, has been
affected by the computer. A new group of historians, the cliometricians, armed with computers, test old theses and attack new
questions which were previously unasked or were considered unanswerable. As a group the cliometricians manifest a very great
deal of confidence in their work which rests on a seemingly more
exact and provable method: quantification through the use of computers.[9] The cliometricians are a minority among historians and
have not gone unchallenged; but their attitudes serve to illustrate
what is going on in the social sciences—economics, sociology, political science—which have always been more amenable to quantification. The computer already dominates research in these fields.
Among those who engage in this research there is a feeling of confidence which is understandable, if not always laudable. With the
aid of the new machine, they have found it possible to control gigantic masses of data in a way which undoubtedly creates a sense
of power and confidence. The machine has seemingly expanded
the province of the human mind. One lone scholar now can achieve
more than a team of researchers. Problems which were unthinkable
or unsolvable now seem capable of solution. Ruth Davis, director
of the Institute for Computer Sciences and Technology for the National Bureau of Standards typifies the new optimism. She predicts

that: " . . . computers will make possible the realization of behavior which is essentially limitless, transcending man and computer taken separately, and that computers will confer on the individual more control over his personal environment than he has ever before been able to exercise." With this prospect in mind she triumphantly concludes: "It is a future worth awaiting."[10]

There exists a distinctive group of social scientists who not only eagerly look to the future but seek to plan it. These "futurists," as they call themselves, manifest the new confidence of social science in a unique fashion. Indeed the enthusiasm of the futurists for technology and their confidence in the abilities of man and in the future earn them the right to the title, the "new philosophes." They are (perhaps unwittingly) the new prophets of the idea of Progress. These students of the future frequently warn of possible catastrophe, yet beneath their warnings lies a basic optimism regarding man and the future. Regardless of differences in bias or methodology, all futurists view man similarly: "   as a being 'in process,' humanized by his capacity to contemplate and judge himself and choose his future, free only if he can build a world which allows him to develop his potentialities."[11] This view is startlingly reminiscent of the eighteenth-century philosophes' belief that man controlled his destiny and would in fact improve both himself and his society.

The most widely read of the new philosophes is Alvin Toffler. His book, *Future Shock,* warns of possible calamity, but in fact Toffler is inclined to believe in the Millenium. Like other futurists he believes in the capacity of man to subject "the process of evolution itself to conscious human guidance."[12] The better world which is envisioned by the futurists will be made possible in large measure by computer technology. Indeed the future world as fact and the planning process necessary to achieve that fact seem dependent on the computer. One of Toffler's major prescriptions for "future shock," for example, is the convening of "social future assemblies" which rely on computer technology.[13] Of this suggestion and similar ones another futurist has been led to speculate: "Pushing these proposals and activities just a bit further ahead and placing them in a computerized cybernetic context, it is easy to envision the emergence of national and transnational clusters of multimedia futurist networks—perhaps focusing upon different problem areas, such as education or transportation—capable of organizing the transfer, storage, retrieval, comparison and creation of ideas about the future with undreamed-of speed and agility."[14] Thus the new philosophes look to the computer as their primary means for defining Progress.

Clearly there is going on at all levels of society a "computer revolution" and that revolution has renewed the belief in Progress. Such faith and hope in the future is probably a necessary and healthy thing, but there are some dangers. The present belief in Progress, as was the case in the eighteenth and nineteenth centuries, appears to be excessively materialistic. That is, the equation of Progress with computer technology leads to an assessment of life which overemphasizes creature comforts. This view tends to measure Progress in terms of gadgets and buying power, while tending to forget questions of justice, aesthetics, liberty, and ethics. Moreover, the effort of the futurists to define the path of Progress with the aid of computers seems open to objections. Their attempts to predict the future are usually based on computer modeling techniques which in turn depend on present perceptions. Such perceptions of the future can be highly inaccurate as they have been in the past. Furthermore, these new philosophes, while paying lip service to the past, are inclined to reject or ignore it. Yet they seem very much concerned with clarifying values for the present and for the future. One is led to fear, therefore, that the futurists tend to define present values in terms of public opinion polls and that values for the future world which they design will depend on computer models derived from such opinion polls. This approach to the definition of values is contrary to humanistic tradition. As a result, some humanists have been tempted to ignore the concerns of the futurists and to become further confirmed in their prejudices against the technology which the futurists praise. Nevertheless, there can be little doubt that computers are renewing the faith in Progress.

It is essential that humanists recognize this fact and that they participate in the definition of the better future which all humanity seeks.

⊒

A Historian Looks at the Computer's Impact on Society

MICHAEL de L. LANDON

A professional historian, because of the wide-ranging nature of his particular field of study—which embraces at its fullest extent every one of the varied activities of all the human beings that have ever lived since records began to be kept—often finds himself engaged simultaneously in two of the major areas of modern scholarly endeavor: one being the humanities and the other the social sciences. All scholarship, properly carried out, consists of discovering what is factual truth and from there going on to point out valid comparisons and valid contrasts that can be shown to exist between those facts. A historian as a humanist is particularly concerned to arrive at a clearer understanding of what it means to be a human being. He or she does so by reading the written records, both factual and fictional, that previous generations of humans have bequeathed to the men of the present; and then adding to those records, for the benefit of his contemporaries and their posterity, his own written conclusions concerning the human condition. A historian as a social scientist tries to apply to man's social activities in the past the same exact research methods that are utilized in all of the "sciences" including the latest advances in technology. By applying them he hopes to arrive at demonstrably provable statements about human societies in the past that can stand up to careful scrutiny as well as any of the findings made by other kinds of "scientists" who employ the methods of technologi-

13

cal research respected in our modern, scientifically-oriented world.

When a historian considers the computer's impact on modern society, therefore, the first question he is likely to ask himself is whether the computer is a tool that can be usefully employed in carrying out his own social function of adding to our knowledge and understanding of the past. But before very long that part of him that is a humanist is going to begin also to weigh and consider the question of what changes are going to be brought about by the increasingly common use of the computer in our everyday lives. How is it going to affect the quality of modern human existence?

A great many professional historians in fact have already hailed the computer as an extremely useful new adjunct to research. Its use has given rise to a whole new branch of the discipline known usually as quantitative history; or, more recently as cliometrics—a word that has not as yet found its way into the dictionaries.[1] Some two years ago Robert P. Swierenga of Kent State University argued in an article that " . . . every history department ought to provide . . . introductory courses in computer programming [including] 'hands-on' experience with computers and their ancillary equipment."[2] And, just last year, the prestigious *American Historical Review* devoted most of one whole number to the pros and cons of quantification in historical research.[3] That certainly proves that there is a great deal of general interest in the subject even though the issue's lead article, by R. W. Fogel, was entitled "The Limits of Quantitative Methods in History."[4] Fogel's was followed by a review article by Charlotte Erickson on some of the most notable recent publications by cliometricians in which she argued that historians "are likely to remain selective and eclectic in dealing with men and motives in other times and circumstances"; even while she was prepared to admit that "in certain fields such as economic and demographic history and the study of large social groups in the past the effort to quantify is essential." And the reason it was essential was that the "large masses of data otherwise closed to the historian" can be statistically analyzed by the computer.[5]

In the field of political history a computer can certainly do a far better job than the unaided human brain of analyzing the comparative ethnic, regional, social and economic backgrounds of the hundreds of members of a legislative body. Likewise it can analyze in much greater detail, and with much greater accuracy, the varied make-up of the millions of voters who elected them; and the factors that caused those legislators to vote as each of them did on the numerous issues that came up for their attention after they had been elected. Also in the field of social history the computer now allows the scholar to study systematically the variations in wealth and the extent of social mobility that were present in the societies of the past. And he can comprehend more profoundly and more assuredly the root causes of revolutions and other historic mass movements. Finally, a demographic historian, provided at last with scientifically arrived-at information, can begin making some very definite statements about past causes and effects of population fluctuations and perhaps suggest some useful answers to the questions that are posed by the problem of too many people in so many parts of the world today.

Already, indeed, enough valuable contributions to historical knowledge based on computer-assisted research, have been published to place the value of the computer to historians beyond any seriously debatable doubt. Peter Laslett, leader of a group of historians at Cambridge University in England engaged in computer-based research, has added immensely to our knowledge and understanding of life in preindustrial Britain in his book *The World We Have Lost*.[6] His colleague, E. A. Wrigley, has amply demonstrated in *Population and History* the good use a skilled demographic historian can make of the quantitative analyses provided by computers.[7] And, here in America, Fogel and Engerman by their computerized analysis of large masses of hitherto unused statistical material in their recently-published work *Time on the Cross* have come up with some radical new findings concerning slavery in the Old South.[8] Many of their conclusions have been roundly denounced by experts in the same field who are dedicated to the use of more traditional research methods. But the figures they came up with have provoked a vast amount of new and valuable discussion of the whole slavery issue.[9]

For a historian who aspires to become a cliometrician Edward Shorter has published a useful manual entitled *The Historian and the Computer* which could well be used as a textbook in the sort of course that Swierenga insists every history department should by now be offering for its majors.[10] Since many historians are not very mechanically adept, Shorter advises his readers to leave the actual task of programming the machine to an expert in the field. For those, however, who believe, like Swierenga, that personal, "hands-on" experience is desirable he states reassuringly that while programming a computer is "somewhat more difficult than taking shorthand" it is "less difficult than repairing television sets."[11] Some historians may fear that moving into the field of quantitative history will mean abandoning intellectual endeavor to become merely a pusher of buttons and a reporter of processed factual materials. But, says Shorter: "There is no question of letting the machine do your thinking for you." In fact, he reminds his readers, a computer cannot think; all it can do is assist one with the large-scale calculations that one has decided oneself are necessary to arrive at the historical knowledge that one seeks. "It is a giant clerk rather than a giant brain."[12]

The by now familiar cliché "garbage in, garbage out" of course applies as much to a historian's use of the computer as it does to its use by any other information seeker. Nor should it ever be forgotten that the computer, like every piece of machinery constructed by human beings, is mechanically fallible and can malfunction or even break down altogether. In that case valid material in can also result in garbage out. Therefore, a historian when the time comes to consider his computer-derived findings must not let himself be so overawed by the mechanical marvel that has produced them that he forgets all of his training in the critical assessment of sources. If they do not fit with what he knows, from other, independent sources, he must reject them; or at least ask himself some very searching questions as to what could be the cause of the discrepancy.

Besides remembering that not every piece of information derived from a computer is necessarily accurate, a historian must always bear in mind that even what is true may not be very new or particularly significant. In all of the social sciences in recent years much electronic energy and hours of computer time have been spent to arrive at findings that can only be described as platitudi-) nous. Few political historians, for instance, can have been very much enlightened by the recently published discovery of one of their computer-consulting colleagues with regard to riots in nineteenth century France: "that people take part in disturbances in order to maintain established political rights or attain new ones."[13] The present writer recalls hearing a few years ago a paper presented by an eager young graduate-student convert to cliometrics who reported at great length how a mass of statistical data fed into his computer had shown that in a certain seventeenth century English city those merchants who began their careers with large amounts of inherited capital were apt to die richer than their competitors who started out with little or none. And the writer himself recalls with some embarrassment a personal foray into the field of quantitative history which after a multitude of mechanically-aided computations produced the not too surprising finding that the Inns of Court of London in that same century recruited more students from the more populous counties of England than they did from the less populous counties. Unfortunately works composed mainly of such trivial platitudes, if they are based on computer research, are considerably easier to get accepted for publication—because publishers, and to tell the truth the buyers of books, are much impressed by the technological modernity of the research methods used to arrive at them—than are far more solid original contributions to knowledge arrived at by more traditional types of scholarship.

That part of every historian that is a humanist may very well incline him to concur with the French philosopher, Henri Bergson, who argued in *Creative Evolution* that quantitative techniques, while they are perfectly adequate for application to inanimate objects, are invalid when applied to animate beings that are continually moving and changing in myriad ways, some of them imperceptible to an external observer. "We see," he wrote, "that the intellect so skillful in dealing with the inert, is awkward the moment it touches the living."[14] And if a living human brain is so inept when it comes to assessing beings possessed of life how much more inept for the task must be the mechanical brain of a lifeless computer? Does the statistical evidence, offered by Fogel and Engerman, that the diet of the *average* black slave in the American South around 1860 was nutritionally superior to that of the *average* free white man in the same period tell us anything at all significant about the comparative quality of the lives that each of them led?[15]

That same historian-humanist, nevertheless, in going after some of the answers that he would like to have about past human societies, occasionally may well find himself confronted with so large a mass of such complex data that, as Charlotte Erickson conceded, he is forced to turn to the computer for assistance. Similarly, when he considers what may be the impact of the computer on the quality of life in present-day and future human societies, he has to admit that it can be a useful, and it indeed may be an essential, adjunct of the good life. For the modern decisionmaker, faced with the vast amount of material available in almost every field of human activity today, like the historical researcher overwhelmed by vast masses of data on the past, is almost inevitably forced to resort to mechanical methods of quantification and information storage and retrieval. Some three-quarters of all the human beings that have ever lived, we are told, are alive on this earth today. The population of the United States in the Bicentennial year was almost 100 times as numerous as it was in 1776. If this enormously increased number of people is going to be adequately governed, cared for and catered to, then much more sophisticated means of keeping track of them all are simply going to have to be employed. Another French philosopher, Antoine Nicolas de Condorcet, the last great optimistic intellect of the Age of Enlightenment—writing just a short while before his own death at the hands of French revolutionaries who represented that same Enlightenment gone mad and turned murderous—declared himself to be not at all alarmed at the tremendous increase in the population of the civilized world that was already beginning to manifest itself in his day. For he was unshakably confident that advances in scientific techniques would enable the leaders of the future to handle easily and competently the problems presented by vastly larger numbers of people than the world had ever known before. Among other developments he anticipated the invention of machines like modern computers. "The strength and the limits of man's intelligence may remain unaltered; and yet the instruments that he uses will increase and improve . . . as the result of a more general and philosophical application of the sciences of calculation to the various branches of knowledge."[16]

A humanist-historian realizes that nearly every human being wishes to preserve intact around himself a shell of privacy concealing as much as possible the intimate details of his personal life. And he understands why people are afraid that the increased use of computers in today's world may in many menacing ways penetrate that shell of privacy as governments and corporations feed into their computers' data banks more and more quantitative information concerning all aspects of people's activities.[17] Because he is a historian, however, he cannot help reflecting that as long as there have been governments those governments have tried to acquire the completest possible quantitative records about their subjects; primarily for military conscription or tax assessment purposes but also often in order to facilitate more efficient law enforcement. And, as long as men have been doing business with one another, creditors have always tried to find out as much as possible about their would-be debtors.

Over 3,000 years ago Moses informed the Hebrews that the Lord had commanded him to "take . . . the sum of all the congregation of the children of Israel, after their families, by the house of their fathers, with the number of their names, every male by their polls. From twenty years old and upward, all that are able to go forth to war. . . . [18] In 1086 King William the Conqueror: "sent his men over all England into every shire and had them find out how many hundred hides [of land] there were in the shire, or what land and cattle the king himself had . . . or what dues he ought to have in twelve months from the shire . . . or how much everybody had who was occupying land in England, in land or cattle, and how

much money it was worth. So very narrowly did he have it inves-
tigated, that there was no single hide or a yard of land, nor indeed
(it is a shame to relate but it seemed no shame to him to do) one
ox nor one cow nor one pig was there left out, and not put down
in his record; and all these records were brought to him after-
wards."[19]

Two generations earlier good King Canute had decreed that
"every freeman above the age of twelve shall be brought within
hundred and tithing."[20] That meant that each Anglo-Saxon adult
who was not a slave had to be enrolled in a group of ten forming
a subdivision of a fellowship of 100 men all of whom were responsible for one another's good behavior and had to produce any one
of their number summoned into court or else risk being punished
in his stead. The manorial rolls kept by the stewards who managed
things for the great landed proprietors of the later middle ages con-
tained a multitude of details concerning every villein or serf's private life, labor and military obligations, taxes owed and criminal
record. That is why during the great revolt in England in 1481 and
during the rural uprisings that occurred periodically in France
from the fourteenth century down through the French Revolution,
a major aim of the peasants was always to seize and burn manorial
records. The same motivation impels many of their modern de-
scendants to want to let government computers know as little
about them as possible; and some to even demand the complete
destruction of all computerized records.

A malefactor of several centuries ago would not have had to flee
any very great distance to get to a region where his past criminal
record was totally unknown and unrecorded. But, on the other
hand, the primitive transportation facilities of those days would
probably not have allowed him to go very far, very fast, away from
those who had known him all his life and were well aware of his
antisocial tendencies. The modern criminal can fly halfway round
the world in a day (assisted by computerized air-traffic control systems). But his description and the details of his criminal record,
retrieved from the data banks of police computers, can be sent over
the wires and beamed by satellite even sooner to every member of

Interpol. The businessman of earlier days did business with comparatively few customers during the course of his entire career. And those with whom he dealt were mostly people of his own community whose financial soundness and reliability were intimately known to him after years of mutual dealing. If by chance they were strangers they usually came bearing letters of credit from people whom he did know. A modern business corporation is asked to extend credit to literally millions of individuals, nearly every one of them totally unknown to its officers, dispersed sometimes over an entire continent. Only from the data banks of the major credit agencies can it acquire the knowledge that will enable it to determine whether the person applying has a reputation for fiscal responsibility.

But a historian may view the modern age's growing use of computer technology as a natural outcome of mankind's perennial efforts at ever more efficient quantification and information storage; and still have to admit that some aspects of our computer age are unprecedented. Never before has so much information been able to be accumulated so quickly and with such mechanical thoroughness. For the first time ever, for example, it is being accumulated by machines rather than by people. Alvin Toffler, in *Future Shock*, has suggested that the computer may in fact make the bureaucrat redundant, his clerical and minor decisionmaking functions usurped by a machine.[21] But a bureaucrat, no matter how narrow-minded and infuriating he may be, as a person can be argued with and explained to; a machine cannot. The same computer planning that provides our nation with a sophisticated defense system in this nuclear age may be overcome by the superior computers employed by an enemy. Computers can aid in apprehending criminals, but criminals can also use computers to plan crimes of unparalleled magnitude.[22]

Perhaps the most infuriating aspect of the computer's role in our modern life is its usual insistence on identifying each one of us by a number rather than by our names. Our given and family names, with all their implications of kinship ties, religious, ethnic and national backgrounds, are a very important part of our sense of identity in a huge and mechanized world. On the other hand when computers do use names instead of numerical digits they tend to sound insincere (as in the case of some major selling campaigns where the name is mechanically inserted into stylized letters), and sometimes they run completely amok. Such was the case recently in Gibson County, Tennessee, where a Mr. Loftin had regularly paid the taxes on a piece of land that he owned; but that did not prevent a computer in the tax assessor's office which knew him as Mr. "Lafon" from declaring him delinquent and putting the land up for sale without his knowledge.[23]

The truth of the matter surely is that ever since *homo habilis* began using primitive tools over a million years ago in the Olduvai Gorge of Tanzania man has been a tool-using creature. And always he has tried to invent better and more efficient tools. The computer is but one of the latest in a long series of mechanical aids that humanity has devised to try to make tasks easier. From the flintstone axe to the atomic reactor most of them have had the potential both for great good and great harm. Neither the historian nor anyone else should regard the computer as a demon to be feared, a god to be revered, or an oracle that should always be believed. Like any other tool devised by human beings during their long history it should be used when it can be helpful, but it should be used with care.

PART II

THE COMPUTER
AND SOCIETY

Direct effects of technological developments are obvious; the indirect effects are more subtle but do raise some important societal issues. The automobile, for example, had direct effects at the turn of the century: geographic mobility, prestige with ownership, elimination of street pollution by horse-drawn vehicles. Later, other direct effects were in evidence: new source of jobs, growth of suburban real estate, prime mover of American economy, noise pollution, traffic congestion, highway deaths. Some less obvious effects are still under study: changes in patterns of courtship, socialization, use of leisure time, creation of a broad middle class and reduction of class differences, changes in education through busing.

Computer technology, although a more recent development, has also had its effects on society. This section offers two chapters which examine these effects. In Chapter 3, Shirley Hallblade and Walter Mathews survey the state of current computer use in both direct and indirect social applications. The authors argue that we are rapidly approaching the Man-Computer Age where computers are a direct tool in the daily lives of a major segment of the population. The fact that we cannot return to pre-computer days raises some issues for society. Looking at the implications for society, the authors focus on four major issues: automation, power, individuality, and privacy. They conclude with concerns for awareness and

23

adaptability in a society experiencing the subtle, side effects of the sophisticated and pervasive technology of the computer.

Edwin Dolin, in Chapter 4, claims that computers are merely one more item in the technological development that has defined humanity from palaeolithic times. Like other items in this series, such as explosives, the computer can be misused. Criminal use for financial gain is an obvious misuse. More important, suggests Dolin, is the misuse made possible by the authority computers have acquired among the uninitiated as machines that think better than a human brain. This authority can be involved in misleading the public about the validity of scholarly theories. It could be used as support for a system of classifying children, thereby leading to indirect controls over individual life by a self-chosen few, or it could be falsely and dangerously comforting at the level of national defense security.

3

Computers and Society: Today and Tomorrow

SHIRLEY HALLBLADE
AND WALTER M. MATHEWS

The beginning of the end of the Industrial Revolution occurred in the middle of the 1950s when two events happened: the balance of the American work force shifted from manufacturing goods to delivering services, and the first commercial computer became available.[1] The first event made this country the first "post-industrial" nation; the second allowed the computer (the twentieth-century steam engine) to become more than just an instrument of science, but a tool of the booming service industry.

The Industrial Revolution freed the human race from the land, creating in two centuries a largely artificial environment. The computer revolution promises to free the human mind; where that could lead in two centuries staggers the imagination . . . but there is no turning back.

The availability and efficient capabilities of the computer have made it a highly attractive tool in coping with the "information explosion." The Organization for Economic Cooperation and Development forecast that "in 1985–87, 6 or 7 times the present volume of new information will be produced." But by 1987 "the degree of automation of information will approach a hundred times that of today." Thus machines will do even more of the work of coping with the avalanche of information.[2]

The computer is also on its way to becoming a household appliance—an attendant infinitely adjustable to our needs, but one to

25

which we will also have to adapt.[3] When we pass the threshold to where computers are a direct tool in the daily lives of a major segment of citizens we will be in a new era in the annals of humankind—the Man-Computer Age—and there is no turning back.

PRESENT

A look at the present portends a "computer-world." Computers are no longer a novelty or a tool restricted to use by a few highly trained professionals. The influence of computer technology is evidenced in many dimensions of society from the spectacular feats of facilitating space exploration to the mundane, practical tasks of processing checks and producing mailing labels.

Applications of computers in society diversely influence the typical citizen. Some recognition of the role of computers results from the manner in which computers directly touch the daily lives of the individual or the family. Other more indirect uses of computer technology form the underlying structure for many systems and functions having wide-reaching, global effects. Not unaffected by the continuing computer revolution, the average person forms some impressions of the nature of computers and their pervasiveness in society while the larger, philosophical issues may never reach a conscious level of awareness.

Direct Applications

Probably the most obvious and ubiquitous evidence of the application of computers is in automation of the "paper shuffling" and related tasks associated with daily transactions between individuals and organizations. An individual's paycheck is now typically prepared by computer. It is generated by a computer recordkeeping and accounting system which handles multiple facets of the firm's internal administrative needs as well as external requirements for records and reports. As money (or its representation) flows through the economic system, further applications of computers are encountered. Banking has computerized most aspects of the processing of checks and maintenance of accounts, facilitating recent moves into such areas as automatic bill payment and installation of electronic tellers. The individual also finds a computerized basis for credit-card transactions and account billings, magazine subscriptions, and contracts with book clubs. It is not possible to use the major transportation and lodging systems without being processed by a computer.

Transactions for the local commuter may also be computerized. The Bay Area Rapid Transit System (BART) in San Francisco is essentially computer-controlled. The fare is based on the exact number of miles each passenger travels and is computed with the use of a magnetically coded card as the passenger gets on and off the system.

A more recent application has moved the computer into the supermarket where consumer purchases are made through automatic reading of product/price codes which generates a printed bill for the customer and provides current information for inventory control and sales trends. An "unmanned" supermarket has recently become operational in Japan and serves as a prototype of an automated merchandising system.

The prevalence and feasible coordination of such computerized systems suggest the inevitability of a system in which a uniform payment principle can be applied in purchase of a variety of goods and services. This "electronic funds transfer system" (EFTS) would bring us from our "cashless" society of plastic (credit cards) and paper (personal checks) transactions that ultimately reduce our bank balance, to a "checkless" society where the use of a computer sensitizing card will allow direct access to bank accounts permitting financial transfers to occur in a computer memory at the time of sale. Use of EFTS is growing daily in our country.[3]

Indirect Applications

Besides their significant role in the daily transactions of the life of the consumer, computers are responsible for the coordination and control of numerous functions and processes in many sectors of society. Some of these applications operate behind the scenes and are perhaps not obvious to the casual observer.

Sophisticated computer systems are in operation for both ground and air traffic control. The flow of surface traffic in many major cities is facilitated by computer regulation. The National Weather Service now prepares and distributes its weather forecasts through a network of minicomputers, and computerized typesetting and editing have revolutionized the printing and publishing fields.

The wide use of computers in industry includes not only the automation of production processes but also applications in operations relating to the design, manufacture, and distribution of products and their components. Computer analysis of needs and utilization of electric power is enabling some companies to realize an energy-and cost-saving by reducing the consumption of electricity.[4]

In the field of health care, computers not only serve as a tool for recordkeeping and administration but also have increasing roles in the monitoring and diagnosis of patients and in control and analysis of laboratory tests.

Computers handle the unwieldy volume of data necessary to maintain numerous programs and the underlying tax structure in the governmental sphere. The federal government's executive branch alone has almost 8,000 computers staffed by over 100,000 employees.[5] Computers audit tax returns and assist in the analysis and design of municipal tax assessment systems. Analysis of public opinion polls and processing of electoral returns via computer provide input for the political process. Recently the legal system has felt the impact of computers through such uses as generation of evidence for litigation and more rapid production of trial transcripts.

Applications in science and technology are numerous, but are perhaps overshadowed by developments in the space program. Even those with a casual interest are aware that space explorations would not have been possible without computers. The United States landed astronauts on the moon before the Soviet Union, primarily because of superior computers for control and navigation.

The capability of computers to model and simulate aspects of the environment allows the study of probable effects of certain actions and provides insights into complex processes or conditions such as pollution control, river flow and water supply. Computers provide a model for the management of Wisconsin's forest resources and assist in genetic analysis for the crossbreeding of livestock.

The educational system has also used computer technology. Computers assist in both the generation and dissemination of knowledge through research and instruction as well as in the variety of administrative functions and services.

Hardly an area of society has not felt some impact of computers. Even sports and recreational activities have been affected. The racing yacht, *Courageous*, which won the 1974 America's Cup carried a minicomputer on board for navigational and tactical calculations. Professional football leagues utilize computers to aid in the process of drafting players, while computerized recordkeeping and communication have brought new dimensions to the activities of the Olympics since 1972.

Growth

Twenty years ago if one looked in the *Readers' Guide to Periodical Literature* under "computing machines," one would be directed to "calculating machines," which was the only major heading referring to computers. Three subheadings would be found there, two of which were uses of these machines: meteorological and military.

Five years ago if one looked in the current edition of the same publication, 24 major headings concerning computers would be found with 62 subheadings—48 of which are application areas.

The growth has been exponential. In 1951, when the first commercially-available computer, UNIVAC-I, was built some experts predicted that 100 similar machines would be sufficient to fill the needs of the country. Now the United States has 134,000 computers, and another 100,000 are spread around the rest of the world.[6] In the U.S. today, ten percent of all business expenditures on new plants and equipment is spent on computers and associated systems.[7]

Since the introduction of commercial computers, the cost of calculation has fallen more than a hundred-fold, calculation speed has increased by a factor of 10,000 and space requirements have shrunk to about 1/800 of their original size.[8] Improvement will inevitably continue. Already a fifty-pound, $10,000 computer is available from several companies, and kits to build small computers for less than $1,000 are selling briskly.

In 1977 general purpose computer installations in the U.S. had a value of over $40 billion. Arthur D. Little, Inc. predicted that by 1980 it will be around $60 billion in constant dollars.

THE FUTURE

If we define the power of a computer as the product of its basic speed and its rapid memory capacity, then, Herman Kahn predicts, during the decade of the seventies alone, this power should increase, in the largest and most advanced computers, by a factor of 10,000. As a result, Kahn says, many of the most extravagant projections made about computers seem likely to be rather conservative from the vantage point of 1980. He continues: "By the end of the seventies the world is likely to look quite different to younger people. For example, it is almost certain that computer-assisted instruction and computerized retrieval systems for information will begin to be ubiquitous in schools and other institutions frequented by the young, at least in more developed nations. For many children the computer will, literally, play a role less than, but close to, that of parent and teacher."[9]

Donald Michael reports what seems obvious: that the long-range stability of the social system depends on a population of young people properly educated to enter the adult world of tasks and attitudes. Once, the pace of change was slow enough to permit a comfortable margin of compatibility between the adult world and the one children were trained to expect. Today, in the age of computers, we are not sure of the appropriate kind of education for the current generation—certainly not a linear projection of what *we* were taught. If we do not look at the long-range needs of members of our society and appropriately modify our educational systems, we will have a population that is more and more out of touch with social realities and occupational needs.[10]

Gruenberger reiterates the fact that only now, in the 1970s, are computers feasible in both size and cost for their permeation of society. He says: "For some people, computers have been around for all their lives. For everyone, computers will be around from now on. We must learn to live with them."[11]

According to a survey conducted by the Institute of Electrical and Electronic Engineers,[12] experts predict that by 1981 computers will be used as the basis of medical diagnosis and traffic control, able to receive information through optical character recognition, and composed of microscopic integrated circuits fabricated using electron beams and X-ray lithography. Over the following three years, computer terminals will become common in general office use, which will also benefit from electronic data files and communications networks. By 1987 Josephson junctions are expected to revolutionize the central processing units of large computers while miniature computers are used to control artifical human organs.

Even now, computer monitoring—telemetering information from tiny sensors and transmitters embedded in the human body keeps recalcitrant hearts beating steadily. In a few years they may transmit information about subtle internal states through a computer to a physician and could even be attached to parolees or social deviates.

James Albus, who worked in computer automation at the National Bureau of Standards, says that "Within two decades it may be practical for computer-controlled factories and robots to produce virtually unlimited quantities of manufactured goods, and to even reproduce themselves at continuously decreasing costs." Already, the introduction of numerically-controlled machine tools to existing industries can result in productivity increases of up to 400 percent.[13]

Possibly the greatest impact on daily life may come from com-

bining computers with sophisticated means of communication to
form data networks. Just as the growth of industry drew great
masses of people together to form overcrowded cities, networks
and computer-coordinated transportation systems may free them
again to seek alternate lifestyles in communities of their choosing.
By creating "computer cities" people will soon be able to enjoy the
benefits of urban jobs, services and culture, wherever they live.[14]

In the Man-Computer Age the computer will be as ubiquitous
as the typewriter, the desk calculator or the telephone. Information
processing equipment in the Man-Computer Age will be as easy
to use as the telephone. A small-sized terminal will be available for
individual use at a reasonable cost, considering the function it performs, and it will be capable of performing mental tasks on a real-
time basis with the availability of all necessary data.[15]

Kahn sees that by 1980 the interaction of man with machine
would be carried to the point where the two will be able to function in a working partnership in many creative enterprises. By that
date he claims, it is likely to be at least in the homes of the richer
families as a convenient central method of regulating temperature,
humidity, various cooking devices, home accounting, and access
to mass media and libraries. Computers may even have the capability to begin to play surrogate mother or at least surrogate baby-
sitter and playmate as well as tutor and/or teacher. Such household
computers might well have access to a large variety of entertain-
ments, and a number of alarm-type circuits to inform the parents
or neighbors when they should look in on what the youngsters are
doing.[16]

IMPLICATIONS

The present state of computers in society and their projected role
for the future have not gone unnoticed by those who reflect on the
implications for life in such a world. Four major issues have been
repeatedly raised about the impact of computers on society: automation, power, individuality and privacy.[17]

Automation

The industrial revolution centered on the supplementation and ultimate replacement of the *muscles* of man and animal by mechanical methods. The computer revolution went beyond this to supplement and replace some aspects of the *mind* of man by electronic methods. Both changes have had widespread implications on the world of work—if not replacing people, displacing them from burdensome, tedious and repetitive tasks—"freeing" individuals for more challenging activities, while productivity and cost are optimized. A corresponding increase in the amount of leisure time available to working people has developed with this decreased need for human involvement.

Norbert Wiener tells us that since machines of the future are going to take away a lot more jobs from humans, we can no longer value a person by the jobs he or she does. We must value him or her as a person.[18]

Power

Information is power, and computers mean information. The centralized accumulation of data permits the concentration of enormous power in the hands of those with access to the computer. The very existence of sophisticated computers leads to a power gap between those trained to use and understand them and those who are not. *See p. 240 What will be*

In another sense of power, computers seem sometimes to dictate how, when and what we do. Systems failures, for example, can create chaos and catastrophe. We have rather recent examples in the area of electrical power systems, and we have the vivid threat of possible intercontinental ballistic missile system failure.

Individuality

This is a value that has been cherished in the United States since its beginning. Being involved in a society that is wired to computers means that our individuality is altered; at times our essence is pared to a bare number.

Computers are especially useful for dealing with social situations that pertain to people in mass, such as traffic control, fiscal transactions, consumer goods, and allocation of resources. They are so useful in these areas that they undoubtedly will help to seduce planners into inventing a society with goals that can be dealt with in the mass rather than in terms of the individual.[19]

Privacy

Issues of individual privacy and confidentiality of communication and personal data are raised by increasing use of computers in data collection and information handling. Some have deplored the trend toward using the Social Security number as a "single identifying number" which serves as the access point in developing individual "data images."[20] The technical capability to integrate several information files into networks of computerized data banks poses further questions regarding privacy. With such networks, personal data provided by an individual for one purpose could potentially be accessed for other purposes.

Societal Side Effects

The direct societal effects of any pervasive new technology mean little compared to the more subtle and ultimately much more important side effects. In that sense, we have not yet felt the societal impact of the computer.

In the same way that perhaps the greater impact of the atomic bomb was felt by those people who lived since Hiroshima and Nagasaki and who are aware of what happened and what might happen, the potentially tragic impact on society that may ensue from the use of computer systems will likely come as side effects and not direct effects. In the case of the atomic bomb and the computer, there is a psychological impact on individuals in which forces which are anonymous formulate the large questions of the day and circumscribe the range of possible answers.[21]

Consider too that computer-based knowledge systems become essentially unmodifiable except in that they can grow, and since they induce dependence and cannot, after a certain threshold is crossed, be abandoned, there is the expectation that they will be passed from one generation to another, always growing. Weizenbaum concludes: "Man too passes knowledge from one generation to another. But because man is mortal, his transmission of knowledge over the generations is at once a process of filtering and accrual. Man doesn't merely pass knowledge, he rather regenerates it continuously. Much as we may mourn the crumbling of ancient civilizations, we know nevertheless that the glory of man resides as much in the evolution of his cultures as in that of his brain. The unwise use of ever larger and ever more complex computer systems may well bring this process to a halt. It could well replace the ebb and flow of culture with a world without values, a world in which what counts for a fact has long ago been determined and forever fixed."[22]

Herman Kahn makes some strong statements concerning the potential pervasiveness of the computer—strong statements, but ones reflecting careful consideration: "As far as I know, despite many popular and sometimes expert statements to the contrary, nobody has demonstrated any intrinsic limits to what the computer can eventually do in simulating or surpassing human capabilities. There is a clear capability for mimicking the appearance and characteristics not only of such human activities as analysis, calculation, and playing games, but of activities which have a large aesthetic, emotional, or seemingly intuitive content. . . . It is my personal conjecture, and one which personally always depresses me as well, that by the end of the century, if not by 1980, the experts will have concluded that the computer can transcend human beings in every practical aspect. I do not know what this means in terms of philosophy, religion . . . and even the democratic way of life."[23]

Time after time science has led us to insights that, at least when viewed superficially, diminish man. Copernicus removed man from the center of the universe; Darwin removed him from his place separate from the animals; and Freud showed man's rationality to be illusion. Man's view of himself is continually being narrowed, but at the same time perhaps made more accurate.

When asked if man is changing his environment beyond his capacity to adjust to it, Norbert Wiener replied: "That is the $64 question. He's certainly changing it greatly, and if he is doing it beyond his capacity, we'll know soon enough. Or we won't know—we won't be here."[24] He also said that the use of computers is irrevocable. It is not merely the fact that computers are being used. It is the fact that they stand ready to be used, which is the real difficulty. In other words, the reason we cannot go back is that we can never destroy the possibility of computers being used.

The most important aspect of the late seventies is less likely to be the actual technological developments of the next decade than an increased understanding of what the emergence of the coming technology, the post-industrial culture, and the computer age are likely to mean.

Many of the people who will first live in this kind of world are alive today. The predicted hundredfold increase in the automation of information by 1987 brings some of the issues closer to us. In 1987, today's first-grade students will be nearing graduation from high school. Will they be prepared to face that world?

L

Computers—For Better and For Worse

EDWIN DOLIN

Human society undoubtedly derives, and will derive, great benefit from computer technology. Every day now, calculations necessary to medical research are being done by computers at astonishing rates of speed, a procedure that is increasing the likelihood of finding cures for serious illness. The use of computers in science, in particular their use in medical research, is pointed out first because medicine seems to be the area in which computer technology can be expected to do the most good for human beings. Certainly health, while not perhaps an absolutely essential prerequisite, is at least an important factor in the exercise of the imagination and skill which differentiate human activity from our fellow animals' instinctive search for food and shelter.

In fact, computers can be seen as simply an additional item in what anthropologists call *culture*, meaning by that word the whole panoply of techniques and tools which make human society distinct from that of other animals. As the prehistorian Grahame Clark has remarked, few paleontologists "would maintain that it is possible to distinguish on purely zoological grounds between those hominids that remained prehuman and those that had attained the status of man. To qualify as human, a hominid has, so to say, to justify himself by works. The criteria are no longer biological so much as cultural," and, he continues, it is the "transmission of the cultural heritage which alone distinguished men from other animals."[1]

37

Thus, from a perspective that looks at humanity as a part of all that is living or has lived, nothing is more decisively and characteristically human than technology, the development of tools which assist their users to live with at least some degree of foresight and control over their destiny.

Technology, therefore, including computer technology, instead of separating us from what we may think of as stone age, primitive and best-forgotten forms of our species, actually, from the perspective of biology, joins us to the palaeolithic hunter with his finely-formed flint handaxe and fire-hardened wooden spear. We are the toolmakers among the animals, and the invention of computers is perhaps, at the stage we are at now, less striking an intellectual achievement than was the development of the concept of how to make stone knives tens of thousands of years ago or the realization that fire could be manipulated for the hardening of spears, for cooking, for warmth and for defense against predators. Thus, since we are partly defined as the species of animal that invents tools, it is natural and probably inevitable that we devise and make use of computers, now that the progress of our ancient, inherited "culture" has put the means to do so at our disposal.

Misuse of Technology

But, given the naturalness of the development of computer technology, does it follow that all uses of computers will be *good* for us as a species? Quite obviously technology has been misused by humanity in the past, for example, in the case of explosives. Readers of *Gulliver's Travels* will recall how Swift depicts the horror of the king of Brobdingnag at the mere idea of explosives and their use in war. "Some evil genius," the king says, "enemy of mankind, must have been the first contriver" (Part II, Chapter VII). He commands Gulliver never to mention explosives again.

This one example, explosives, is enough to make the point that technology can undoubtedly be used for ill as well as for good. We may thus take it for granted that technology per se is not an unqualified good. Judgment and self-restraint are essential with regard to any technology, if its potential for harm is to be kept within bounds.

Two Categories of Misuse

What of computers? What possibilities do they pose of dangerous or improper use? We might tentatively divide these possibilities of misuse into two broad categories, one comprising criminal activities and the other comprising noncriminal activities that, nevertheless, are dangerous to the health of the body politic.

Criminal Misuse

There is something vaguely comic about conversion of a computer to criminal ends, at least when these criminal ends are confined to moneymaking. Something of a game atmosphere seems to be involved, as when a gambler thinks up a way to beat the system in Las Vegas. If a programmer now and then is clever enough to outwit something so important and establishmentarian as a *computer*, we are perhaps inclined to admire him as an heroic figure and wish we could do the same. Recently, a programmer is said to have directed his company's computer to put any fraction of a cent that turned up during daily transactions into a special account which the computer was instructed to "forget." The programmer reportedly succeeded with this scheme for a long time before he was caught. Those fractions of a cent, in a major business, add up fast.

Another story, this one not hearsay, but from the media, has to do with an accountant who got himself one million dollars by programming the computer to record higher payments for raw materials than the company was actually paying; the excess cash went into the accounts of dummy companies. This accountant even built into his program an instruction to let him know how much he could withdraw from the dummy accounts without attracting attention.[2]

The total annual loss through this form of computer crime is put at $300 million,[3] a small sum compared to what the future probably holds, when there will be more computers and when the device known as Electronic Funds Transfer System is in widespread use. Electronic funds transfer, if it actually is set up, will tend to eliminate cash. Payment will be by means of individual plastic cards that can be used at terminals in retail establishments or in one's home phone. The charges will be handled by a computerized network constantly adjusting one's bank account. Elimination of the problem of cash, dirty old coins and bills, is an enticing prospect. On the other hand, there would then exist a complete record of one's financial transactions at a central location, a record available to anyone who could get at it. Perhaps more serious, a computer technician obviously could get away with enormous amounts of money in an electronic funds transfer system. No matter what the security measures—voice-prints, fingerprints, what-have-you—the challenge would find people who could overcome the obstacles. The same people who are clever enough to devise systems will be clever enough to get around the safeguards that are supposed to protect the systems. Besides greed, the simple sporting aspect of computer crime is probably going to turn out to be an irresistible lure.

A trivial and simple, but instructive, example is offered of the power of technological devices to challenge people, particularly specialists, to combat. To prevent theft libraries have developed a magnetism-sensitive tape fitted into a book. If someone tries to leave the library without checking out a book properly, the tape sets off an alarm and locks the exit gate. This is reportedly an effective device, but attempts to beat it are most often made at engineering colleges, where students see the system as a challenge to their professional capacity.[4] If students are intrigued by this elementary sport, think what heights they will soar to when confronted by the challenge of a computer!

Noncriminal Misuse

A humanist's response to computer crime of this sort is probably going to be along the line that, while antisocial, it is not so serious a misuse of the new technology as is, potentially, the noncriminal type. The potential for noncriminal misuse of computers is connected with their claim to a mysterious and imposing authority, an authority based on the idea, widespread among the uninitiated, that computers are not only accurate calculators but also somehow capable of thinking for themselves on a scale beyond the grasp of the human mind. As remarked by a weekly news magazine, "people tend to accept any computer printout as sacred truth."[5] The word *sacred* conveys the quasi-religious veneration that is directed toward this piece of technology.

Spurious Authority

Such an atmosphere of authority can cloud the discussion of scholarly issues, even where one might think the intellectual sophistication of those involved would be proof against the emanations of divinity surrounding computers. Consider the case of *Time on the Cross*,[6] the recent important and controversial book on the question of the efficiency of slavery in the antebellum South. The book's findings are based, in part, on very expensive computer work. Many people were impressed by the statements regarding the alleged economic efficiency of slave labor, largely because these statements were claimed to be based on lengthy and painstaking computer calculations. Then along came numerous critiques of the book's computations by other experts with equal credentials who asserted that the authors of *Time on the Cross* were wrong, precisely where they seemed most authoritatively right, in their figures.[7]

The lesson is obvious. The fact that scholars say they have reached their results through the use of computers is no reason to consider the case as proved. One must wait until other experts indicate whether the input was adequate to the problem, well thought out and correctly programmed.

Credulity of Businessmen

Even hard-headed, pragmatic, bottom-line businessmen are apparently susceptible to this naive impulse to believe in the omnipotence and omniscience of computers. In a letter to *The New York Times* the president of a computer company points out that, contrary to the opinion of some, stock exchange specialists and floor brokers could not be replaced by a computer. The writer, in describing an imprudent faith placed in computers by some businessmen, remarks that "the data-processing industry has been justifiably criticized in the past for being too ambitious in applying its systems expertise to non-routine tasks. In many of these cases, after great expense no significant cost savings were realized and the quality of service was not improved."[8]

Earlier in his letter this computer specialist makes what seems to be a crucial point. "A computer, while working at incredible speed, can only respond to the instructions of its programmers and it cannot take even the simplest step without these precise directions. Consequently it can apply no test of reasonableness unless that test has been previously specified and programmed."

These two cases of susceptibility to the authority image of computer technology among scholars and businessmen are relatively trivial. They were brought up merely to illustrate the existence of a quasi-mystical attitude toward computers even where one might least expect it. More serious is what might happen if certain developments in the psychology of human development are pushed to extremes.

Specialists in the area of infant psychology have been challenging the idea that newborn babies are almost totally incapable of perceiving and understanding the world around them. These scientists have gone so far in the assertion of the innate activity and individuality of babies as to claim possession of the data and theory necessary to project the basic personality traits of an infant seven days old, including how he or she will react with the environment. In connection with this research the experts have developed what they refer to as a "neonatal behavior scale" to help make this projection of basic personality traits together with a prediction of style of interaction with the environment.[9]

Personality Typing

This research is probably on the right track and is not itself at issue here. However, one could be concerned about its possible application along the following lines. A "neonatal behavior scale" and other devices are used to type infants of seven days or two months or the like. The accuracy of the typing is defended on the grounds that thousands, even millions, of pieces of data have been put into a computer to produce a so-called sophisticated discrimination between variables and so forth. The infant is then assigned to a certain personality type with an authoritative-sounding piece of nomenclature—perhaps an impressive looking code with numerals, letters and other symbols. On the basis of this typing, decisions are then made about the child, for example, what kind of toys he or she should have to compensate for or enhance supposed personality defects or advantages or what sort of attitudes toward the child the parents should adopt under given circumstances. Later, one style of nursery school or another and one style of academic training or another would be prescribed on the basis of computer-assisted personality typing and prediction of interaction with the environment. The result of all this could be a self-fulfilling prophecy. The child could, in effect, be getting the message that he or she was expected by everyone to act a certain way and do a certain thing. We could be programming people. Rather, we could be trying to do so. But so great is the need for faith in a scientific method for making children good, happy and productive that there may be a movement to turn the job of bringing children up over to those great authority figures, the scientists, and their authoritative apparatus, the computer. This is a danger that should resolutely be guarded against, because whatever "neonatal behavior scale" or the like is developed, no system for typing infants and children will be able to avoid oversimplification and bias. Any such system will just be one more scheme to impose the ideas of a self-chosen group of experts on the rest of society.

Dubious Use in Strategy

There is one final danger from the authority image of computers. This has to do with the role of computer data-storage and calculation in the planning and execution of national defense policy. It is obvious that, while computers can be of immense help in logistics and weaponry, they are positively dangerous in the area of strategy.

Let us remember the words of the letter to *The New York Times* quoted above: "A computer, while working at incredible speed, can only respond to the instructions of the programmers and it cannot take even the simplest step without these precise directions. Consequently it can apply no test of reasonableness unless that test has been previously specified and programmed."

The application to defense policy is plain. The computer will produce the results that are put into it by the strategists who devise the program. Even with every safeguard against bias the subjective element in a program of this type is unavoidable. The public that puts its faith in a national policy because it is told that this policy is based on conclusions confirmed by computer technology will be deceived. Perhaps the public will never be asked to base its confidence on such a faith. But we should remember the longing of human nature to be consoled and reassured. And each one of us has a human nature.

A humanist, mindful of the complexity and weakness as well as of the strength of human nature, will take his or her stand against any movement to put one's trust in computer technology. Human beings, who have created computers along with the rest of technology, are too complicated to be measured, "understood" or forecast by this or any tool.

One of human nature's well-known aspects is the inclination to find gods in peculiar places. The computer is not, perhaps, the most likely candidate for a new god. But the future always produces surprises. A humanistic response to the prospect of our complicated future and its technological development is to warn as resoundingly as possible against false and deceiving gods.[10]

PART III

THE COMPUTER AND PEOPLE

The chapters in this section explore the more subtle philosophical and psychological issues raised by computer technology. Robert Bergmark, a philosopher, considers the role of computers in a humane society in the context of the age-old philosophical question of the distinction between persons and things. Tom Kibler, from his background in computer work, explores person-machine relations and the role that fear plays in the acceptance of new inventions and technologies. From the perspective of a linguist, Roger Johnson examines the appeal of the computer-generated printout as a functional communication device but also as an object with certain aesthetic qualities and appeals. Arlene Schrade explores the effects of technology in creating an expanded role for woman in society and in making possible a better quality of life for all humankind

In Chapter 5 Bergmark expands his argument that the debate over the proper role of computers in society is often a debate over the proper role of persons in society. He urges that computers should be recognized as the tools they are—spectacular tools, to be sure, but tools nonetheless—and used as such. They should be used to enhance the quality of human life, not debase nor dehumanize it. Computers can provide vastly improved means for carrying out human ends. However, Bergmark asserts, only persons can determine what those ends ought to be, and only persons can feel the weight of responsibility for making that determination.

45

Kibler, in Chapter 6, begins with the observation that in the Western world, acceptance of and dependence on machines and machine products has often occurred without people's conscious awareness. Yet there have always been people who have fought against the use and growth of various mechanical devices. As individuals and as groups, however, we no longer ask if all machines or if science in general are good or evil, but instead ask if a specific device is the best one, in the best form, for our particular purpose. This finer questioning, rather than general condemnation, asserts Kibler, comes from a better understanding of various machines and their capabilities. However, each major invention and scientific discovery brings with it some of the old fear of the new and unknown. Computers are an example of an invention that has brought back some of our fear.

In Chapter 7, Johnson asks, "Is the medium really the message, as Marshall McLuhan figured?" In applying this question to the computer generated data profile he notes that, as a means for communicating, it has, among other qualities, something to tell and a way of telling it. Besides being useful and thus attractive automatically to those who value utility, the printout is a functional representation, a mimetic object. Thus, Johnson asserts, at the same time that the printout is a tool, it is also a plaything, a gratifying object, with traditional aesthetic qualities and appeals. He explores the attractiveness of the printout from three aspects which it shares with the appeal of certain kinds of poetry.

In Chapter 8, Schrade pursues the idea that woman's expanded role in society is based upon the maxims of cultural anthropology, science/technology and the prevision–decision sciences. She focuses particularly on implications for the role of the individual woman, both physically and psychologically, and on the necessary adaptive and coping mechanisms in a highly technological society.

5

Computers and Persons

ROBERT E. BERGMARK

We live in a troubled society. The symptoms are many and the diagnoses varied, but they who would insist that all is well would immediately have their judgment, if not their sanity, called into question. We agree that all is not well; we disagree on the causes that have brought us to our present condition and on the steps that need now to be taken to rescue us from this condition.

Our special task here is to ask in what ways and to what extent our technological civilization in general, and computer technology in particular, has contributed to our troubles, and how such technology can be controlled in the future, and indeed made use of, as we undertake the task of working toward a more humane society.

1. Persons and Things: Socrates versus Democritus

At the very heart of our problem lies an issue that is as old as our civilization itself. It has to do with what it means, basically, to be a person rather than a thing. It was Democritus in Greece in the fifth century B.C. who, in a position paper, laid the foundation for all future science and technology: the world is a world of things, not persons; of quantities, not qualities; of mechanistically understood events, not meanings or purposes or values. According to such a view a person is an outgrowth, a product, an epiphenomenon of the world of things. The world consists of matter in motion.

But Socrates, a contemporary of Democritus, had difficulty in accepting such an assumption, and it was Socrates who laid the foundation for all future humanistic belief: the qualities and dimensions of human life found in experiences of love, of commitment, of duty, of mutual trust, of values, are not reducible to the world of things, but somehow the world of things is infused with possibilities of actualization of the true, the beautiful, and the good. According to such a view a person, in the midst of his web of meanings, purposes, and values, is a significant clue to what the world is all about. Persons are what matter. Things are to be used by persons in the pursuit of humane ends.

For the past four hundred years, ever since the new birth of science in the work of such persons as Kepler, Copernicus, and Galileo, educated people have found themselves choosing sides between Democritus and Socrates, between a mechanistic world view and a humanistic world view, between science and the humanities, between physics and poetry. Thus, when now we seek to determine what sort of impact computer technology has upon our society, it is no isolated issue we raise, and any worthwhile answer to the question must surely deal with it in this larger context.

The followers of Democritus have no difficulty in coming to terms with the computer. It is a machine, but so are they, and so is the world. They speak of computers as constituting a "new species" with which the human species must "cooperate."[1] They speak of "intelligent machines" and "artificial intelligence."[2] They speak of machines that "learn" and "solve problems."[3] But why not? A brain is a computer and a computer is a brain. The world consists of various energy systems which differ from one another in the final analysis only quantitatively, and quantities constitute the grist of computer mills.

The followers of Socrates, however, find it easy to feel threatened by the computer. Unable and unwilling to assume that a brain is a computer and a computer is a brain, and insisting upon the significance of qualities of human experience that have not at this point been reduced meaningfully simply to quantities, they read the literature on the computer written by the followers of Democritus and they fear for the future of human society.

2. *Computer Literature and Its Problems*

Indeed, it is this literature on computers and not computers themselves that arouses this sense of dread and foreboding. Computerization has meant the elimination of many tedious tasks, easy and rapid access to immense quantities of all kinds of information, and elaborate and complex computation without which, for example, there could have been no travel to the moon. Computers in one field after another have provided us with tremendously improved means for accomplishing our ends. But only persons can determine which ends are worth pursuing. Computers cannot handle that problem. Thoreau, when told of the invention of the telephone and the telegraph, called them improved means to unimproved ends. The computer is an amazingly improved means for doing quite a variety of jobs, but the evaluation of the quality of the ends lies outside the province of the computer's competency.

But the literature seems to suggest that the computer is in the process of displacing persons. Alvin Toffler, for example, views "progress" of science and technology as inevitable, and persons must simply adapt or perish.[4] Technology and the demands of engineering determine what must be done, and human beings must comply. This is what causes "future shock." Toffler is a devoted follower of Democritus. To be a human being is to be a body. To be a body is to be a machine with replaceable parts. What can be done determines what will be done. If we can colonize Mars, then we will colonize Mars, whether or not it will serve humane ends. If we can develop human beings with gills for living under water, then we will do it regardless of the ends served. If we can manipulate genetic codes, it will be done. If we can create machines that will make decisions for us, we will abdicate in their favor.

Commenting on such an understanding of how the future will unfold, Philip Slater writes, "Leaders of alien civilizations in space fantasies often have motives that seem hilariously trivial, but the joke is on us since those fantasies are simply projections of our own culture. It is in *our* culture that people's lives are threatened or destroyed because some unknown person is consumed with dispassionate scientific curiosity, or mechanically carrying out some bureaucratic procedure, or obeying an order whose premises have been forgotten."[5]

An even more dramatic illustration of this type of literature appeared recently in *The New York Times*. In February, 1976, in its magazine section, *The New York Times* carried an article with the title, "When the Computer Procreates."[6] Combining prurient appeal with scarc tactics, the title seemed to meet the standard of the usual Sunday supplement feature. But *The New York Times Magazine* is not the usual Sunday supplement, and the author of the article, Jeremy Bernstein, is not without credentials in the field of physics.[7] Bernstein, after reviewing at length the work of Turing and von Neumann in their attempt to develop "thinking machines," says, "The most profound impact of the computer on society may not be as much in what it can do in practice, impressive though this is, as in what the machine *is* in theory, and less to do with its capacity as calculator than with its capacity for self-replication."[8] Warming to such a thesis, and allowing his imagination to run at will, even while giving the impression that he is writing as a scientist, Bernstein says, "It now seems conceivable—in principle, at least—that perhaps with the addition of some primitive biological components (who knows what!), the process can be further developed to the stage where self-reproducing automatons can be made that are compact and, acting in concert, can do just about anything."[9]

What is the lay reader to think when he reads such material? He certainly must believe that inevitably, in the not too distant future, human beings will be confronted with a new species of self-producing automatons, far more intelligent and far more powerful than humans, and with whom persons must either learn to accommodate or become extinct. This is certainly the sort of thinking on which science fiction, such as the film "2001," thrives, but is it scientific?

Joseph Weizenbaum, Professor of Computer Science at Massachusetts Institute of Technology, responding to Bernstein's article, calls that article "a fundamentally harmful contribution to the science and society debate."[10] Weizenbaum objects to the suggestion of the inevitability of such a technological development and points out that Bernstein does not argue for such inevitability on the basis of scientific developments but simply asserts it as though he had received it by divine revelation. Such a development will arise not because some society wants it, according to Bernstein, but simply because it is going to happen. In the face of this, Weizenbaum asks, "Is it really so astonishing that ordinary people feel powerless in the face of a science and technology for whose course scientists themselves acknowledge no responsibility and which they themselves characterize as self-determining?"[11]

Essentially, Weizenbaum is claiming that the article by Bernstein is fraudulent. "It is simply and plainly not true *in any sense*," says Weizenbaum, "that real computing machines are now almost self-replicating. Nor is it at all clear that, even if we wanted to achieve it, we could ever build practical self-replicating computers."[12] Weizenbaum, himself a computer scientist, is not willing to abandon Socrates and follow Democritus. Persons matter. Persons need to plan for their own well-being and for the well-being of other persons. The world is not simply a series of mechanistic events, with all events completely explainable in terms of antecedent events. Rather, persons have responsibilities for themselves and for their societies.

Fred Hapgood, commenting on the literature of the past fifteen years which has grossly exaggerated the capabilities of computers, and citing the story entitled "Latest Machines See, Hear, Speak and Sing—And May Outthink Man," which appeared in the June 1973 issue of the *Wall Street Journal*, writes, "What is striking about these stories is the determination of their authors to believe. They seem never to notice the highly artificial environments or the extremely simplified nature of the problems which allow the computer programs they describe to show even the modest success they have to date."[13]

One of the more brilliant exposés of the hyperbolic nature of much computer literature, and one of the earliest, is the book by

Mortimer Taube, *Computers and Common Sense: The Myth of Thinking Machines*.[14] In this book he deals with such problems as mechanical translation from one language to another, machine learning, and linguistic analysis. He recognizes that much of the work of the human mind as well as of the human hand can be mechanized but that machines can deal only with that which can be mechanized. He rejects the basic thesis of Democritus that persons are nothing but atoms in motion, even as he rejects the nineteenth century materialism of Ernst Haeckel who, in *Riddle of the Universe*, saw persons as nothing but an epiphenomenon of the physical order described by Newton, and as he likewise rejects the twentieth-century materialism which sees persons as nothing but highly complex digital computers. Such "nothing but" theories replace one another *seriatim* and seem always doomed to a relatively short life. It is worthy of note that Alfred North Whitehead, after working for more than fifty years with mathematics, logic, and scientific theory, rejected all "nothing but" theories and developed a philosophy of organism which emphasized not disparate events but process, not isolated parts atomistically understood but wholeness, not a mechanical concept of linear cause and effect but a total organism of interrelated dynamic activity.

3. Computers Are Not Persons Nor Are Persons Computers

Joseph Weizenbaum expresses considerable concern over the negative effects of the computer on society and cautions the computer scientist against exaggerating its accomplishments. "Most of the harm computers can potentially entrain," says Weizenbaum, "is much more a function of properties people attribute to computers than of what a computer can or cannot actually be made to do. The nonprofessional has little choice but to make his attributions of properties to computers on the basis of the propaganda emanating from the computer community and amplified by the press. The computer professional therefore has an enormously important responsibility to be modest in his claims."[15] More than this, Weizenbaum warns against substituting a mechanistic perspective for a humanistic one. If questions are always put in mechanistic and technological terms, their answers will be given in mechanistic and technological terms. If answers are to be humane, then the questions to be asked had better arise out of a humanistic perspective and have to do with the basic issues of human values, human meanings, human purposes, and human ends. Writes Weizenbaum, "The fundamental question the computer scientist must ask himself is the one that every scientist, indeed every human, must ask. It is not 'what shall I do?' but rather 'what shall I be?'" Socrates would concur wholeheartedly. (Such an act of wholehearted concurrence, by the way, is not possible for computers. Computers may concur, in a sense, but never wholeheartedly. Only persons can act wholeheartedly.)

May Brodbeck, in her presidential address to a meeting of the American Philosophical Association did a brilliant job in drawing the distinction between computers and persons, between robots and humans.

Consciousness alone distinguishes men from machines. Men have reasons for their behavior. Without consciousness, there is neither freedom nor morality. Freedom is a moral ideal because the *feeling* of freedom is desired by men. When all is said and done, and there is much to be said and done, the last appeal is to the effects of the actions on the inner life of man. Morality is only applicable to beings that suffer and enjoy, that consciously prefer one state of affairs to another. A moral agent acts and knows that he acts. A robot merely acts. A robot may exhibit choice-behavior, but it has no preferences. Since it has no feelings, it doesn't really care. A man cares. To make a moral choice is to choose consciously among alternatives that have consequences for human sentiments. A robot can kill a man, but it cannot sin. It cannot violate a moral law, because it cannot consciously act in accordance with one. It literally does not know what it is doing. We do not forgive it for this, for we do not judge it at all. We do not punish a robot, though we may destroy one. A robot is not free because it cannot literally choose to do one thing rather than another. Neither is it unfree. It can be prevented from doing something but it cannot be forced to act against its will, because it has no will. A robot can do everything a man can do. But it cannot be everything a man can be. It cannot, in particular, be conscious. That we know, as well as we know anything in this life and on this earth.[16]

4. Computers Are Tools To Be Used By and For Persons

At the beginning of this article we said that our task was to ask in what ways and to what extent our technological civilization in general, and computer technology in particular, have contributed to the troubles we face in society, and how such technology can be controlled in the future, and indeed made use of, as we undertake the task of working toward a more humane society. We have dealt implicitly with this task. It is now time to be explicit.

At least a portion of the difficulty we find ourselves in as a society is a result of listening to Democritus and neglecting Socrates. The Democritus outlook encourages us to develop a thing-perspective toward the world, toward ourselves, and toward other persons. Such an outlook encourages us to develop societies with an overwhelming concern for property values. It encourages us to measure success in terms of possession of things rather than humane relationship with other persons. It makes it possible for us to refer to computer capability as "intelligence," computer programming as "learning," computer printouts as "decision-making." It makes it possible to depersonalize and dehumanize the whole fabric of political, economic, and social activity.

At least a portion of the solution to our difficulty is to begin paying more attention to Socrates. The Socrates outlook encourages us to be concerned about persons, their joys and sorrows, their fulfillments and their frustrations, their pleasures and their pains, and their search for meaning and purpose in their lives. It encourages us to develop societies that are supportive of humane living rather than concerned exclusively with bank accounts and the gross national product. It makes it possible for us to agree with John Dewey who said over half a century ago, "Government, business, art, religion, all social institutions have a meaning, a purpose. That purpose is to set free and to develop the capacities of human individuals without respect to race, sex, class or economic status."[17]

The computer is a tool. It is a spectacular tool, to be sure, but nonetheless a tool. It is not a person. It is not involved with meanings, purposes, and values in the sense in which persons are. Tools can be used by persons for good or evil ends. The computer can be used for spectacular good or spectacular evil. Whether it is put to good or evil use is not dependent upon computer technology as such, but rather upon the quality of the society, and the quality of the persons in that society, in which the computer is found. The problem we face is the age-old problem of developing a society in which personal character will be nurtured and supported. The presence of the computer makes the development of an adequate solution to that problem spectacularly urgent.

6

While Debating
the Philosophy
We Accept the Practice

TOM R. KIBLER

In 1832, *The Working Man's Companion No. I* was published. Its purpose was to explain why machines are helpful and good. A review of the book, published by the *North American Review*, opens with the question, "Is the influence of machines on society good or evil?" In 1832, this was a valid question. Today, however, this question is no longer meaningful. The question is no longer meaningful because the Western world is so permeated with machines and machine products that it is impossible to conceive of going back to a totally nonmachine age.

There have always been people who have fought against the use and growth of various mechanical devices. In the mid-nineteenth century people fought against the steam engine. At the turn of the century it was the automobile and a little later, after the Wright Brothers, the airplane. "If God wanted man to drive, fly, etc., He would have . . . " was the rallying cry of those who raged against the evils of mechanical advances.

But while in books—like Mrs. Shelley's *Frankenstein*, songs—like "John Henry, the steel-drivin' man," and legislation— like the Connecticut law that all horseless carriages must be preceded by a man carrying a red lantern—individuals have fought against machines and science, in real life the gadgets developed by science have been accepted. While people were debating the good and evils of the automobile, they were using the mechanical apple peeler.

While the use of airplanes was debated, electric refrigerators and electric lights became commonplace. While the values of nuclear reactors are argued, microwave ovens are used.

Although most individuals use the gadgets and eventually accept the major scientific advances, there are groups who reject technology with the fever of religion, often in fact incorporating their rejection as part of their religion. Interestingly enough, none of these groups rejects all technology, but rather pick and choose those aspects of technology that they wish to reject and those they wish to accept. The Amish reject electric and gasoline power but accept and use steam power. Christian Scientists reject modern medicine but accept the rest of our mechanical society. Even the organic farmer rejecting chemical fertilizers, pesticides and herbicides is accepting tractors and other mechanized farming tools.

The point is that we, as individuals and as groups, no longer ask if all machines, or science in general, are good or evil, but instead ask if a specific device is the best one, in the best form, for our particular purpose. This finer questioning, rather than general condemnation, comes from our better understanding of various machines and sciences and their capabilities. However, each major invention and scientific discovery brings with it some of the old fear of the new and unknown. Computers are an example of an invention that has brought back some of our fear.

II

The stored program computer was first developed in the late 1940s, but the fear of computers did not begin until the early 1960s, and the real concern for the social impact of computers did not begin until the early 1970s. Much of the reason for the delay has been the "behind the scenes" nature of the computer. However, in the 25 years it has taken society to develop a serious concern about computers, they have become a firmly rooted fixture in our society, and even more importantly they have become an indispensable tool.

In the mid–1940s when von Neumann and a few others were

doing the initial development work on the first computers, the ENIAC and the EDVAC, their goal was not to develop the general information tool that is today's computer, but rather to develop a specialized mathematical tool to aid in the solution of series of equations. These first computers were developed, under the impetus of World War II, to solve ballistic research problems.

However, because of their large size and cost, the early computers stayed primarily in research corporations, government installations and very large businesses, far from the public view. It wasn't until the early 1960s with the introduction of the IBM 1401 and 1620 families of computers that computers started to impinge on our daily lives.

The 1401 and 1620 families of computers were small business and scientific computers that dealt with such business practices as payrolls and inventory control. About 16,000 of these machines were sold between 1960 and 1964 (Bell and Newell, 1971). It was with the introduction of these and similar machines that many people's lives began to be touched by the "output" of computers.

Thus, while science fiction writers were inventing gigantic scientific computers that could rule the world, it was the small business computers, doing payrolls and gas bills, that touched the lives of most individuals. It was these small machines, programmed by experienced and often not so experienced programmers, that first brought to our language such phrases as "the computer made an error"; "we have had to do it that way because the computer requires it"; and "it will take longer because the computer is down." It was the fictional stories of computers running amuck, as did HAL in the movie "2001," and the use of the word *computer* for a collection of human mistakes that brought about doubt as to whether people controlled computers or computers controlled people.

Furthermore, it is impossible for people to believe that complex computers can be reliable when the less complex machines they are familiar with are so unreliable. How can a computer guide a rocket to the moon when the Coke machine steals my dime? How can the IRS program a computer to properly evaluate my tax return when the auto mechanic can't fix my car so it doesn't stall? If companies can't build a color television that doesn't produce green people, how can they produce a computer that gives the right answer?

But we have landed men on the moon and have landed automated probes on Mars. Thus, obviously, we can produce machines which have a high degree of accuracy and reliability if necessary. Further, the ground computers which have made space flight possible are the same computers which do payrolls and checking accounts. The difference is in the price we put on accuracy and reliability. Business views its consumers as much more willing and able to put up with mistakes than does NASA. Thus NASA puts in the effort and money to have reliable, error-free machines while others don't.

III

NASA and the space program have given people more than the realization that computers can be as reliable and as error-free as people care to make them. Another by-product of the space program has been the miniaturization of the electronics needed for onboard operation of spacecraft. This miniaturization, and the corresponding price reduction, has led to widespread acceptance of computers and computer-dependent devices. The ENIAC, which weighed 30 tons, occupied several rooms and had tremendous "fear power," had essentially the same computation power as the Hewlett-Packard 65, which weighs 11 ounces, easily fits in the palm of a hand and has little or no "fear power" (*Datamation*, June, 1974, p. 26).

Miniaturized stored logic devices are becoming as commonplace as can openers, electric razors and toasters. We find digital watches everywhere—giving not only accurate time but dates, elapsed time and simple math calculations. Automobiles have small computers to improve gas mileage and lower pollution emission. Most new large buildings use small computers to monitor heating and air conditioning in order to save fuel costs. Hospitals use minicomputers to monitor the critically ill and to help perform and analyze laboratory tests. Mini- and microcomputers are becoming so common that no one gives them a second thought.

IV

Widespread acceptance of small computer devices and the ability to build relatively error-free systems—if we choose—does not mean automation is without problems. There are still a number of areas of computer use that demand concern. These problem areas are not inherent in computers but rather are problem areas that have already existed but are magnified by the ease with which computers manipulate and store information.

Privacy is just such an area. Privacy has always been a concern in this country. Federal and local governments have always maintained information on their citizens. Computers just make it easier to maintain and distribute large volumes of information. Thus, computers make easier both the use and the abuse of large data files.

Electronic funds transfer is another possible problem area. Ever since the invention of the telegraph and the telephone, it has been possible to transact limited amounts of banking by wire. Credit cards have eased much of the need for carrying cash. However, with the advent of the computer and the computer network, it is now becoming possible to develop a completely cashless and checkless society. There seems to be nothing inherently good or evil about electronic funds transfer; however, it is a change which has much social impact and needs to be considered on its own merits.

While there are problem areas dealing with computer use, there are also areas in which computers are needed and have not been applied to their full potential. While computers will continue to promote change in our society, numerous other factors are also promoting change. Many of these factors are complex and have far-reaching effects: the relationship among increasing population, food supply and decreasing fuel supplies; or the interactions of pests, pesticides, food supply and environment.

These and many other problems are not amenable to simple armchair analysis. J. Forrester (1969) has suggested that many of these problems may be counter-intuitive, that what seems to be the best solution can often be the worst. For example, when one has a pest the intuitive reaction of many is to apply a pesticide. If the pest gets worse you apply more pesticide. But, as the gypsy moth problem in New England has amply shown, the application of pesticides often can have a greater impact on a pest's predators than on the pest and, therefore, can actually make the problem worse. Only by the analysis of the actual factors involved can one understand a problem and make a reasonable decision as to a solution.

Computers can be useful in this analysis because of their capacity for the manipulation and tabulation of data. However, the capacity of computers to simulate or model complex relationships will have a much greater importance in decisionmaking in the future. For to model or simulate a problem means that one must understand the interaction of the factors involved. Thus, computer simulation can help people to understand complex problems and to point to possible solutions.

While concern is definitely warranted in a number of areas—some because computer use is too prevalent and others because it is too limited—we have, nonetheless, come to accept the computer and perhaps take it for granted. Thus, while the debate goes on as to the social impact of computers, we have become a society dependent on the computer.

7

Printout Appeal

ROGER JOHNSON, JR.

"Do you like computer printouts?"

"What do you mean, 'like them'? I use them in my job. They are part of my job, tools."

"What if printouts suddenly became unavailable? How would you feel?"

"I suppose we could manage, but less effectively, less efficiently. I couldn't get a handle on things as quickly. Nobody could. But the question is wrong. You don't 'like' or 'dislike' a piece of paper with numbers and charts on it. You just use it if it helps get the job done."

"It has to be accurate?"

"Of course. If it weren't, it wouldn't be any good at all. They say 'garbage in, garbage out,' and it's a fact."

"Does it have to be clear?"

"Depends on who is reading it. Yes, it ought to be clear, unambiguous. But what is clear to one person might not be to another."

"Pertinent?"

"Well, it might be informative in a general way, but, yes, a printout would have to bear on a set of data or nobody would ask for it. You don't just go to the computer people and say, 'Tell me all about what we're doing this year.' You ask for specific information. When the information comes, it's automatically pertinent."

This dialogue is a fairly accurate composite of several conversations between me and persons in positions of management who regularly use computer-generated data profiles. Would that undergraduate students of literature could respond with the same sort of no-nonsense answers, rejecting the like-or-dislike distinction and seeing clearly the status, effect, virtues, intention and limitations of the thing under discussion. Of course the question of liking or disliking is too superficial to be permanently interesting, whether applied to a computer printout, a short story or a hamburger, for the question rarely yields information about the object under scrutiny, but rather about the person. For example, when someone says that he does like baroque art, he has revealed nothing about that style of art but has said something very definite about himself. This is an observation worth remembering in the following discussion, as is the composite dialogue, since it touches on a number of the qualities of a data profile that give the object its appeal.

Is there indeed any such thing as "printout appeal"? The answer must be affirmative for this analysis to continue, but the answer is neither obvious nor universal. Many persons who use printouts seem to reject the question or to answer it negatively. The widespread presence of the things has nothing to do with appeal, they assert, but rather with utility. The rejoinder is that utility has an appeal and that the printout is forever wed to the value system that affirms utility. Furthermore the printout is a real document, admittedly not the system or reality being managed, but a functional representation, a mimesis, of that reality. No one seriously believes that money lacks appeal because it only represents another, somehow more real, accumulation of valued items. On the contrary and despite the well-intentioned efforts of economics teachers, the bills and coins themselves have tremendous appeal, as does a well-written history book, which is, after all, merely an organized reflection of the larger reality. The appeal of the book, money, the printout or almost any other mimetic object is clearly wrapped up with our interest in what the thing represents, but our interest is often focused and maintained by the organizing power of the thing doing the representing. Neither the larger reality nor our handle on it can be entirely isolated.

The appeal of the computer-generated data profile to managers is based on its utility to them, but not limited to utility. At the same time that the printout is a tool, it is also a plaything, a gratifying object, with traditional esthetic qualities and appeals. The attractiveness of the printout has three bases to be discussed here:

1. It includes a "self," an image of its creator.

2. It has utility within the system where it occurs and a set of conventions that signal esthetically the quality of utility.

3. It makes concrete and portable the values, perceptions and presuppositions of the system that causes its generation.

The appeal of the data printout shares its bases with the appeal of certain kinds of poetry, so that the data profile turns out to be suspiciously like a poem in several respects. This is a most disturbing analogy for some managers who use printouts regularly, but the disturbance rests in a misconception of poetry. Strangely enough for the uninitiated, the analogy seems satisfying to programmers. The partial identification of printout and poetry is a telling one, and refinement of it will yield valuable information about the nature and limitations of computer-generated information. We can begin with the first basis of appeal and take up the others in order.

The Personal Touch

Putting "self" into a product is a familiar but somewhat mysterious process. There is currently in this country a craze for antiques, or simply for old furniture and objects. As these items become more difficult to obtain, there is a movement toward setting high value on handmade furniture, handcrafted pottery and tapestry, and the like. We value these objects partly because there is or was someone who put himself into the production of them. The care, conscientious love and pride of the skilled cabinetmaker become incorporated in the fine table he fashions for himself, and all of these are somehow perceived by the person who seeks out the table and treasures it. This kind of value is largely esthetic, and it need not be sentimental. For example, there is great appeal in some tools, an appeal that derives from the consideration that went into their design and production: wood chisels, good handsaws, articulated socket wrenches, putty knives, professional paint brushes, even the Fuller Brush broom and certainly any efficient can opener.

Computer people also can put themselves into their product, and the audience or user can perceive the care, concern and—above all—cleverness of the person who designed and produced the data profile he holds in his hand. Frederick Brooks, the "Father of the IBM/360," wrote that a programmer takes great joy in his work, an emotion ranging from the simple joy of making things, through the complicated satisfaction of working out puzzles, to what he calls "the delight of working in such a tractable medium."[1] When the originator of the program that handles the data attaches such value to his work, then that value stays with the process and is incorporated in the final product, the profile itself. How does this happen? Perhaps in no more than the user's fleeting notice of clarity in presentation, his gratification that misleading averages or whatever were not included or were given subordinate positions in the final array, that, in short, "they took some care with this one."

Not all such value is communicated naively. Some computer people are much aware of the appeal of the instrument that finally reaches the hand and eye of the user, and they are at times disturbed by the awkwardness and unattractiveness of their alphanumeric communication with management. Graphics may come to the rescue, giving a more appealing product, and such modes may also be employed quite self-consciously, as is revealed in this exhortation: "The use of graphics may become the key to involving management and other personnel in computer operations, because the dialogue can be made simple, fluent, and seductive."[2] One thinks of a medieval bishop presenting his message through the commission of a stained glass window or a pietà, or Colgate pushing its latest toothpaste with pictures superficially "simple, fluent, and seductive," especially seductive.

A more subtle but no less attractive insertion of self into the computer printout is seen in the printout's inclusion of personal quirks and presuppositions derived from the programmer. Whether the inclusion is ultimately a positive or negative factor in making the end product appealing, it is obvious that it gives a human dimension to the document, one coming directly from the creator of the program. An example would be one of the many printouts from the program written by Jay W. Forrester dealing with urban growth and government. Forrester put together an apparently brilliant program to model urban dynamics and explained his procedures and conclusions in the book appropriately called *Urban Dynamics*. The trouble is that some of his conclusions rankled city planners of seemingly more liberal persuasion, since Forrester's innocent presuppositions would lead to a city heavily industrialized, with high-cost housing, populated in the main by upper middle class managers and executives, with no welfare system to speak of and practically no unemployment. How does he arrive at this utopia? Very simply stated, he makes a model incorporating "the idea that—all other things being equal—a city which is more attractive for unskilled workers will tend to have more unskilled workers." In his view the healthy city has full employment and an absolute minimum average per capita tax rate. These simple presuppositions get incorporated in the conclusion, with startling results.[3]

Does this kind of study have esthetic appeal? It certainly does, and the more so for its inclusion of the personal bias of the programmer. Of course the work must be otherwise finely organized, but, as this remark by L. Kadnoff shows, the appeal is there: "Despite these criticisms of Forrester's conclusions, I would argue that his model-making is so brilliant and beautiful that his ideas are certainly worthy of examination and further development."[4] Kadnoff rejects the conclusions but accepts the model on esthetic grounds.

Obviously, when a programmer's values coincide with those of the user, the appeal will be more direct and the user's delight more pointed. To speak of this now, however, would be springing to the third basis of the printout's appeal before analyzing the basis of appeal found in utility. Suffice it to say for the inclusion of self in a printout that we all have a positive feeling for a job well done. Users, or anyone for that matter, appreciate care and cleverness evident in a thing, and they have a special affection for the aim that hits its mark.

The Appeal of Utility

In the dialogue between me and that hypothetical manager, I was hard pressed to make a distinction between utility and appeal. There is actually no reason to make such a distinction. In the first place, attractiveness can indeed have a strong element of the practical. In the second place, a special kind of appeal, esthetic appeal, and utility have always been partners, especially in the visual and tactile arts, where harmony of form and function is a traditional virtue. A cubic airplane would hardly be a beautiful one, nor would it fly very well; a wrench with a knobby handle would be both unpleasant to hold and awkward to use. A movie that did not give its audience the escape, thrill or insight it sought would be both useless and bad, and that latter conclusion would be an esthetic judgment. This is not to say that everything useful is also beautiful, but merely that in many instances the two qualities are closely related.

When we speak of something's being useful, we mean useful for some end, useful for bringing about some effect in the world around us, in other people or in ourselves. The data profile is almost universally assumed to be useful, as was illustrated in the initial dialogue. What is less recognized is the fact that objects often thought to have only esthetic appeal are or were likewise utilitarian. Recognition of this is very illuminating for understanding the status and appeal of the printout, for the printout is currently making a pilgrimage from work to play, from pure tool to pure art, a journey that will doubtless never reach an end but which has already begun.

Ancient peoples often sought to control nature with poetry and song, making rain fall or stop, making the ground or the women fertile, or curing ills at home while inflicting them on enemies. Old Saxon tribes used to recite a poem to get rid of pain in the abdomen. It began, "Come out worm, with your nine little worms. . . ." The whole verse enticed the worms out of the marrow, bones, flesh and skin. It was to be repeated, apparently three times, while the victim held a little box over the pain. At the end of the recitation, the box was snapped shut, tied to an arrow, and shot into the dark woods with the worm and its nine offspring, who were causing all the trouble.[5] South Sea islanders used to navigate great stretches of open water with the aid of chants passed down as oral poetry. Likewise the computer printout has the intent of affecting the world around us, organizing it and giving us a means, a handle, one often hears, for manipulating it.

When utility and esthetics come together, as in medical and navigational chants or in the religious poetry of Old Egypt, the art form begins to take on a more or less fixed aspect. It becomes rigid. This happens over a period of time and simply makes the information carried in the art form easier to recollect, more accessible. The set form is defined by so-called conventions, such as the convention of perspective in two-dimension art, the convention of beginning an epic in the middle of the action or the convention of rhyme in chants. In time the conventions become the mark of the art form or the tool, if the form still has utilitarian value, and the users or audience begin to value the conventions both for their own sake and for the accessibility to information they afford the audience through their inherent capacity to organize. Computer printouts have esthetic appeal in exactly the same sense that magic spells and chants do. Their conventions—the clear arrangement of figures in columns, for example, or the reduction to quantification, the bottom line, or the pretty green and white striped paper—signal the user that the needed information is present and accessible.[6] The real world can be managed, and here is the means by which to do it. Some of the conventions are, by the way, coincidentally similar to the conventions of magic formulas: both tend to be repetitive, compact, cryptic, stylized, and clear to the initiated but mysterious to outsiders. Users of printouts seek these conventions just as the viewer of a picture seeks the convention of pespective. If the expected convention is wanting, the object lacks—what shall we call it?—beauty.

Celebrating Values

The last basis of the printout's appeal is its making concrete the values, perceptions and presuppositions of the system that causes its production. Forrester's study, *Urban Dynamics*, was considered brilliant and beautiful by at least one person who strongly disagreed with the conclusions. Had Forrester's conclusions been more in line with reigning sentiment concerning the topic of his study, the study's appeal would have been immeasurably greater. It is simpleminded, however, to seek the basis of appeal in the plain conclusions of studies. We all like what agrees with us, but one would hardly be prone to value the data profile because in this or that instance it confirmed one's prejudices. Likely enough, the printout has demonstrated to every manager with much experience the inaccuracy of his personal conclusions drawn from insufficient data. Rather, the printout incorporates virtues that are more obtusely appealing to management.

In the composite dialogue, the manager was quick to see and point out the characteristics of the data profile that make it "good:" accuracy, clarity and pertinence. To these can be added constancy of form, conciseness, simplicity.[7] In the eyes of the user, the data printout has no frills. It is, in the modern jargon, lean and hard; the fat has been trimmed off. It is tight.

These are the virtues of the printout and at the same time the virtues of good management. With very little modification, a description of a good printout could apply to an effective manager: "He always knows what he is talking about and has his facts straight. You can understand him; he gets right to the point without wasting words and time. He talks our language. He sees the real issue and can reduce complicated situations to manageable problems with realistic solutions. He is not erratic. Although he gets on well with people, he is a hard man with no fat about him. He runs a tight ship."

By incorporating the value system of management, the computer printout achieves perhaps its most striking esthetic appeal. To find parallels in history, one need only consider any art form subsidized by a moneyed or otherwise powerful class. The art form will almost inevitably reflect and celebrate, to one extent or another, the value system of the subsidizer. Of course there are always those who will satirize as boldly as they think they can get away with, but even such negative reaction must incorporate, make concrete, the notions of value held by the subsidizer, if only to diminish them. Louis XIV got his poetry as he would have prescribed it had he been sufficiently apt to express his esthetic desires. He paid for it with favors and the incredible power of the court, a poetry now called classic and to be found in the great plays of Corneille, Racine, and Molière. Refined, balanced, sensitive, Christian, luxurious, authoritative, highly disciplined—these were the virtues Louis wanted for himself and France, and these were the characteristics of the literature he subsidized. He got poetry that affirmed and celebrated his view of the way things were or ought to be. In a similar way the Viking lords fed and housed minstrels who gave them epic tales of adventure and exploration, mysterious and strong verse that reflected accurately the preoccupations and values of the subsidizers. The church, also, has always sponsored the production of esthetic objects; and always, for better or worse, the values of the church have found expression in that art. This holds for Baptist television programs as well as for the frescoes of Michelangelo and the religious tapestries of Constantinople.

There is no reason to believe that managers cause printouts to be a certain way any more than there is to think that printouts produce a certain sort of manager. But the document does indeed make concrete managerial values, perceptions and presuppositions. For example, in asking for bushels of corn produced per cultivated acre in this and that county, the manager is causing the generation of a document reflecting his professional concern. This insures that the printout will be pertinent. He is also promulgating a value system that affirms high yield per acre as a good thing, and he will find that value system reconfirmed in concrete form when the printout is in his hand. Causing the printout brings to focus his perception that corn production is going on and is important. He assumes that the information will prove useful and that it will eventually affect corn production. In making all these notions concrete, the printout celebrates them, just as the court poet celebrated and sometimes extended the ideas of the court. Such celebration gives the printout a great appeal to the managers, and the appeal is, once again, esthetic.

The appeal of the printout is, then, more than just utilitarian in the narrow and commonly accepted sense of the word. The printout is more than an innocent and neutral tool of management society, even as the automobile is more than society's bland tool for transportation. The printout will shape the information it incorporates and delivers, as poetry does, and it can run the same risks that poetry runs in transmitting information that is true of reality and true to it.[8] Brooks has already found evidence of decadence in programming, although he does not call it that,[9] and we can all see the havoc that results from confusing the printout and the system it represents—a problem often encountered, in slightly different terms, in the study of poetry. But these and other risks are fun if they are recognized. Knowing why there is printout appeal helps us recognize them.

8

Sex Shock: The Humanistic Woman in the Super-Industrial Society

ARLENE SCHRADE

Preface

The nearly noninflected, highly distributive modern English language retains only two tenses, the present and the past. The past is a trivial tense, indicative. The present extends toward the future, at times substitutes for the future. To express future time, the ways of English are wayward and many. Auxiliaries and strings of catenative constructions march toward infinity. I wonder, then, if this means the English language is future oriented. Communication itself is anticipatory and predictive as well as purposeful and normative; " . . . it [communication] always refers either to the future itself or to that imminently impending future we call the present."[1] If I become too optimistic about the futuristic inseparability of the English language and American culture, I need only muse on the search for an elusive neuter pronoun. It seems as if the language suffers not from future shock but from sex shock. I fear the society suffers from both.

In contemplating the future, I choose optimism over pessimism, utopia rather than doomsday, although ruminating on the words of Kenneth Clark, I do wonder sometimes: "(. . . and one must concede that the future of civilization does not look very bright.")[2] It seems reasonable, though, to show some faith in humankind . . . "for men are adaptable, and their adaptability means constant ability to change and develop the powers of their mind."[3]

72

Toffler calls for utopian and antiutopian concepts looking forward to the super-industrial society, collaborative utopias, indeed "Utopia factories" to use his words.[4] I answer the call with a mini-utopia in the name of womankind, plugging in to the industrial factory with a super-industrial thesis.

The Science of Prevision

The inadequate but evident concern with the future has developed a science of prevision (*prevoir pour pouvoir*).[5] Unlike the ancients' reliance on magic and divination, the science of prevision is rational and rigorously scientific. It is based upon the theory of information, that beliefs contain a high degree of probability. Bell contends there are stable factors and hidden parameters possible to discover.[6] Previsionists calculate, analyze and determine the future, basing their science upon statistical susceptibility, trends, rhythmical and cyclical events, and psychological and sociological limitations. Difficulties arise due to independent variables, unforeseen events and improbable contingencies, but this modern science, self-correcting, and with the aid of technology (particularly the computer, necessary in light of the information explosion) can foretell much of the future.[7]

Science/Technology

To the ancient Greeks science was *theoria* or contemplation, *episteme* (knowledge for knowledge's sake) their special province. Relatively unimportant to them was *techne*. Galileo and Newton regarded science as knowledge, but not until the nineteenth century was technology truly born. Auguste Comte, the father of applied science " . . . realized that the purpose of science was not to contemplate the universe and its laws with detachment, but to discover how to apply the laws of nature so as to influence the world, foresee events and provide for the future."[8] This is what modern science has partially accomplished (providing for the future remains to be seen), thereby granting power to technology.

Although most of the major industries (steel, auto, aviation) remain nineteenth century institutions,[9] modern twentieth century industries have emerged from physics, chemistry and biology (pure theoretical science); electronics, computers, optics, polymers,[10] new energy, eugenics, cloning, birth technology, the green revolution and the mind control[11] stagger contemporary society. No longer does the dichotomy between pure and applied science exist. Theory thrives for technology, and technology is born from pure research. These twentieth century technologies and industries, in turn, have developed and changed transportation, housing and health, spurred underwater and space exploration, pushed environmental technology, produced robots and humanoids, data processing and a combination of machine and computer, called automation, which has profoundly influenced the world. And the prime characteristic of it all is acceleration. Where research in science-based technologies will lead humankind in the distant future promotes fascinating and fearful speculation.

The new technological revolution, however, is destroying an ancient argument, that of the schism between science and the humanities. For centuries, academicians and intellectuals have debated not only the relative importance of each but the very definitions and the dividing line between them. J. L. Jarrett has devoted a book to this argument, discovering some differences between science and the humanities, but miring himself in the mud of overlap. His not-so-new discovery is that natural, physical and social science constitute "science," while religion, literature, the arts and music are the "humanities," philosophy and history meandering somewhere in the middle.[12]

From this tenuous foundation, definitions of the scientific and the humanistic fare poorly. Jarrett's best effort is: "Once again, the point can be made by contrast with the scientific sort of attitude, which is severely, austerely cognitive. The humanistic attitude— we are not saying it is better or worse, but different—is not in this way austere, though it is not anticognitive. It tries to be at once responsive to the sensuous, emotional, moral, and spiritual, as well as cognitive aspects of the products it addresses itself to and of the process in which it participates."[13]

Oh, well, my own definition is whereas in the past science has devoted itself to the laws of nature, both physical and natural, the humanities have concentrated upon the entire realm of things human, whether natural, physical, spiritual, aesthetic, moral, or cognitive. Humanities, humanistic, human deal with the ultimate in total existence. The science of today and of the future is therefore both scientific and humanistic; for by freeing humankind from the physical and natural world, its technology demands that society turn its attention to the fuller range of human considerations. For the first time, science is essentially humanistic. I choose to call science/technology the humanistic sciences.

Cultural Anthropology

Anthropology, the study of humankind, is the stage where the sociological drama plays itself out. *Culture* is defined as: " . . . more than a collection of mere isolated bits of behavior. It is the integrated sum total of learned behavior traits which are manifested and shared by the members of a society."[14]

Crucial, then, is the idea that culture is learned, thereby ruling out any biologically conditioned forms of behavior. Many lesser creatures, such as the ant and the bee, maintain social organizations controlled by instinct. In other words, various ants or bees are produced and by biological instinct perform certain duties in the social system. Even animals such as wild herds band together under leadership, while the higher forms of apes such as the chimpanzee have forms of nascent culture. Only humankind, however, has the capability to create and maintain culture. This culture is realized by a person's complex nervous system, his ability to think or rationalize, his extended memory span and his use of verbal symbols.

Cultural patterns and behavior become habits, and these, in turn, tend to extend themselves unconsciously into the individual. Each person looks at the world through the rose-colored glasses of his own particular customs; he cannot go beyond his own stereotype of what is true and what is false. "Man, all down his history, has defended his uniqueness like a point of honor."[15] Thus, anthropology awards persons the degree of objectivity necessary to look at their beliefs in relationship to those of the rest of the world. "There is no social problem it is more incumbent upon us to understand than this of the role of custom. Until we are intelligent as to its laws and varieties, the main complicating facts of human life must remain unintelligible."[16]

The study of different cultures bears importantly upon present-day thought and behavior. Modern existence has thrown many civilizations and sub-civilizations into close contact. This contact will not only not diminish, it will increase. There has never been a time when society stood more in need of individuals who are genuinely culture-conscious, who can see objectively the socially conditioned behavior of other people without fear and recrimination.[17]

Real culture is what people actually do, *ideal* culture is what people say and believe they should do.[18] Overt behavior is an internalized process including thinking and dreaming. "Covert culture controls perception, because it sets attitudes and beliefs. These may be translated into overt action, but not necessarily so, or directly. There may be conflicts of standards in the covert culture which permit only one of the standards to be translated into action. Attitudes, too, may be verbalized into overt expression without attaining realization in full behaviour."[19]

An attitude is a point of view held toward something, whether a person, a group, or an abstract idea. The attitude may be mental and therefore remain unexpressed, or it may manifest itself in outward or overt expression. At this point it becomes behavior. An attitude can be the way someone feels toward a value. Both attitudes and values are culturally conditioned and not biologically inherited.

And so, each human society passes on to its children its own particular value system. Values themselves are professed beliefs whether stated explicitly or implicitly. The individual has his own values and each society has what is called a "dominant value system."[20] "The ways in which a society answers these questions about truths and . . . human experience are shaped by its continued evolution. . . . Our value system tells us what is important within that mountain of stimuli, that is, what things are real, true, and good.

It says to us, this perception makes sense; this one, nonsense. The result may be a xenophobia and an ethnocentrism, euphemisms or narrow-mindedness. They may, on the other hand, result in world-mindedness."[21] At times individuals find themselves at variance with the cultural values of their society. This is normal. Many now question the dominant value system in the United States.

Children learn their values and develop attitudes at a very early age, and so, encultured by the training, their behavior continues throughout their lifetime and in turn influences the next generation.

A culture is never consistent. Each individual is unique, influenced by his experience and the patterns of his culture. There is usually a conflict between the general characteristics of a society, called tribal or national traits concerned with the "good" person, and the individual personality or self. When this conflict cannot be resolved there are psychopathological implications.

Sociology

According to Toffler, the super-industrial society exudes change, acceleration, transience and novelty.[22]

Since humankind's gigantic step from barbarism to civilization, thousands of years ambled by through agricultural societies. Then the industrial age skipped along for a scant 100 years. Now the United States teeters on the edge of the super-industrial society characterized first by a service economy,[23] and eventually by a mad dash through an experience economy.[24] When physical needs finally disappear, psychic or psychological dimensions of life take precedence. In a society ruled by a service economy, human, professional and technical services proliferate.[25] In an experience economy, the search for quality of life by aesthetics, simulation, and whatever seems vital to humankind after basic needs and human services are met, will rule the society.

In a society hurtling toward the future, professional, technical and managerial roles will expand. Technology will liberate humans to all but thinking, planning and watching.[26] The middleclass, white collar group will become the norm and evolve ultimately into a democratic leisure class only. Education will change its curriculum, methods and organization, concentrating on technological education and continuous plug-in, plug-out educare.

Accentuated change in organization, information, space (places), time, science/technology, things and interpersonal relations will permeate all of life.[27]

The Decision Sciences

G. L. Shackle describes decision as "the choice of a future goal through an act of creative imagination, rather than a choice between present advantages."[28] When planning and prevision combine, the science of decision is born. Since the sciences of decision are rational, they must fulfill three conditions: 1) they must base themselves upon the sciences of information in general and upon prevision in particular; 2) "since pure information and decision do not form a continuum and it is necessary to jump deliberately from one to the other, this jump should be made in accordance with ethics and commonsense"; and 3) the logical validity of value judgments must be recognized along with the ethical propositions formulating them.[29]

Since rational decisions must be taken in isolation as expedients to avoid difficulty, these rational decisions need to depend upon previous information and probable results predicted by means *of* information and supported *by* information. To respond to the difficulties arising from changing reality, a new science of administration must emerge to invent solutions in advance.[30]

The Individual Woman in the Super-Industrial Society

First, some postulates must be stated.
1) There will be a new society. (To some extent there *is* a new society.)
2) Technology is neutral, neither good nor bad.
3) The society will be de-shocked.
4) Woman's role in this new society will be an expanded one.

The science of prevision reveals future society to present society. Naturally the future affects all humankind, but I am concerned directly with the individual woman, both physically and psychologically. The physical and the biological science-based technologies will transform both her inner and her outer worlds.

More and better automation will radically affect her relationship with goods and services. Computers (eventually digital computers in her home) will invade her work, her thinking and gradually do her thinking for her. Holography, optics, polymers and new sources of energy will join the movement to alter her house and home, her transportation, her occupation and her children. Ultimately cyborgs, robots and humanoids will be as familiar as friends, relatives and household appliances. Every crevice and corner of her once familiar life stands exposed to the future.

Pioneering efforts of birth control have opened but a narrow crack in the door of things to come. Eugenics, birth technology and cloning will wreak havoc with former concepts of woman's own body and those of others. Her food will be determined by the green revolution and by the cloning of animals.

All of this will, in turn, force radical changes in her physical dwelling, in her concept *of* and relationships *with* family, friends and coworkers. Lifestyles will proliferate, the world of work will demand her attention. In a service economy, with brute strength no longer important, middleclass, white collar work will welcome female as well as male, diminishing stereotyped visions of household roles.[31] The post-service economy will bring experiences in total contradiction to all that has gone before.

Psychologically, woman will be bombarded by an ever increasing accelerative pace of life, by change and mobility, by transience and novelty.[32] The community and the world will loom as familiar as her bedroom and will consume her energies.

What will future woman become? In the past, she has always belonged to someone; to a father, a husband, children, a boss. In the future, like man, she will belong only to herself. She will become unprotected (and therefore vulnerable), equal, transient, choice- and novelty-ridden and, above all, free. What must she be like to survive? She, like man, must be responsible, adaptable and participatory—in essence, a mature, individual human being.

The sciences of decision teach that planning for the future must be based on information and prevision, with choices made ethically and commonsensically.

On the personal (psychological or private) level, future woman must learn to cope, to formulate her own decisions. She will not be able to rely on anyone but herself, the ultimate in total individual freedom. She must learn to adapt, to adapt to change at a more and more accelerated pace. She must be able to *deal* with mobility, transience and novelty. In all, she must choose. She will be free to choose to be a mother or not to be a mother, free to purchase and/ or determine offspring, free to choose her own lifestyles, free to be or not to be a wife, to be one of several wives or to have several husbands, to have one or more families, to be a surrogate parent, to be single or to be a single parent, to be married once or have a series of marriages or something yet to be imagined; she will be free to work or remain at home, and if at home, free to determine what to do with her new leisure time. Her sought-after and new-found freedom will be her blessing or her blight. Technology frees her. Society enslaves her. Future society and inner self must keep up with technology and free her as well.

In the public, societal sector, decisions must also be made. With an early model such as Sweden's[33] pointing the way, government must help woman take an equal part in the affairs of society. The legal and judicial arenas must opt for equal opportunity laws, provide for health, family and educational services, and intervene in environmental and communications affairs. Business and industry must cooperate to allow woman full participation at every level, including decision making itself. Education, too, looking ahead instead of back, must provide her with whatever she, the society and technology demand. "Education does not necessarily result in changed opinions or altered points of view, but it should result in understanding and tolerance, respect for rational discussion, and the acquisition of the techniques and discipline needed for critical analysis. Discipline refers to means, not ends. It refers to rigorous and scholarly enquiry and to a respect for relevant evidence."[34] Since all people are motivated by their society's value system and guided by it, a reasonable assumption is that the schools should attempt to aid students in a rational understanding of all values; theirs and others. Inculcation of values is not the issue, but the teaching of what one should become—not what one is. In this way education is a moral thing.[35]

Anthropology teaches that culture is learned behavior, so that alternative ways can be learned, unlearned and relearned. Only humankind can create and maintain culture (so far), and it must learn to create and maintain culture by direct decision and not by chance. Social and economic dislocation and loss of direction necessitate careful planning.[36] "Furthermore, just as an individual can exercise conscious choice among alternative life styles, a society today can consciously choose among alternative cultural styles. This is a new fact in history. In the past, culture emerged without premeditation. Today, for the first time, we can process to awareness. By the application of conscious technological policy—along with other measures—we can contour the culture of tomorrow."[37] Society must make ethical, human decisions based upon commonsense to contour future culture.

Cultural universals and alternatives will remain with the society, but they themselves will change. The evidenced values will be different and will continue to change at a cosmic clip. Specialties of groups will no longer be the same, nor will the groups themselves. Specialties groups will group, re-group and group again. Attitudes and behavior reflecting overt and covert phases of culture will also slip around.

A society eludes control. Education and the law can be altered, but it remains to be seen how an entire society can be changed and learn to cope with continuous change. Over one hundred years ago America's black slaves were freed, and for some years now civil rights have existed; yet, the real and ideal cultural traits of individuals and of groups choose to render blacks invisible. Women, too, have been invisible, but the society cannot for its very survival continue to condone invisibility regarding any individual within its folds.

McGeorge Bundy claims that what is just in a society is what is fair for every individual.[38] John Rawls's notion of what is fair is deceptively simple and brilliant. He suggests that all persons entering into a social contract do so under a veil of ignorance, not knowing whether they would be born black or white, man or woman, rich or poor. Rawls's principles are:

> First Principle: Each person is to have an equal right to the most extensive total system of equal liberties for all.
> Second Principle: Social and economic inequalities are to be arranged so that they are both: a) to the greatest benefit to the least advantaged, and b) attached to offices and positions open to all under conditions of fair equality of opportunity.[39]

This is an ethical and commonsense model for decisionmaking.

The Sex De-Shocked Future Society

Perusing the writings of the feminist revolution, I find them irrelevant for the future. "Women must rebel" maintains Shirley Chisholm, "all discrimination is eventually the same thing—antihumanism."[40] What Chisholm fails to realize is that women will not need to rebel. The future itself will be rebellion. And it is senseless to argue for or against antihumanism in a future bombarded with freedom, democracy and humanism. Mary Lou Thompson echoes the point that women have great responsibilities, with their protection withdrawn; and no longer content to sit on the sidelines and knit, they must take part in the decisions that count.[41] Future woman has little option. She will make decisions that count or perish. People first, then women, says Betty Friedan. "Women have to share in the decisions of all."[42] I say it is inevitable and nondebatable. "The real sexual revolution is the emergence of women from passivity, from thingness, to full self-determination, to full dignity. And insofar as they can do this, men are also emerging from the stage of identification with brutality and masters to full and sensitive complete humanity."[43] Men and women will both emerge or fail to survive in the super-industrial society. Roxanne Dunbar encourages the idea that instead of fighting a lone battle, women must force society to "allow us to be free to build the kind of society that meets basic human needs. Female suppression is not petty, but a widespread social disease."[44] No oppression is petty. And the only kind of future society that will survive will meet basic human needs whatever they are or will be or can be or ought to be, and go beyond. Alice Rossi's hybrid model for the society is as she terms it " . . . a radical goal which rejects the present structure of society and seeks instead a new breed of women and men and a new vision of the future."[45] This, she contends, will be a "restructuring to bring the world closer to the fulfillment of individual human needs for both creativity and fellowship. It is a desire for a more meaningful sense of community, a greater depth to personal relations across class, sex and racial lines, a stress on human fellowship and individual scope for creativity rather than economic efficiency in the bureaucracy, heightened interest in the humanities and social sciences from an articulated value base and a social responsibility commitment to medicine and law rather than thirst for status and high income."[46] I find that Rossi and the other feminists have been upstaged by technology, and their goals, however noble, have been or will be disposed of.

In post-industrial societies, there will be greater independence of women, not only for ideological reasons but for the simple fact that the society provided for the first time an economic base for female independence.[47]

Clare Booth Luce wonders about the failure of present women to leap up the ladder alongside man.[48] It is not important, however, that women are not numerous at the top of the present pyramid—for the pyramid is crumbling. In its place is the uneven, squishy circle of a new organizational structure.[49] Technology and progress are changing administration, too. A Luce thesis is that all persons serve the male dominated society and always have. All minority groups are at the bottom, and on the lowest rung of all are black women.[50] Sad, perhaps; inhuman, yes; but irrelevant in the face of the future. If marriage collapses, says Luce, so goes the economy, for the homemaker has served her purpose well.[51] Given the future concepts of marriage and family, this statement, too, is totally irrelevant. The agricultural and industrial economies are collapsing and with them all semblances of the past.

The ethical decisions to be met and made will revolve around the most moral manner of dealing with the future, not the past or the present!

Technology, the hero (or villain) of the present and the future is indeed neutral. It appears willy nilly in capitalist and Communist societies and will appear in the Third World as well. Aranguren maintains that tyranny cannot be produced by machines, only enforced by the men who use them, that machines increase man's power for good as well as evil. He further states that ethical decisions cannot be eliminated by automation, that humans would be responsible for their renouncing the human condition.[52] The opposite view is taken by Kenneth Clark who believes, " . . . in a world of action a few things are obvious—so obvious that I hesitate to repeat them. One of them is our increasing reliance on machines. They have ceased to be tools and have begun to give us direction. And unfortunately machines, from the Maxim gun to the computer, are for the most part means by which a minority can keep free men in subjection."[53] I must reject this pre-industrial, nostalgic view, for it evades reality. Machines of the technological super-industrial age will be neither slaves nor masters. Their relationship with humankind will be a collaborative one. And so, at one point of time in the near future, there will be a colleague-like partnership between human and machine, science and the humanities, and pure science and technology; not a two-sided coin or a two-headed monster, but complementary colors on the color wheel. This is truly humanism (or machinism).

The most challenging and critical crises, however, come in the attempt to close the economic gap between rich and poor within super-industrial societies and the wider economic gap between them and the rest of the world. This can only be accomplished by a world effort. Perhaps peace, planning and "psych corps"[54] could roam the world. Aranguren maintains this effort is essential. Kurt Waldheim, fourth Secretary-General of the United Nations, contends that the United Nations must be that vehicle.[55] All men and women must direct all efforts to create and maintain a super-industrial supra-world.

Symptoms of underdealing with the future are evident: apathy,

violence, over-choice and over-stimulation.[56] Humankind's adaptability is in question, its ability to decelerate and tame technology
is in doubt. Society is at an incredible crisis in human history when
the need may be to control evolution itself.

Viktor Frankl, in his philosophy of logotheraphy, advises humankind to look to the future, not to the past. Life has always been
riddled with choices to be made.[57] The future increases and acceler-
ates them. Highet believes human history is a process of learning.
He urges the world to believe that humans are adaptable, that they
can deal with change, that it has brought them from savagery to
civilization and will take them further still.[58]

And so I come full, squishy circle to my optimistic miniutopia
for womankind and, therefore, humankind. Perhaps it is not mini,
but midi, maxi or mighty; whatever the utopian level, it is an an-
drogynous one. I do believe that in order to survive, future society
will be forced to drop class/minority concerns and focus on total
humanity, a sort of "united we stand, divided we fall" idea, leaving
sex for better things.

If humans are at present using only one-third of their incredible
brain power, I am sure they *will* use the other two-thirds. I wonder,
though, what happens when they use up all three-thirds of it. I
often think as I watch Olympic atheletes break record after record,
jumping higher, running and swimming faster, lifting more—where
is the limit! Surely, there must be one! And so, surely there must
be limits to humankind's adaptability. Where the upper and outer
limits are I do not know. I cannot believe, however, that humankind is necessarily without those limits. All evidence tells me otherwise. When and if humans are no longer needed and they cannot
adapt, like the dinosaurs they too may become extinct. Machines
may then take over the world. A world of robots, humanoids and
computers would be eminently more efficient.

The English language may be future ready, but it is not yet sex
ready. In all of Toffler's brilliant books, the male dominated language is evident. It is even a problem in my paper. If the language,
like society, is to survive in the near and distant future, it must
develop a new concept of gender. If language and society, insepar-

able, can adapt and if language reflects that society, there is hope. Some day, though, when communication between machines is the norm (also eminently more efficient) there may be a post-super-industrial world.

PART IV

THE COMPUTER IN USE

Computer technology has been applied in many sectors of society, changing the way we do things. This section offers a representative sampling of these application areas through four perspectives. Professors in education, communication, social work, and art offer their views on uses and implications of computer technology in their respective disciplines.

The field of education has seen many applications of computer use. In Chapter 9, Patricia Campbell presents a brief history of computers in education and then focuses on computer-assisted instruction (CAI). The initial growth of CAI is discussed, as is the slump in computer use in education that occurred in the late 1960s and the rebirth of computer use in the early 1970s. Campbell also examines "what's been happening" in educational computing and hypothesizes some trends in computer use in education, including the increased use of minicomputers and the development of dialogue CAI.

From the perspective of a "media ecologist," David Guerra examines how computer technology interacts with electronic media. Beginning with the premise that "every communication system and process is connected with every other communication system and process in a complex network," he identifies the elements and environments of computer technology and the media, their interrelationships, and the effects on the media system and the individuals within it. Guerra concludes that awareness of the effects of such interrelating technologies indicates a need for people to learn how to live in our evolving communications environment, to cope with possible impacts before they occur, and to be the assessors of our technological destiny.

As a society moves toward provision of a greater number and diversity of services and programs for its citizenry, utilization of computers has become a growing trend. Gary Mooers (Chapter 11) traces the impacts of computer technology on the social welfare sector, identifying several problem areas which merit concern. Among problems identified are the reliance on naive or misleading data, difficulties of realistic measurement in a multivariable situation, resentment of computers by agency staff, the possible depersonalizing effect of computer management, and the question of maintaining confidentiality with the existence of large data banks. Mooers concludes that solving these problems should come through proper appraisal of computer technology as a tool, with such assessment done in the context of social work values. He suggests potential value in the use of computers which can enable the social welfare sector to provide humane and efficient services not previously possible.

The field of art, as well as other humanistic disciplines, has traditionally been viewed as somewhat apart from the domain of science and technology. In Chapter 12 Margaret Gorove presents an interesting perspective on this view in her examination of the impacts of computer technology on the field of art. She first examines computer impact on art as a profession, focusing on the changing definitions of art as artists utilize the new materials and subject matter brought about through technology. She goes on to analyze the effects of computer technology on the exposure of society and individuals to art.

9

Computer–Assisted Instruction in Education: Past, Present and Future

PATRICIA B. CAMPBELL

In the late 1950s the concept of computers as tools in the educational process was introduced. Although at this time the idea of computer–assisted instruction (CAI) was being considered by only a few scientists and even fewer educators, its potential was great (Atkinson and Wilson, 1969). CAI looked as if it might cause the dreams of American educators to come true by giving students a personal instructor, who would have infinite time, patience and capacity to remember each student's correct and incorrect answers.

During the early 1960s the concept of computer-assisted instruction grew rapidly, encouraged by educators' interest in programmed instruction, the mushrooming of electronic data processing and, most importantly, by massive influxes of federal money (Atkinson and Wilson, 1969). One of the earliest recipients of federal money, Patrick Suppes at Stanford University, was originally funded in 1963. By 1965 he had developed and was field testing CAI in arithmetic computation. In Suppes's programs elementary school children were given problems like 2+5=? or 3×5=? and asked, via the typewriter-like terminal, to type in the correct answer. If they got the answer correct, they went on to the next problem. If they got the answer wrong, they were given another chance. If they missed the problem three times they would then be given the correct answer and given a new problem (Suppes and Morningstar, 1972). Suppes's project in following years also developed "drill and practice" CAI programs in reading and spelling.

By 1968, research and development in CAI had become big business, Harvard had established a CAI laboratory, universities like Florida State and Harvard were using CAI to help teach courses like physics and chemistry, and computer companies like RCA and IBM were developing CAI materials (Hansen, et al., 1968; Stolurow, 1967). As more people got involved in research and development in CAI, the methods used became more sophisticated. The original process of drill and practice was augmented by tutorial programs where, if the student gave the wrong answer, that answer was analyzed and the student was given remedial instruction to try to correct misunderstandings. Stanford University's logic course and IBM's statistics course were two examples of the earlier tutorial programs (Odeh and Cook, 1969). At this point people working in CAI research and development also started investigating the possibility of using CAI for simulation and gaming. Schools that did not have, for example, a betatron or an electronic microscope could have a computer terminal with a CAI program to simulate these important, but expensive, pieces of equipment. CAI was seen not as a replacement for hands-on experience but rather as a supplement that could both give more students experience and catch and correct student error before the student tried the actual equipment. IBM's physics laboratory course was an excellent example of the simulation type of CAI (Lindsay, 1969).

As the 1960s progressed, CAI research and development continued to grow at a phenomenal rate; the Defense Department started funding CAI programs in foreign languages for use with soldiers, while companies like IBM started developing and using CAI courses for training their customer engineers. Also federal agencies started funding CAI programs to be used with disadvantaged children, to see if the computer could make a contribution to equal educational opportunities (Wells et al., 1974). During the late 1960s people started experimenting with offshoots of CAI, like computer-aided testing, where the computer developed and administered the test and then scored and analyzed the results; and computer-managed instruction where the computer-scored tests, kept track of student progress and often even assigned outside readings and assignments to the student (Gardner, 1972).

At this time people started adapting CAI for use with special students. Rochester Institute of Technology started using CAI very effectively with deaf students while other universities used CAI with rural students to allow them to take courses like physics or calculus, that otherwise would not have been offered in their sparsely populated areas.

By the end of the 1960s there were CAI courses in physics, chemistry, electronics, medical diagnosis, spelling, reading, logic, arithmetic, statistics, geography, English, grammar, Russian, German, French and Chinese, among others (Atkinson and Wilson, 1969; Allen, 1973). Studies were finding that students in CAI courses had more positive attitudes toward the subject and learned faster than they did with lecture instruction (Jamison et al., 1974). Many scientists and some educators started talking of the not so distant future day when children would have computer terminals in their homes and would learn most of their cognitive skills from CAI.

However, in the midst of the CAI boom, some clouds appeared on the horizon. The basic component of these clouds was that while CAI research and development were moving at a rapid pace, few people were actually using it. When the federal government stopped paying people to develop CAI, they stopped developing new courses and even stopped using the ones they already had. Without the incentive of federal money, CAI was just not being used. There were two basic reasons for this lack of use: cost and fear. Computer-assisted instruction, in the 1960s, was expensive. For example, the well-funded CAI effort of the University of Illinois, PLATO (Programmed Logic for Automatic Teaching Operations), cost about ten dollars per student hour. This meant that if a student spent ten hours a week on PLATO, the cost was $100 a week for that student alone. Thirty students spending ten hours a week on PLATO would cost about $3,000 a week. The problem was obvious; school systems and universities just could not afford to use computer-assisted instruction. There were, of course, cheaper systems, those using teletype terminals rather than light-pen-equipped cathode ray tube (CRT) terminals, but the research found that, in general, these cheaper systems were not as effective in terms of student achievement (Jamison et al., 1974).

While cost was a major deterrent to widespread use, there were several other technical problems with CAI. One was the noise. One teletype terminal makes enough noise to interfere with concentration; twenty teletype terminals make enough noise to drive the average student out of the room in a very short time. Noise, of course, was not a problem with the CRT terminal with its visual, television-like, displays, but flickering was. Even on the best of CRT terminals, the displays flickered on and off with great speed. Although the flickering was not noticeable during the first five or ten minutes of terminal use, by the end of thirty or thirty-five minutes of terminal use, noticeable eye strain developed. Both problems, noise and flickering, were unresolved during the 1960s.

Another problem with CAI was the lack of course materials. The newness of the field, combined with the lack of copyright protection and the absence of royalties, did little to encourage people to develop CAI courses. Course authors could not be sure if they would get any money or even any credit for their efforts. Many qualified people felt that their time and work were better spent on an effort with an established reward system.

While CAI had its cost and technical problems, they were not its most serious problem; the problem that had the most negative effect on CAI during the end of the 1960s and the beginning of the 1970s was fear. Teachers, as they began to be aware that computers might have classroom uses, began to fear that computers and particularly computer-assisted instruction would replace teachers; and that the human element of education would be gone. This fear was groundless because CAI was not viewed by developers as a replacement for the teacher but rather as a supplement, much the way textbooks or learning activity packages are used as supplements. However, even though the fear was groundless, it was real; and it caused some teachers to respond in unusual ways. One teacher's response to the fear of CAI was to "try to invalidate the results of research studies dealing with CAI." An example of this was found in California in 1966–67 where the effect of a daily ten-minute drill and practice CAI session in arithmetic was being assessed. The researchers discovered that in one of the schools being tested, the group not having drill and practice scored significantly higher in math achievement than did the group that *had* the drill and practice. Subsequent investigation found that in that school, teachers had, without telling researchers, introduced a daily twenty-five minute period of noncomputerized drill and practice so that "the computer wouldn't beat them" (Jamison et al., 1974). This practice of teachers in the control (or nonresearch) group doing extra work so that CAI or some other innovation would not do better than they has become so widespread that researchers have coined a name for it, the "John Henry" effect, named after the "steel drivin'" man (Saretsky, 1974).

Teachers' fears of CAI came out not only in their response to research but also in their union contracts and negotiations with school boards. Teachers just did not want to deal with CAI in their classrooms, and their resistance, combined with the high cost of CAI, insured that the spread of CAI from the research and development centers to the classrooms would be minimal.

As the news of the lack of implementation of CAI came back to the developers and the funders, repercussions began to be felt. In 1969, IBM stopped all of its CAI research and development efforts in both hardware (machines) and software (course development), and concentrated on CAI only for training their own employees (IBM Internal Memo, 1969). Other industries like RCA followed suit; and as federal grant money was reduced, so were CAI research and development efforts in universities. By the early 1970s, the University of Illinois's PLATO, funded by the National Science Foundation and Control Data Corporation, was the only well-funded major CAI carryover from the 1960s.

Just about at the point when scientists and educators were beginning to think CAI was a good idea that just didn't make it, the ramifications of a technological revolution in computers came into the picture. Miniaturization of computer components caused the price of computer hardware to fall drastically, even in a period of high inflation ("Computers, A New Wave," 1976). For example an electric calculator that was priced at just below $100 in 1970 now sells for below ten dollars (Kibler & Campbell, 1976). This price drop has also been felt in CAI systems. In 1968 a drill and practice CAI system in arithmetic cost more than most school systems could afford; in 1976 a calculator-based learning aid called the "Little Professor," with more than 1,600 drill and practice basic math problems, is sold complete, hardware and software, for less than twenty dollars ("News From the Industry," 1976).

This price drop is causing an increased use of computers and an increased teacher-student familiarity with them. It is a poor college or junior college indeed that does not have its own computer or at least does not have several computer terminals that have access to a computer. Today more and more high schools and vocational-technical schools are getting computer terminals and often whole minicomputers to do their own data processing and to teach their students data processing. Even many elementary schools are getting computer terminals that are able to hook up with the school district's computer. The calculator boom is also contributing tremendously to new awareness and familiarity with computers. Currently there are literally millions of calculators in use, and people who were, and often still are, terrified by the concept of a computer, would not think about going to the grocery store, the golf course or to class without their calculators. And calculators differ from computers in degree rather than in kind.

This new awareness is now being channeled into education. The EXXON Education Foundation's IMPACT program worked to do this with its two programs, EXPERSIM and TIPS. TIPS, which is a combination of computer-aided testing and computer-managed instruction, gives students periodic tests, scores and analyzes the results and assigns the student both new and remedial work. Students are then tested on the new work and re-tested on the remedial work at their next testing time. One of the advantages of this system is that one does not have to be a computer programmer to adapt TIPS to a particular course, so that teachers are able to use the program without much outside assistance. EXPERSIM, a simulation program, also attempts to use as little outside help as possible in its adaptation to specific courses (EXXON Education Foundation IMPACT Program Portfolio).

The EXXON Education Foundation encouraged interest in these programs by offering interested schools and colleges funds to assist them in setting up the program. Learning from the National Science Foundation's mistakes of the 1960s, EXXON required that the schools and colleges indicate their commitment by agreeing to fund the faculty time necessary for initial implementation of the program (EXXON Education Foundation IMPACT Program Portfolio).

The National Science Foundation (NSF), long-time funder of CAI, has also decided that it is time for computerized education to sink or swim, depending on the commitment of users (Magarrell, 1976). NSF is putting its two major CAI systems, PLATO and TICCIT, in the market place. PLATO, which can give individualized instruction to up to 500 students at once is marketed by Control Data Corporation, in three different ways. PLATO can be leased by the hour at learning centers in major metropolitan centers; PLATO terminals connected by long distance telephone lines to a central computer can be leased, or the entire system can be leased or purchased at a cost of five to six million dollars (Magarrell, 1976).

TICCIT (Time-shared Interactive Computer Controlled Information Television), a system using modified color television sets, connected to a small computer for two-way student-computer interaction, is also going on sale. Although the details for marketing TICCIT are not worked out to the extent that they are on PLATO, it is estimated that the program cost should be between seventy-five cents and two dollars per student hour. It is also estimated that with wide usage, the per student hour cost could fall as low as fifty cents (Magarrell, 1976).

Both EXXON and NSF have been saying that CAI has come of age and it is now time for educators to make some decisions about whether it will be used or not. Many of the earlier problems with CAI have been solved or at least minimized. CAI per student-hour cost is less and is continuing to decrease while teacher instruction per student-hour cost continues to rise. Noisy teletype terminals are being replaced by silent impact printing terminals; flickering CRT terminals are being replaced by higher resolution CRT terminals or by PLATO's flickerless plasma terminal. Computer companies like Control Data Corporation, are establishing royalty programs, based on the volume of use, for authors of CAI materials, to encourage the development of more courses. Finally and most importantly people's greater awareness and familiarity with computers is reducing some of the fear of CAI that has been generated in the past decade.

If educators make the decision to use CAI in the schools, then there will be some interesting developments for both CAI and education. The first major trend of the future will be away from large expensive computer systems like PLATO's 5–6 million dollar effort and toward minicomputer systems like Digital Equipment Corporation's CLASSIC (Classroom Interactive Computer), a complete self-contained unit that sells for under $8,000 (Berry and Richards, 1975), or even toward systems like Texas Instruments "Little Professor" which costs less than $20. Large computer systems, if used at all, will spend part time on CAI and part time on the business end of educational functioning as Xerox's ACES (Administrative Classroom System) currently does, or they will be used to power series of minicomputers which will do the actual CAI ("Teachers Should be Dedicated, Not Computers," 1975).

As computer systems become smaller and cheaper, they will more and more come to be accepted as classroom tools, much the way other classroom technology like casette tape recorders, motion picture projectors and televisions, are being used and accepted. Once teachers get used to these new teaching aids, more of them will become involved in adapting CAI programs to their own use and also in writing their own CAI programs. As CAI authoring languages become easier to use and as audio tape casettes gain usage as ways of storing CAI programs, teachers will lose much of their fear of the unknown that currently stops teachers from writing CAI. In the near future, more schools will start holding in-service training to show teachers how to write CAI programs and will give release time and increment credit to encourage teachers to write Learning Activity Packages (LAPs).

As more and more people write and use CAI programs, the quality of the programs should increase as well as the quantity. With user encouragement, work will continue on the development of dialogue CAI, where the student and the computer can interact, more according to the student's needs than the machine's. With dialogue CAI, the student will be able to ask the computer questions and respond to computer questions in a narrative or essay format rather than in an objective or short answer format (Kibler & Campbell, 1975).

Another offshoot of CAI in the future will be the increase in programs like the LOGO project at Massachusetts Institute of Technology. Here elementary age children become immersed in a "computer culture" and learn how to manipulate the computer in order to both answer their questions and have fun. With this type of computer use in education, the children don't learn by using already programmed CAI, but rather learn through designing and programming their own programs (Solomon, 1976).

The combination of dialogue CAI and programs like LOGO will very much change the tone of computer use in education. Students will use the computer to find out information that they want to know, either by direct query to the machine or by developing programs that can get at the answers that they desire. Under these types of computer use, the great bases of information, or data banks, that have been collected on a myriad of subjects will be open for student use and learning.

It is entirely feasible that within the next five to ten years small portable computers will be as available and accessible as calculators are now. Students of all ages will then be able to have a personal computer capable of functions that most school districts cannot today afford to provide (Kibler & Campbell, 1976).

The student of the not so distant future will be one who cannot imagine education without computer use. The computer will be the aid that helps students brush up on weak skills, the library that answers student informational questions on a wide range of topics, the instructor that presents students with new materials and skills and the tool that students can program to meet their own needs.

10

Computer Technology and the Mass Media: Interacting Communication Environments

DAVID M. GUERRA

The vagaries of societal change induced by our speeding technology have been focused on by such theorists as McLuhan, Toffler, Ellul, and DeFleur. Claims of shocking changes, dehumanization, media petrification, retribalization, and other uncontrollable effects are common warnings. Whether traumatized or cauterized, we are apparently under assault from the varying influences of the technology we have created.

Technology, though, is a neutral force, and can be viewed for its "potential and limitations" systematically.[1] It is an instrument or method of reaching a desired end. It is with intention and purpose machines are developed, although unintended effects often result, along with unanticipated spin-off technologies.[2] These machines, then, are both processes in our communications environment and the media of that communication.

The computer is both a communications system and a process. When it is called on to interact with the environment of the mass media, results are both planned and unwitting. What is the nature of these effects on each of the mass media, and, particularly, on the individuals involved in the interaction? How are we to determine the implications of these effects on individuals in the future?

MEDIA ECOLOGY AS METHODOLOGY

We can answer these questions and improve on our perspective of the interrelationship of the computer with the mass media by using the methodology of the media ecologist. The ecologist would suggest that "all communication is environment" and start from the premise that "every communication system and process is connected with every other communication system and process in a complex network, and that the study of communication process is the study, not of elements, but of elements in relationships."[3] The media ecologist would analyze in the context of "how" one communications environment or system, computer technology, within another communications environment, the mass media, interrelates with that system.

This methodology, then, asks us to look at and identify the significant characteristics of computer technology as a whole, the subsystems that are a part of it, the larger system, i.e., the mass media environment it operates within, and the interrelationships between them.[4] Computer technology as its own environment plugs into and interacts with certain of the mass media producing change, and varying sometimes unexpected effects. We will later mention these mediating influences affecting the individual and the social process.

Computer Technology as Environment

The computer as a technological system has its own subsystems which help to define it as a communications environment. These generally definitive subsystems, i.e., each having a particular function within the total system setting them apart from one another, serve to "define" the computer environment by signaling certain behavioral traits. And it should be noted that "variations" in subsystem functions will determine the "range of permissible behaviors within the environment."[5] The interrelationship of these functional subsystems sets down then the structure or boundary of the total computer environment.

The elements or subsystems of the computer environment would include the company that builds, sells and maintains it as well as the process of building, selling and maintaining and all the individuals so connected. The designer, engineer, programmer, salesperson, console operator, systems analyst, each with a particular function, are elements of the total environment. Even the buyer and other receptor personnel, as well as the buying and using of the machine, are all subsystems.

The electronic or physical makeup of the computer, how it operates, its specific purpose, how it interacts with, for example, the programmer, or fulfills the requirements of the designer, or functions as a problem-solver or decisionmaker are all significant elements of the computer's technology. Even the space program is an element because its interaction contributes to the sophistication of the computer. The information processed, the message resulting and how it is used are all subsystems of computer technology. Each of these definitive elements with its particular function that establish its specific boundaries enables us to focus in on and define each subsystem. These elements joined together or interacting with one another create a new boundary, the focused definition of the computer environment as a whole.

Mass Media as Environment

We have suggested that there is a larger system, the mass media environment, which the computer plugs into. The definition of this technology is, as well, determined by the nature and function of its subsystems. Specifically, the focus of this study is on the radio and television media. The elements of these technologies are to some extent similar, particularly since each is an electronic system of mass communication. Each is a medium and a process for transmitting information.

The subsystems of both media would include the owner and licensee, the license, and the regulations and regulatory agency that enforces them. The process of regulating, applying for a license, ascertaining community needs and interests, building the facility, buying, installing, operating and maintaining the equipment are all significant elements. The conceiving, producing and broadcasting of programs, and all the individuals who are a part of these processes, e.g., the program manager, producer, director, crew personnel, engineers, graphic artist, disc jockey, announcer, news director, writer, reporter, station manager and other personnel are subsystems. The audience, listeners and viewers, their feedback, the ratings and measurement organizations are also part of these media systems. Of course, there are numerous other subsystems, but it suffices to say that all of these elements, significant as they are, are clearly defined by their specific functions or traits. Then, viewed together, interacting with one another, they bring into focus the radio and television environment as a whole.

Interacting Communication Environments

The primary design of this writing is not so much to view the myriad of elements or their interactions within the electronic media and computer environments, as it is to show the interrelationships of the computer and electronic media environments and the effects of that interaction. Computer technology functions as a mediating influence, and master of impact, dictating change in the ever evolving environment of the electronic media. The more sophisticated the computer technique the greater the potential impact. Toffler supports this contention when he states that "each new machine or technique, in a sense, changes all existing machines and techniques, by permitting us to put them together into new combinations. . . . Indeed, each new combination may, itself, be regarded as a new super-machine."[6]

The computer has become a significant force in changing the traditional operating function of radio and television and has had profound impact on both the individual and the media systems. In what ways has computer technology generated social change through its interrelationship with the electronic media environment? What have been the consequences of this combination of technologies? And in what ways has the technology of the computer in speeding up the media environment affected interpersonal relationships? We can best answer these questions by taking a look at the specific interactions of the computer with the electronic media.

In the following examples of computer/mass media interrelationships, keep fresh the concept that it is the "how" we are most concerned with—how the environment of the computer interacts with the environment of the various media—and, significantly, with what effect both on the structure of those communication systems and on the individuals who are a part of the interaction.

Computerized Radio vs. the Human Factor

Computer-controlled automation of radio stations has quickly caught on in the broadcasting business. In fact, one prediction suggests that by 1986 70–80 percent of radio broadcasting stations will be automated. Broadcast station owners are in business to make a profit—a significant reason for the apparent successful integration of the technologies. This interrelationship has been called a "quiet revolution" because the implementation of automation is not necessarily recognized by the listening audience except in the improved quality of a station's "sound." That is the second significant rationale for an owner investing large sums in automated service. Of the more than 7,000 radio stations, approximately 1,000 have become automated. What does this mean to these stations? "Disc jockeys spinning records on turntables in front of live mikes have been replaced by banks of tape decks, cartridges and audio clocks for time checks, all controlled and played automatically by a computer . . . " or at times by a simple automation system.[7]

The capability now exists for stations to operate without humans on the premises, and some stations have gone almost that far. The Federal Communications Commission, which regulates broadcasting, requires a licensed engineer on duty at all times. Nevertheless, we are a minute step from complete and very sophisticated mechanization. The computer is programmed to monitor the automated system, take corrective action, play the prerecorded audio tapes, allow for live program insertions, operate twenty-four hours a day, seven days a week, if the station is so licensed, and perform numerous other functions for the broadcast operation.[8]

Although saving money and improving programming quality have been the primary concerns of station owners in turning to automation, the impact on station personnel has been significant. McLuhan states, "With automation, it is not only jobs that disappear," but "complex roles that reappear."[9] In an effort to make more money some stations have let go the majority of their announcers, putting the remaining chores in the hands of the one or two staff members. Yet, the consensus seems to be that on the whole most jobs are not eliminated at these stations. What occurs is a forced redefining of duties for the affected broadcast employees. Instead of either firing individuals or choosing not to go with automation, station owners disperse workers into other areas of operation, e.g., into the production of pre-recorded material for the new system. Certain "low level clerical positions are being eliminated," but there is apparent optimism among most personnel.[10]

Some radio employees "resent the computers and [are] not . . . able to adjust to new methods of doing jobs they feel they have been performing well for years." One of the important responsibilities of the automated station owner is to advise his workers that the system is "not a rebuke for poor performance." An apparent benefit of automated radio for the worker has been the reduction of the "pressure cooker" environment common in broadcasting operations.

There are other apparent advantages, including higher wages to some employees, announcer's programs being heard seven days a week even though they work five days, disc jockeys moonlighting on automated stations and so on. "A lot of broadcasters see automation as making better jobs for guys who deserve to stay in broadcasting and weeding out guys who shouldn't be there anyway."[11] This is no doubt true to some extent, and could be a plus for the station, but it needs to be carried out with human concerns to minimize the creation of new and more complex problems.

The Computer and the Business of Broadcasting

The computer is also revolutionizing the business end of the broadcasting industry. Both radio and television stations across the country have computerized their inventory and billing systems. Broadcast advertising is big business, a billion dollar business;

therefore when the technology can save the station money and turn it into profit, with the minimum of transaction error, it is welcomed with open arms. Traditionally, broadcast stations have to "keep track of hundreds of advertisers who purchase millions of different time periods for thousands of different commercials, with the prices of the time slots changing continually with fluctuations in audience ratings, seasons of the year, and days of the week." The laborious task was "makeshift" at best and "rife with errors," which meant "extremely slow payment by advertisers and agencies while their own workers check and double-check station bills."[12]

The computer is programmed with all of the station's inventory and billing data—a push button away from recall. Affected directly by the computerization are the station's sales department personnel. It has apparently eliminated, again, some clerical staff, while at the same time redefining the responsibilties of the sales personnel and giving them more available hours to sell time to advertisers with more accurate station sales data. The station may save as little as $1,000 or as much as $20,000 per month, depending on its size.[13] With computer/broadcasting interaction traditional jobs that would have developed in a growing company are being eliminated, and new positions and responsibilities are developing.

Computers and Cable Television

Cable television systems have grasped the technology of the computer as well, at significant savings, while "effecting meaningful improvement in operations." Computerization gives cable management greater control over its system, through "instant access to status of subscriber accounts; daily balancing of payments, new subscriptions, disconnects, reconnects and service charges; fast monthly zero-balancing; breakdown of revenue received by franchise area; and status reports on all subscriber transactions." There are numerous other benefits of the system with the "net effect that the manager or operator knows what is happening and therefore can take steps to control it." Yet, with these positive aspects, including the cutting of office costs and greater profitability, "the new system needs fewer employees than before." Traditional jobs in "payroll, accounts payable, general ledger and inventory control" are now done by the computer. In this interaction the remaining office personnel need not be skilled on the computer, but may simply be clerical staff. The technology further enables the "optimum utilization of the highly-paid installation and maintenance staff."[14] The potential impact of cable communications cannot be overemphasized. Besides "democratising broadcasting . . . cable technology could alter the whole social and cultural process of televised communications."[15]

Another interrelationship between the computer and cable communications is the "two-way interactive cable system," providing home or classroom terminals capable of sending return data signals. The Spartanburg cable project involving adult education, day care training and social service agency intercommunications is an example of classroom interaction. In the two-way interactive system as many as twenty-seven different services could be provided the individual cable subscriber at home. They might include, "catalog shopping, ticket ordering, alarm monitoring, opinion polling, instruction with voice feedback, information retrieval from various sources, auction sales, facsimile transmission of publications and mail, computer time-sharing access, videophone, and electronic voting," among others.[16] These are products of the interacting environments, and each as well is an interacting element, changing the life style of the indvidual and the traditional environments of the home.

Computer Cable and Privacy

With such a "wired city" structure the question of invasion of privacy is quickly raised. A Rand Corporation study suggests that tapping into one's cable connection is not a realistic fear because use of the system in that manner would result "in a far greater danger of exposing the 'tap' than present techniques." Yet there is a more "subtle invasion of privacy issue" that warrants attention. "If a record is compiled of each subscriber's individual uses and choices of the services available, resulting in a knowledge of his activities, interests, and preferences, that constitutes unauthorized invasion of privacy." There are others who fear such a system "will be operated in ways which maximize the flow of such information to business and government, rather than to limit the information to the aggregated data that protects individual privacy."[17]

International Computerized Broadcast Systems

Computer technology is interacting with broadcasting facilities both in this country and throughout the world. A prime example is NHK, the noncommercial Japanese broadcasting network, which as early as 1968 installed one of the most elaborate computerized systems in the world. The "science-fiction" like computer system, which has eliminated from the daily operation an estimated 1,800 telephone conversations and 5,000 memos, performs four primary functions. It serves as a "communications link" between the NHK broadcast center and its studios five miles away; "an information retrieval system storing program schedules, budgets, inventories, etc."; "a simulator working out personal assignments and studio schedules"; and "a master switching control which selects in sequence studios, cameras, tape machines, station breaks, etc., and automatically puts them on the air."

The 1,200 radio programs and 640 TV shows in production at the same time are planned and supervised by a staff of about twenty, who also monitor the programs while they are being broadcast. NHK's president has stated that the computerization has "reorganized the entire broadcast organization so that 'the mechanics of running the organization would be looked after by machines so that our people could do human work.' ". [18]

The Media and Computerized Election Analysis

The U.S. broadcasting networks make extensive use of the computer in some of the ways already pointed out. One significant interrelationship between the computer and the networks not yet mentioned is in national election analysis. At least two of the network-broadcasting election centers make use of predetermined data on sample voting precincts which consider political and demographic factors and include population density and the ethnic vote. During the Wisconsin Democratic primary in April, network broadcast analysts decided to project Morris Udall the winner over Jimmy Carter because the computer data indicated he had been consistently maintaining a slight lead. As it turned out the lead shifted to Carter, who eventually won by one percentage point. "What had begun as a piece of cake for the sophisticated network computers ended as an omelet for all," claimed *Newsweek* magazine.[19]

The computers were correct, the human factor had failed by misjudging the data, in the pressure to announce a winner at an early hour. That pressure forced newspaper reporters to accept the early network projections favoring Udall and proceed to file their stories. The chain reaction began with newspapers across the country carrying the inaccuracy. "Newspapermen were particularly mortified that instead of relying—and going wrong—on their own judgment they had taken their miscues from the rival TV medium."[20] This "variation" or erratic behavior by subsystems, i.e., the over-stepping of their limited boundaries and the interaction with one another, produced considerable overall system error and instability. Several election analysts "agreed it was a triumph of precise computer science over fallible human judgment."[21]

The Interaction Pervades

Television and theater production facilities have begun to acquire computerized lighting systems which have markedly improved the "entire lighting flow of the production." The lighting control memory saves time in rehearsal and in the technical phases of production, and saves on "person-power." The system needs only one well-trained lighting operator to handle the new technology with all its intrinsic and complex production abilities.[22]

Even in the field of satellite communications where investment approaches the one billion dollar level, computer technology plays an integral role. Communicating by satellite is an alternative to terrestrial communications systems and may be generally more economical in reaching distant populations. A recent proposal to the FCC by a consortium of four giant corporations called for "a radically new kind of communications network," whose technology would be "based entirely on ultrahigh-speed digital circuits and computer-based switching." The satellite network "will offer such new services as secure, encrypted voice and data transmission and faster data transfer speeds that match the internal operating timing of computers. Automatic error detection and correction techniques will increase accuracy a thousand-fold over present terrestrial switched services. . . ." Even "private-line phone calls and ordinary traffic from switchboards and data terminals" will operate in the system.[23] Satellite-cable interconnection is also underway with the construction of ground terminals or earth stations picking up and sending audio–video transmissions.[24]

The interaction of the computer within and outside of the field of telecommunications has been formidable and pervasive. Besides the radio and television applications already discussed, and including satellite transmissions, there exists computer graphics, computer-controlled telephone exchanges and data and message switching, display of worldwide weather data in color images, computer-assisted instruction, computer updating of the telephone book on a daily basis, computer typesetting, pagination and news-transmission services as well as other new computerized electronic systems. All of these developments have profoundly speeded up our information flow.

Interacting Environments and the Information Fallout

The increasingly sophisticated computer interacting with the media is contributing not only to the advancing technology but also to the production of overwhelming amounts of information. We are bombarded daily with useful and useless data; "as the amount of information transmitted increases, the number of forms, channels, or processes through which it is reported expand: more media, more communications, more output."[25]

Coping with the Information Explosion

How do we maintain an acceptable quality of life with "*more* information at *faster* speeds" invading our senses?[26] One method which has following among the masses is escaping to the technology of the television set with its requirement for "depth involvement."[27] It is an "absolute distraction," states Ellul in his criticism of the medium. "Man seeks . . . a total obliviousness of himself and his problems," to avoid a great deal of the weighty information flow.[28]

Fuller suggests that we "sort" through the information, discarding what is unimportant and unnecessary.[29] The news media help us with that process through headlining stories, summarizing and providing commentaries. We should demand only "authentic information," advises Mumford, in attempting to cope with the information flow.[30] There are, of course, other methods, each serving as a possible answer for the individual who needs a strategy for coping.

The computer is the ultimate sorting and recall device and an invaluable tool in the decisionmaking process. As the benefits of its problem-solving and other uses reach the individual, she will be better able to deal with the information explosion in her ever-changing environment. As long as the computer is programmed for the good of all society and the technology is used in the same manner, the people can be instrumental in both the direction and the pace of change. We need to gain control over the accelerative thrust of technology[31] and futurize our concept of education.[32]

Effects of the Interacting Communication Environments

Looking over the rather phenomenal changes taking place in our society through computer technology's interaction with the media environment as envisioned here, we cannot escape two significant conclusions: that technological changes are benefitting the technological system, and these changes, mediated influences, if you will, are having profoundly positive as well as negative effects on the individuals in their way.

McLuhan suggests that we are becoming centralized and retribalized, losing our traditionally honed individuality developed from the printed word.[33] On the other hand, Ellul declares that "the electronic media individualize by directing us to interact with the ma-

chine in lieu of the human." This is dangerous, believes the sociologist, because it may be "destructive of personality and of human
relations."[34]

Innis, McLuhan, Toffler, Ellul and other theorists have written
that the "coming of new media to a society makes a tremendous
difference in the lives of people and in the social process," that, in
fact, the effects are sweeping.[35] DeFleur disputes that concept and
argues that scientific evidence indicates the media have "little direct influence on people." But he diagnoses the apparent dichotomy
as " . . . two approaches operating on different levels of abstrac-
tion."[36] It is apparent that both concepts are valid in their own ways.
The research, though, clearly indicates that, in the changing environment of our society, the mass media as they increase in sophistication and interrelate with such advanced technologies as the
computer are significantly affecting each of us.

Conclusions

What is intended to be and is advantageous for some is often
traumatic for others in the myriad of effects brought on by the high
speed changes and forced reorientation in our always changing and
increasingly complex system. In an effort to ensure a better quality
of life for both existing and future generations we need to be aware
of that technology and the fact that it has an impact not only on its
intended beneficiaries but on the unintended as well. We have been
aware for years of the intentional nature of television to reach the
masses. Now there is "the desire to use the technology for oneself."[37]
And "even the beneficial impacts on those the technology is intended to benefit may have further consequences that are not considered at the time the technology is introduced."[38]

We need to be the masters of the technology we create. Even
though it is neutral in substance, the technology can be directed to
benefit some and disenfranchise others. Individuals in society must
have decisionmaking responsibility in setting the direction the
technology travels and how it is used. They are a part, an integral
part, of our communications environment in which all systems
and processes are interconnected and interrelating. "How technol-

ogy develops from now on is then not only a matter of some autonomous process directed by remote engineers. It is a matter of social and cultural definition, according to the ends sought."[39] It is how we, the affected individuals in an impacted society, choose to use the technlogy that determines the effects of that technology.

"We are entering a period in which the whole communications system will be in a process of constant flux."[40] The individual needs to reassess this system: determine where we are, where we may be going and what kinds of effects will result. Ellul speaks to this point when he states: "It seems clear that there must be some common measure between the means and the ends subordinated to it. The required solution, then, must be a technical inquiry into ends, and this alone can bring about a systemization of ends and means. The problem becomes that of analyzing individual and social requirements technically, of establishing numerically and mechanistically the constancy of human needs."[41]

The future demands that we learn now how to live in our evolving communications environment, to cope with possible impacts before they occur. Assessment of our future is vital. One methodology for technological assessment suggests that we need to: identify and refine the subject to be assessed; delineate the scope of the assessment and develop the data base; identify alternative strategies to solve the selected problems with the technology; identify the parties affected by the selected problems and the technologies; identify the impacts on the affected parties; evaluate or measure the impacts; and compare the pros and cons of alternative strategies.[42] But who is to do this appraisal? Toffler emphasizes, and rightfully so, that it must be the people who do the reassessing. "The time has come for a dramatic reassessment of the directions of change, a reassessment made not by the politicians or the sociologists, or the clergy or elite revolutionaries, not by the technicians or college presidents, but by the people themselves. We need, quite literally, to 'go to the people' with the question that is almost never asked of them: 'What kind of a world do you want ten, twenty, or thirty years from now?' We need to initiate, in short, a continuing Plebescite on the future."[43]

11

Computer Impact
and the Social Welfare Sector

GARY R. MOOERS

The year is 1983 and the president of a prominent professional social welfare association is addressing his colleagues:

You will be pleased to know that all decisions made by our master case managers are based on a comprehensive data bank of material that can be computerized, centralized, and made available to you at a few moments' notice. That is true, of course, only for the data collected after 1975. As some of you oldtimers may recall, a unified code for reporting data was only established in 1980.

The unified code requires that the diagnostic category, the type of service offered, the length of service, the techniques used, and the relative success of the service be fed into computers. Not only has this provided ongoing records of service to the individual, but it has enabled the field to assess which types of treatment seem most successful for which types of clients. Naturally, but perhaps regrettably, this has led to the eclipse of certain treatment approaches that proved to be statistically unsuccessful.

With complete profiles of the client and worker on computer tapes, simulated interviews can be played back in seconds. By feeding the computer a few "what if" questions, we can be told the most successful responses or questions. Certain clients—particularly those who are suicidal or on probation—will have to have a videotaped interview each morning for five minutes. The computer analyzes the content and voice patterns and warns if an immediate personal interview is needed.[1]

This somewhat satirical projection of a "future-shock" type of computerized social welfare system indicates the staggering impact that computers and related technology are making in the social welfare arena. The fictional 1983 speech appears much more plausible when one picks up the local paper and reads the headline: "Psychiatric patients talk to computer."[2] The article goes on to briefly describe an experimental program in Salt Lake City where a computer is programmed to administer various psychiatric tests, analyze the responses, and print individual summaries which the researchers claim are more objective than summaries prepared by professional staff. Time will tell whether this program will be successful in the long run, but it clearly illustrates just one of the many uses of computer technology in the provision of human services in the 1970s.

It is apparent that the extensive use of computers and the seemingly endless tasks that they efficiently perform are rapidly changing modern society and the social welfare mechanisms within this society. The ramifications of this technological revolution are, in all probability, unknowable at this time, and it will be many years before the effects of computer technology on social welfare systems and services can be realistically assessed.

To some social welfare educators and professionals the advent of the computer offers limitless opportunities to modify and streamline the existing social welfare structure. As Gruber notes, "the systems science, the management sciences, and the information explosion open new vistas for social management and control. Some see in these possibilities the acme of rationality and efficiency, a kind of technological utopia that blots out the last vestiges of man's irrationality and capriciousness."[3] While not all social welfare spokesmen are this optimistic, most would certainly agree that increased reliance on computers is the wave of the future in social welfare programs. One source cites "the burgeoning computer technology just beginning to be felt in social work,"[4] while another notes its impact in "welfare, education, health, urban planning, corrections, law enforcement and other fields involving social management."[5] It seems reasonable to assume that in the very near future, all professionals in the social welfare field will be expected to knowledgeably participate in data collection, analysis, and utilization.

It now appears obvious that computer technology has moved

past its initial pioneering contributions to the physical sciences, space and defense industries, and the private business sector, to programs focusing on services to people. This trend has not been viewed with universal approval, and many professionals have attempted to ignore or minimize the changes occurring in the social welfare field. Weiss notes "an important reason for the history of neglect of even the most sophisticated system has been data overload. Too much information is spewed out—more than decision-makers want, need, or can digest."[6] This overwhelming amount of data, coupled with valid ethical concerns and a natural resistance to change, has led many experts in the field to view the technological advances in computer systems as a decidedly mixed blessing.

Rationale for Increased Computer Use

In spite of these reservations, conditions are such that increasing utilization of computer systems is assured. "The United States is moving slowly but inexorably toward a welfare state."[7] Rising public demands for services and administrative and judicial decisions liberalizing eligibility requirements will continue to expand along with the inevitable accompanying bureaucracy. If proposals for a guaranteed annual income, full employment programs, and national health insurance are passed into law, then the expansion will proceed at an even more rapid pace.

"With this expansion, managing resources has become a grave problem."[8] The funding and management of these expanded social welfare programs has become increasingly complex and costly, particularly in regard to programs and services provided by the federal government on a national basis. It is extremely doubtful that many of these programs (e.g., Social Security) could be successfully administered without computerized information systems which provide data to assist in accounting, planning, decision making, priority setting, and evaluation.

This expansion and proliferation of services and bureaucracies has been enormously expensive and has inevitably cost more than was anticipated. An important, if obvious, point is that the great bulk of social welfare expenditures comes from the public treasury.

The rapid increase in expenditures in the social welfare area had generated a call for efficiency and effective cost controls. "When resources are scarce as they are in the social welfare field—it becomes increasingly important to allocate them with a purpose and a plan."[9] Financial scandals and evidences of mismanagement in some social welfare programs have caused an aroused public to increasingly question expenditures and to demand maximum performance for their tax dollars. Suchman well states this insistence on accountability: "a better educated and more sophisticated public is less willing than ever to accept the need for community services on faith alone."[10]

The demands for accountability and the means to feasibly measure this concept have only recently arrived on the social welfare scene. "Social work programs traditionally have been carried out without systematic accumulation of information concerning their operations or outcomes and hence have had little accountability."[11] The pressure upon agencies and programs to be accountable is not only applied by the general public but also by funding agencies. Purchase of service contracts which are often sought by competing agencies or organizations certainly put a premium on the documentation of effective service delivery. The quite justifiable expectations that services should be delivered at a reasonable cost is leading to increasingly sophisticated computer management systems which enhance efficiency and produce data for evaluation.

The demand for accountability simply requires that service delivery organizations must be prepared to document their activities in terms of what they are doing, what are the costs, and what are the results. Hoshino and McDonald succinctly state this evaluative process: "Agency goals and objectives need to be operationalized, and measurable indicators of achievement need to be developed. These measures of output can be incorporated into the agency's information system. The agency will then be in a position to evaluate program effectiveness."[12] It is apparent that the process described above is greatly facilitated by computer technology. Without this tool, it is doubtful that any meaningful large-scale assessment could be completed in a reasonable amount of time.

Common Computer Tasks

As previously discussed, computers are continually playing a larger role in the delivery of social welfare services, and it seems appropriate to examine some of the diverse tasks they are now performing in the modern service delivery system. Perhaps the most frequent utilization of computer technology involves the routine processing and accounting functions which every program is required to accomplish. Anyone who has been employed in a public welfare department, as this writer was for a number of years, is familiar with computer printouts containing current caseloads and is acquainted with the procedures necessary to have the computer open, close, or change the status of a case. "Relevant data may be processed to develop a computer system that will handle most accounting procedures presently necessary, with considerable reduction in time and effort by administrators and clerical staff."[13] This type of computer usage is invaluable, and it is difficult to imagine any of the large social welfare organizations being able to function effectively if this type of technological support were withdrawn.

Another advantage that computers have brought to the social welfare sector is a vastly increased potential for empirical research. Social workers (the predominant professionals in the social welfare field) have not traditionally been overly productive in the area of research, and much of the relevant research produced has come from universities and colleges. This situation has the potential for rapid change now that "present computer technology brings research within the range of almost every practicing social worker and statistical packages or 'canned' programs make the computer even more useful to agency staff."[14]

Computer usage in program analysis and evaluation is a swiftly developing and essential aspect of computer technology in the social welfare arena. The previously mentioned need for accountability has necessitated the gathering, analysis, and interpretation of data by information systems in order to improve and modify service delivery. Weiss notes that "Information systems have the capability to analyze a wide range of program conditions (for example, length of service, referral flow, and unit costs) against the outcomes that ensued for clients. If the data are selected and arranged with care, they can provide regular guidance that is enormously useful for decision making."[15] Anderson cites the "promise held for knowledge building, examination of effectiveness, and innovation in service delivery."[16] It seems clear at this point that the evaluative components of computer technology will assume an even greater role as methods improve and knowledge advances in this relatively new endeavor.

While computer technology has swiftly established itself as an essential and indispensable servant in accomplishing the goals of effective service delivery, it has come with such speed that many of its ramifications and complexities are not yet fully understood. Almost any technological advance has unintended and unforeseen consequences or spinoffs (e.g., development of the "pill" and its effect on adoption). A number of professionals in the social welfare field feel strongly that we need to closely examine the whole area of computer management and technology so that we can better understand this phenomenon and knowledgeably counteract the problems which inevitably arise.

Problems and Criticisms

A number of serious problems have already been identified, and these warrant careful consideration. If computers are to achieve the high potential predicted for them, each problem will need to be identified, analyzed, and alleviated. Even a brief review of the literature reveals that this process is well underway. While no one is advocating a retreat to the pre-computer era, reflective voices are pointing out deficiencies and suggesting solutions to various aspects of computerization.

One problem frequently alluded to is the problem of meaningless data. "Administrators may find much of the data poured forth by these systems to be irrelevant, unreliable or both."[17] Since social welfare agencies have the mandate to help individuals, it is frightening to contemplate the idea that decisions affecting people's lives might be based on erroneous data. This problem is exacerbated when decisionmakers place an inflated value on data and are unaware of its limitations. Supposedly "objective" measures of performance are extremely difficult to determine in a field where all the variables affecting a situation are seldom if ever known.

Hoshino and McDonald lucidly comment on this problem: "Agencies should not consider computer utilization as a panacea to the problem of accountability. The acronym GIGO—garbage in, garbage out—is still the first law of computer analysis. The computer opens the door for the use of many complicated statistical procedures and applies them to large files of data. But without some knowledge of these procedures and competence in applying them to the specific problems at hand, a glut of worthless data and studies will be turned out."[18]

It is obvious that data can be either of immense value or useless at best and misleading and destructive at worst, depending on its accuracy and ability to measure what it was intended to measure. Perhaps Hoffer has best stated the central issue and major obstacle to obtaining relevant and meaningful data in a field crowded with complex variables: "No one has really been able to get to the central question of what information we really need for management purposes. In many cases, there is a need to restructure or reorganize data and present it in a different framework so that more cogent questions can be asked and answered."[19] Until questions can be devised which will consistently produce accurate answers and valid measurements, a healthy scepticism toward much of the social welfare data seems to be in order.

If social welfare data is often inadequate, it seems germane to consider how we formulate the questions to be answered. Thompson faults the "assembly-line approaches to problem solving which vastly underestimate the complexity of the units with which they deal—people—and they fail to take adequate account of emergent situations."[20] He also faults the insistence on mathematical forms of measurement and implies that other models might well be more useful.[21] Another criticism is offered by Bonney and Streicher concerning the "hour interview" between social worker and client which is sometimes viewed by computer management personnel as a social welfare standardized unit of output or production. "This designation is problematic, however, because it is not a standardized unit of production. It is unlikely that every interview hour is equally productive in its contribution to the resolution of interpersonal problems. Thus it is extremely difficult to conceive of a method of quality control that might resolve the problems inherent in any attempt to measure the productivity of the more creative and interpersonal types of professional work."[22]

Another problem concerned with data collection involves the social workers who must provide the information which goes into the computer. "Practitioners are likely to resent the increased paperwork required and may resist or subvert detailed reporting of data that might adversely reflect on their performance."[23] The resentment of the paperwork involved seems nearly universal, particularly since the burden of data collection falls upon those workers already busy providing direct service to clients. This writer once observed a group of disgruntled caseworkers discussing various methods of how to "foul-up" the computer. They finally instructed the computer to change the client status of an elderly senile nursing-home resident to that of an unwed mother in need of counseling concerning her unborn child. The deleterious effect upon the accuracy of that agency's data is apparent. In far too many agencies there is an unceasing demand for information concerning objectives, goals, diagnoses, and outcomes on each client. This demand made on frequently overworked and harried workers can only lead to frustration and inaccurate data reporting. Less time-consuming data reporting is obviously needed if the total cooperation of the workers is to be achieved.

Another problem in the social welfare field is how to minimize the depersonalizing effect of computer technology in an already impersonal modern society. This problem concerns both employees and clients of social welfare agencies. Computers, with their ability to efficiently process information and rapidly make it available, often work against local decisionmaking, autonomy, and innovation to meet local needs. "It seems probable that computerized decisionmaking and information systems will slow down or even

reverse the trend toward decentralization. Both of these technological innovations encourage recentralization. They do so by
eliminating one of the compelling reasons for decentralization—
management's inability to keep up with the increasing size and
complexity of the enterprise."[24] The beneficial effect of computer
technology can be effectively nullified if it results in rigid centralized decisionmaking which thwarts local efforts to solve differing
problems in different locales.

Two authors are particularly concerned about current efforts to
utilize technology to solve problems. Abels warns that computer
systems are "deaf and blind to human values" and decries the fact
that "the man behind the computer—the man who really makes
the decisions—will be a manager, a systems analyst, and not a social worker."[25] Gruber is particularly vociferous concerning this
problem, as he foresees a possible "new form of collectivism that
subjugates the person under the new order of control and efficiency."[26] These gentlemen may be unduly alarmed, but we must
insure that the computer assists in solving problems and not in
creating new ones.

The proliferation of computerized data banks has been viewed
with concern by some authorities. Fein comments, "It is generally
agreed at all computer installations that confidentiality of information is a sensitive and important topic and some attention has
been paid to it. Individual agencies can guarantee confidentiality
when they alone deal with their data, but planning for safeguards
has not proceeded for systems with purchase of service or third
party payments tied into them. Confidentiality is an area in which
good intentions must be formalized for the protection of clients."[27]
Reid also recognizes the threat to confidentiality of professional-
client relationships but is hopeful these problems can be solved or
minimized in time.[28] The data banks with their often sensitive personal information (e.g. psychiatric labels concerning mental patients) must be guarded closely so that the clients' right to
confidentiality and privacy is protected.

All the problems discussed above should be of great concern to
all individuals since the lives of every citizen have been or will be

influenced by occurrences and trends within the modern social welfare system. The problems of irrelevant data, depersonalization, and confidentiality must be resolved if computer technology is to fulfill its unlimited potential as a positive force in ameliorating and alleviating problems in this society. These problems are complex and will not be solved overnight. However, they have been identified (which is perhaps half the battle), and definite efforts are being made to reduce and minimize these problems. One inescapable fact is that though these problems pose serious difficulties for the social welfare sector, the absence of computers would create many more serious problems than we face today.

The computer and its trappings have grown in importance and will continue to exert more influence in the future. Computer technology is an integral part of the provision of social welfare services, and it is here to stay. Even the most vocal critics of computerized management do not suggest eliminating this form of technology. The challenge to social welfare professionals now seems to be: How do we best maximize the efficiency and effectiveness of this very valuable tool?

Putting Computers in Perspective

Perhaps what is needed is a new appraisal of what computers actually are and what they can and cannot do. Many people hold computers in awe because of a lack of understanding of their nature. Computers are machines (albeit complex, intricate and marvelously useful machines), and they do only what we build and program them to do. They cannot tell us what to do, but they can aid us in performing needed tasks and accomplishing specified goals.

Rosenberg and Brady see the whole range of computer technology as being an important means of improving services as long as it is not viewed as an end in itself, and social work values are the base from which to use this technology.[29] Abels also sees the potential value in computer management and data systems but suggests that the social work profession assume more responsibility in these areas, so that computer managers understand human and social problems as well as management techniques.[30] Both articles imply that the problem lies not with the computer but in how we have viewed and utilized it.

Vondracek, Urban, and Parsonage provide perhaps the best perspective on computers that this author has read. "Concerns about dehumanization resulting from an automated intake procedure can be laid to rest by looking at the computer as a tool, no different in principle from a typewriter or a dictating machine. If properly used, an automated system can increase rather than decrease the level of humanistic concern in human services systems. In sum, it appears that the judicious use of technology in the human services field holds great potential for releasing humanitarian concern where it has been buried under red tape and paper work, and for giving it new life where it has been pushed aside by excessive workloads and other demands."[31] The crucial statement made by Vondracek and his colleagues is that a computer should be viewed as a tool and not as a mysterious object to be feared or revered.

One of the hopeful developments within the social welfare sector is the growing awareness by social work eduators that computer technology can no longer be ignored and left out of the required curriculum. The understanding and skilled usage of computer technology may soon be as important to social workers as are basic interviewing skills. Anderson indicates that social welfare professionals will soon be expected to participate in both feeding and using data systems and advocates the presentation of the basic features of information systems within schools of social work.[32] Hoshino and McDonald also suggest a stronger commitment by the schools of social work to "imparting knowledge of information systems, statistical analysis, and data processing."[33] Social work education has moved rapidly in this area, and it seems safe to say that new graduates are much more knowledgeable in this area than were graduates of only two or three years ago.

The field of social welfare and the computer have their problems to overcome, but these do not seem insurmountable, and one hopes that Reid is correct in his prediction: "The growing reliance on data, while creating some novel and difficult problems, should have a salubrious effect on a profession that has far too long relied on its convictions for its credibility. The way forward for social work, like medicine, will be in the development of empirical foundations. The next decade should see some sizeable strides in this direction."[34]

12

Computer Impact on Society: A Personal View from the World of Art

MARGARET GOROVE

The humanistic issues raised by the impact of computer technology on society have been much discussed in generalities that raise yet more generalities and with questions that raise but more questions. It is realized that no pat and easy answers can be found, yet world organizations as well as local civic groups recognize the need to pinpoint the broad ramifications of technology on our daily life. The events that have occurred within our lifetime have not been sudden since hindsight allows us to see their seeming inevitability from the time the Industrial Revolution first began. However, it does seem formidable to realize that the advent of atomic energy, man's walk on the moon, photographs from Mars, massive dispersal of computers, televisions, jets and numerous other developments foretell yet even more to come in the near future. It is remarkable that men and women are such adaptable creatures that they can absorb it all and seek to put it in order.

The field of art has been chosen for investigation not because it will provide any answers but because, as a reflection of society, it serves to demonstrate how technology has become finely enmeshed in every aspect of our life. To detach the arts of painting and sculpture from their intricate interrelationships with other areas of humanities and sciences is an impossible feat, but the attempt is perhaps justified if it brings understanding a little closer. One can hope to control and direct only that which one understands to some degree. For the sake of analysis, the many ramifications of the computer impact on art have been divided into examinations of the changing profession of art itself and the impact this has had on society in general, though admittedly each has felt the effect of the other.

It would be wise at this point to clarify certain basic terminology. Both art and technology are often referred to as part of the "common good" that can enhance the quality of life, but it is generally agreed that the term "common good" will remain a laudably vague concept based on certain undefinable universals until it is applied to a specific locale where the social, economic, and political circumstances are taken into consideration. To seek the "common good" by using "computer technology" opens further complications, inasmuch as the latter term enters all streams of life today, and to a great extent many examples of generalized machine technology have simply become more sophisticated with computers. The question of "technological shock" and whether we have passed it or whether it is still to come is not discussed, since it seems academic in view of the fact that the way of tomorrow is always paved with the past; and it is reassuring to note that human beings always manage to surpass old "world records" simply because it is within their nature to rise to challenges.[1]

Computer Impact on Art as a Profession

We find that long before such a field as sociology existed, the visual language of art was used to depict the times and the society, sometimes badly, sometimes well. As thinking, feeling, and at times inexplicable creatures, artists have always been part of their societies and, knowingly or unknowingly, revealed it. In surveying the profession of art today, one comes to the conclusion that technology changed the traditional definition of art when it brought new responsibilities by providing the artist with new subject matters and materials.

Defining "Art." The whole question of "what is art?" has been raised from early Greek times, and probably earlier, yet no definite answer is possible. It is a question that is settled by society; and in the past, society was guided by religions, monarchies, or dictatorships. Until a little over a century ago, mankind appeared content to have art defined as the application of certain finishes and techniques to "proper" subject matter,[2] but that standard has changed; and the most frequent question asked by art students today is "what is art?" Traditional definitions no longer seem appropriate, and the underlying basis for this can be traced to technological advances.

Technology began to affect art indirectly when it freed people from the necessity of excessive manual labor and allowed the broadening of the literate base that, in turn, created the political and economic systems which broke down the strict social order of earlier centuries. This is a sweeping simplification, and, admittedly, there are vast numbers who seem to have been by-passed by this technological and social revolution. But, for much of the world, this broadening of the scale of literacy has resulted in a concern for the "common good." For the artist, this process resulted in the loss of the traditional patronage of religions, monarchies and nation-states, and, as part of the sweep toward egalitarianism, the artist began to pursue the subject matter of everyday life. No longer tied to "story telling" with historical, religious, moral, or mythological implications, artists first turned to the daily life of the people around them for subject matter, but in a short time found themselves supplied with new materials that opened up a vast array of other potentials.[3] At this point the inter-relationships become fogged, but it would appear that art would never have changed so profoundly without the new materials offered by technology in the twentieth century. For this reason, a brief survey of the materials and their implications seems necessary before a discussion of the integration of subject matter and materials.

The Materials of Technology. Art has always been intimately associated with technology, for the materials utilized have adverse chemical reactions when improperly made or applied. Until the fifteenth century, the major medium or liquid solution with which powdered organic colors could be mixed was water, which lent itself best to relatively flat forms. When fifteenth century artists developed oil paint for their use, what we call Renaissance art became possible, since only with oil paint could one achieve great depth and subtle interplay of shadow and light. At this point artists began to utilize canvas rather than wooden supports, making paintings into more easily portable objects. Oil remained the dominant medium, being improved during the mid-nineteenth century when the chemical industry provided a wider range of ready-mixed colors at reasonable prices. Today this industry is fully computerized and provides the artist with prepared color combinations based on both organic and inorganic compounds. Machines and computers not only check the permanence of new colors, but keep local art store inventories up to date.

The biggest impacts of technology on the painter today show up with the brand new mediums of synthetic or plastic-based paints, most often called polymer or acrylic. In existence since the early years of this century, it was only about twenty years ago that they were approved as permanent for artists' use. While their potentials are still being explored, they nearly dominate the art market, since a large majority of contemporary painters utilize them in preference to oil paints. One is hesitant to form opinions at such an early stage, for it must be remembered that it took over a century for artists to explore the potentials of oil paint after it first appeared. Hindsight will probably show, however, that plastic-based paints are affecting the style of art today as much as the introduction of oil paint affected artists in past centuries.[4] The implications of this medium will be explored later, but let it be pointed out that, since it can be applied to nearly any material or shape, and withstand dampness and sudden changes in temperature, it is agreeable to rapid, large-scale mural paintings; since it can be applied with a roller or spray gun, it allows the artist to eliminate any individual brushstroke; and since it is mixed and cleaned with water and rapid drying, it has had an important influence on the growth of painting as a hobby.

In sculpture, far-reaching changes have also taken place due to the advances of technology. While the traditional materials of clay, wood, stone, and metal have remained, with modifications, new techniques and new materials of plastic and light have fascinated artists from the beginning of this century.

Artists, in their exploration of the new subject matter of daily life, began to utilize the industrial materials of iron and "junk" metal, welding them together in free-form. Until this development, monumental sculptural pieces were of stone or bronze, both of great expense and enormous weight. Today, by combining the discarded materials of industry and welding them together, it is possible to have large-scale public works at relatively low cost and without the problems of excessive weight. But again, in sculpture as in painting, perhaps the most important development has been the utilization of plastics. Not only of lighter weight than metal, they provide a transparency and allow the artist "to draw in space." Large-scale sculptural groups that would otherwise be immovable without heavy cranes are easily portable when made with plastics. We also find that since this new material can be transparent, the possibility of light becoming part of a piece of art has been explored. Today many contemporary sculptors are concerned with the integration of color, light, and sound, that, with the help of computers, respond to individuals or to the environment.[5]

The social implications of these new developments will be discussed later, but, apart from the obvious potentials relating to public art and environmental work, we find problems arising as to the extent future artists need to be technically trained in electronics and science, and further question the trend of society since the sixteenth century to divide art into compartments easily identified as painting, sculpture, or architecture, since in many art works these are fused.

The Integration of Subject Matter and Materials. When the so-called "freeing" of art from its bondage to literature left the artist in search of new subject matter at the same time that new materials were becoming available, the inevitable result of an overwhelming number of "isms" came about—impressionism, post-impressionism, cubism, futurism, rayonism, realism, and functionalism, to mention but a few. It is startling to realize that people are still talking about the impact of technology on art when over sixty years ago artists began asserting that the automobile was more beautiful than the *Victory of Samothrace*; that the art of the future had to be based on light, speed, and time; and that artists must be trained technicians working for the common good.[6] It is not the aim of this paper to review the many styles of art that are part of our society today, but it must be understood that what might appear to the casual art gallery visitor as "over-choice", or a multiplicity of styles with seemingly no coherence, can be regarded as the end result not only of the new materials that allowed the artist to seek new spatial relationships, but also of that rise of literacy and personal freedoms which we know as democracy.

The Amount of "Self" in the Artist's Work and its Ethical Implications. There is a general tendency to feel that, since art is a very personal matter, the artist has been rather undisturbed by much of the talk about "computer society," "technological shock," "loss of individuality," and the multitude of other phrases utilized today in trying to analyze the effect of technology on our times. Yet a survey of the art world seems to indicate that all of these factors are present. Artists, being a part of their society, and liking to think that they have an added sensitivity that attunes them to things of which others are not aware, have reflected their time. There are those who use art as a type of therapy for the expression of "self." While not to be demeaned, and indeed there are now graduate degrees being offered in the field of "art therapy," for the most part these artists wish the emphasis to be on emotion rather than intellect. They would seem directly opposed to being a part of the computer society; and some so much resent their placement with art market stock reports, computerized files in museums, and other occurrences on the art scene today that they deliberately create art that is self-destructive to emphasize the importance of the act of creation—the assertion of "self"—rather than the object itself as something to be kept, catalogued, and viewed from afar.[7] Fearful that technology will distort human nature, and regarding it as an obstacle both to artistic creation and another's perception of it, they forget that historically artists have long found expression with the assistance of technology.

On the other extreme, we find artists who desire to reflect the world around them, seeking the precision and clarity of machine forms undisturbed by any personal feeling. Some artists retain all their original work, selling only mechanically-produced reproductions of their work which computers have helped to devise.[8] One wonders if the artists who are seeking to become part of the production process portray society as it exists or as they would like to see it exist—perfect with no blown fuses.

Needless to say, as with society itself, the majority of artists are somewhere between these two extremes. But even within this group there arise many major questions, as a search for ethical standards in the art profession continues. Perhaps foremost in the minds of many artists is the question of how much individual as opposed to machine labor is needed in a piece to make it a work of "art." Is it enough to simply design it on graph paper and send it to a factory to be built?[9] Should artists feel guilty when ignorance or economics prevent them from utilizing in their work the latest developments of computers, electronics, and a myriad of other innovations? Even if such specialized equipment is not available, questions arise with photography, reducing/enlarging machines, and other devices which have lightened the need for "craft" on the part of the artist. For the last half-century, some have held that since the IDEA is the primary force behind art, the methods matter little and that a knowledge of basic forms, the ability to draw a figure, and so on, is not necessary because machines can perform these functions as well as they produce the paints within tubes that once the artist had to hand-grind.[10]

While each artist seems to find personal solutions to the problems raised above, all are aware that the biggest impact is yet to come as computer technology becomes a more integrated part of life. Like most people, artists become aware of the computerization of life only when their names are lost in a file or when a bill that has been paid keeps being returned. Little attention is paid to the fact that computers play a major part in supplying people with materials, art books, catalogues, and many other things. Yet the artist is very much aware that in the United States alone nearly 400 million prints "suitable for framing" are produced each year, most with a process of offset lithography that gives only partially true colors, but some with the better process of collotype which has true color but no brush marks. That these millions of art prints surround one in daily life cannot help but affect the production of artists. The recent trends in art toward flatness of almost a reproductive quality might well be traced to the fact that this proliferation of "fine-art" prints coincided with the development of plastic-based paints that permitted the elimination of brushstrokes. The artist often ignores these facts, taking refuge in the realization that, while some prints even simulate brushstrokes, the difference between an original and a reproduction is obvious from the surface texture. But what of the future as processes improve? What will be the distinction between a reproduction and an original if computerized machines can produce several hundred painted "multi-originals" of a painting? Such is possible if an artist applies chemically treated paint to a specially treated canvas plaque and the resulting painting is passed through a computer which analyzes what color, glaze mixture, and texture to apply in successive layers to each of the "multi-originals." Since the original is destroyed in the process, only the "multi-originals" are left. The implications not only for the artist but for museums and public collections are enormous. Such a device is in existence, under patent, and several leading artists have worked with this process, signing each piece as a "multi-original" in order to allow their work to sell for less and thus make it more widely available to the public.[11]

While the long-term effect of such developments on society in general will be discussed later, some of the more immediate effects on the artist's profession must be considered. To some artists the idea is abhorrent and unethical since it takes away the individuality of the piece. To others it is the answer to the art market's needs for more first-quality work at reasonable prices; and since the art market is no longer national but international, larger productions of a good work of art would not adversely affect the market. But this would only be the case if proven artists of high caliber utilize the process. An artist's nightmare could easily result if "multi-original" works of indifferent character flooded the market at prices less than the cost of the materials used by an artist to make one original work. The question also arises as to who decides which artist will be invited to use the machine, and in this connection it must be recognized that today an intricate economic relationship exists between art galleries, auction houses, art critics, and museums.

If development of such processes seems to have formidable implications for the future, so also will the impact of holography, television art, and other computerized or electronic devices that at times enter into the field of public domain. Holography utilizes laser light to "reconstruct" precise, realistic, three-dimensional images of an object.[12] While the potentials for public museums are discussed later, it is interesting to observe that when artists use it as a new medium, most critics choose to ignore the fact that they are viewing special photography or holograms of the original work — in other words, a sophisticated type of reproduction. No doubt this is due to the fact that holography is in the experimental stage and extremely costly and there is always a tendency to find costly things "original." We find the same problems arising with respect to developments in televised work, mass media, and cybernetics, for discussions focus on their effect on society in general. Few ponder the position of the artist who is faced with possible "over-exposure"; the task of determining when a work is actually art or only a reflection of it; and the personal need to distinguish between art and entertainment.

Certainly there are no easy answers for the artist regarding the amount of "self" needed to make a work of art, but then we know from experience that only time distinguishes between true art and "picture-making." For an artist today to spurn technical assistance would seem foolhardy, and one is aware that even the venerable Renaissance masters utilized rudimentary machines and had numerous assistants to help them in their art productions.[13] Today we find that some artists utilize technological developments to a small extent, while others heavily rely on them. It would appear that the situation is similar to the housewife who is asked to supply a cake—some start from scratch, some reach for the ready-mix and others go to the local bakery.

The Place of Art in the Humanities. Art has been included in the field of "liberal arts" for only about 400 years. For this we owe thanks to Leonardo da Vinci and his fellow Renaissance men, since it was through their efforts that art was lifted out of the "manual labor" category and put on an equal status with literature.[14] While no one today questions the placement of art within the humanities, not many artists have lived up to Leonardo's standard that they should be knowledgeable in all allied fields as well as in mathematics and science. Maybe artists are finally coming close to this ideal, however, since during this century America has witnessed the entry of art into university complexes. Forty years ago only about thirty colleges offered degrees in art while today over 400 have artists on their faculties and many universities offer not only undergraduate degrees but graduate studio degrees as well.[15] A majority of the young artists at leading galleries in the United States hold graduate degrees in art. In other words, they had to take all undergraduate college requirements and then additional history, research, and studio work. Many leading artists in America are associated with a university in some way or for some part of each year. The reasons for this are complex, but the primary impetus seems to stem from the fact that there was an immediate build-up of science programs within universities after World War II, and this was substantially increased after Sputnik. Simply put, there arose a feeling that a large dose of "art" would counter the accusations of "science-orientation."

While artists might have entered into higher education as a counterbalance to science, we find that they have stayed and probably will stay. The number of private art schools has declined as costs have mounted, and one rarely encounters an artist who can be self-supporting solely on earnings from art. Photography, amateur painters, and "fine art" reproduction have shrunk the artist's potential market at the same time that the cost of materials has risen. Apart from economic considerations, there is a further asset to being affiliated with higher education, since it is a cultural milieu that is almost a microcosm of society. While artists have other artists in their own areas, they are also in closer contact with other disciplines, most importantly for this discussion, with science-oriented fields. The inevitable effect of this would seem to be closer collaboration between art and science, yet many problems remain. It is interesting to note that most of the leaders in kinetic art and cybernetics began in engineering or an allied field and only later turned to art. Others have produced such work only when collaborating with technicians who could supply the knowhow to carry out their ideas.[16] It would appear that the art instruction of today has not moved as rapidly as the development of new materials. The traditional academy method of teaching art declined at the same time that mass production of artists' materials began, and greater emphasis was often given to the development of a personal "style." Often only a perfunctory review of new materials is given to the young artist, due to the prohibitively high cost of computers, laser beams, complex photographic equipment and other devices. However, such complex equipment can be found within university complexes, and it seems but a matter of time before fuller cooperation and integration will enable artists to become familiar with these materials even before cost-breakthroughs make them more widely available.

Another aspect of the contemporary student's education that bears consideration is the impact of audiovisual aids that are utilized in teaching. In the past, possessing only small black-and-white reproductions of major art works, the artist would often undergo great privations to seek out originals and learn directly from them. Today this burning desire seems to have been tempered by wide exposure to films, reproductions and slides of uniform size, texture, and tactile feeling. While students are more informed than earlier artists about the historical aspects of all past styles, their own work is bound to reflect the changes in teaching methods, and, conversely, eventually the work will reflect a rebellion against those methods.

At least another quarter of a century will be needed to evaluate the full impact of the aspect mentioned above, but it is apparent that the youth receiving art training today is exposed to ideas and fields of technics never encountered by earlier generations. About thirty years ago, it was still common to find discussions on the incompatability of art and science, but today the emphasis seems to be on the various ways that the artist and scientist can cooperate on providing for the common good. One can never be sure of the ultimate result, but it must be remembered that nothing is achieved without the loss of something else, and artists who are integrated into the technological life around them must face the question of whether the sheer lack of time to do all things has lessened the knowledge of craft; or whether it has opened new doors that enable artists, in a multitude of different ways, to apply technology with human sensitivity. Whatever the answers are, it remains clear that the role of artists is undergoing a great change that is reflective of the changing society of which they are a part.

Computer Impact on Society's Exposure to Art

A look at a hypothetical American community might help to avoid the problem of over-generalization in discussing how individuals have been affected by the changes in art at the same time that they have helped bring about these changes.

On a typical day, one can drive down a street, passing advertising billboards of brilliant color and design; turn at the corner near the local art association building; notice the repainting of an old Victorian house that had nearly been torn down a year earlier; stop at the local recreation center which is advertising its courses in rug weaving, pottery, and landscape painting; pass by the local museum which is displaying works by a neighboring painters' guild; stop by the supermarket and find that for a $10 purchase and a coupon one can get a free "fine art" reproduction; return home and turn on the television to the educational channel which is giving a course on basic drawing; switch channels and find that Kenneth Clark's *Civilisation* series is being sponsored by the local electrical company; open a magazine which features an article on "American Art Today"; open the local newspaper and find the design for an "environmental" fountain that is to be built in front of the new county library that will have a special "art browsing" room; open the mail and find a free 30-day trial offer of a "beautiful art book that you can display with pride"; listen to the children remind you that they need new crayons and are supposed to bring an assortment of colored paper and fabric scraps for an art project in math class. One could go on with many more examples, such as the friend just returned from a trip who found that the time passed quickly at the airport because the waiting room had been turned into "living art" with colors and music responding as viewers pushed buttons on the computer; or that another friend just returned from having encountered in a European city square a cybernetic sculpture that whirled, spun lights and sound, and seemed to bow to passers-by.[17]

Perhaps only in the last two instances would the average person stop to reflect on the extent that art has infiltrated everyday life. Ordinarily we do not think about it. We also do not think about it as being directly related to technological advances. But in retrospect, we find that technology, much of which has recently been computerized, is turning out the billboards, books, advertisements, and reproductions; is providing art materials in easy-to-use form for home hobbyists; is developing mass communications; and is also providing the impetus for preserving our past and treasuring our ability to create with our own hands.

Public Collections of Art. Public museums have been developed on an extensive scale only within the last hundred years. While computer impact has been felt in everyday operations of filing, cataloging, and collecting, it is in the area of museum display that the effect on society is most clearly evident.

What would be the result if local museums could display "multi-originals" by leading contemporary artists alongside holograms of major works of art from the past? If the holograms were such that visitors would not realize they were "reconstructed" until they attempted to touch them, a solution would seem to have been found to allow all people to have access to the masterpieces of the world. While this would seem to be for the common good, a question arises as to the human tendency to regard those things which are easily accessible as "less." Often our notion of what is "great" stems from the fact that it is not commonplace but found amidst mediocre, good, and nearly-great pieces from which it stands out.[18] There is also the question as to which "masterpiece" should be available to all. While this century prides itself on being liberal, examining all areas historically and objectively, it has its bias like all centuries. Each age, in seeking to find itself, picks out certain art from the past which seems to tell it something or, in many cases, reflects its own preoccupations. This selectivity allows the next generations to "rediscover" their own masterpieces.

These problems are intimately associated with present-day concerns of museums as they seek to determine the allocation of their limited facilities and funds. While such issues lie outside the scope of this discussion, it is seen that the application of further technology in museum displays must be constantly adjusted to what is loosely described as "human nature."

Technology in Public Works of Art. The developments in technology and new materials have assisted the production of public art. The actual revival of interest in this field seems to stem from two main factors: the reaction arising in society against "machine-orientation," which brought about an interest in humanizing environments; and the fact that today many business concerns and public organizations are concerned with their "image."[19]

While the science of computers is far from perfected in art works, questions involving invasion of privacy have potential impact. The all-controlled environment attempts to link sound to color (which is light), adjusting both to the individual's response with the assistance of computers and sensors.[20] Experiments are continuing to perfect such developments, but little mention is taken of possible dangers. Certainly an environment that would respond to an individual's feelings is not always the best solution if severe depression were being undergone, and is it wise to leave the choice of environment in the hands of an individual? Also, the potentials of controlling or directing human motivation by planned environments is not too far-fetched for contemplation. As with all things, developments in this area could be used for the betterment of mankind, enhancing humanity, or they could be utilized as tools for making individuals but part of a more easily manipulated technological society.[21]

The "Humanizing" Aspect of Technological Art. While the above factors must be kept in mind, the aim of much present-day environmental art is to provide a "humanizing" element. This apparent contradiction—the use of technological art to bring about a humanizing of the technological landscape—is also found in the attitude of many artists who deliberately allow their work to be applied to table mats, T-shirts, curtains, and other transient elements of material life. While this seems in keeping with the trend toward egalitarianism, it raises the same question found in the examination of museum display. Does human nature ever value that which is readily available?

Another aspect that borders on this consideration is the revival of interest in handicrafts and folk art. This would seem to stem from society's reaction to the surrounding industrialization, making it comparable to the growth of craft interest in the mid-nineteenth century when the impact of the Industrial Revolution was first being felt. A further factor influencing its growth, however, is the re-definition of art, which no longer has "noble" subject matter done with "noble" materials and often emphasizes the IDEA rather than technical skill. It might be noted that a certain ambivalence on the part of mankind is found with the admiration of handicrafts since machine-made products that contain flaws are labeled "imperfect" and sold for less, while the irregularities of a handmade object are admired. In the same manner a photographic mural on a public office building seldom provokes comment, but an original work, which is immediately apparent because of its tactile qualities, usually elicits strong opinions.

Some Approaches to the Future

While many other facets of this subject of computer impact on art could be explored, space would seem to demand some type of conclusion. It is obvious that society is undergoing many changes as computerization increases; and while one would like to consider such changes to be for the common good, history would seem to show that human nature, in its endless struggle to understand itself, makes many mistakes along the way, often denying its own ambiguity. Certainly technology and art are inseparable, for both are part of life. But to claim, as some have, that they will soon be completely unified is as far-fetched as to claim that they cannot exist together or that a precise verbalized definition of art and what constitutes the ideal form can be agreed upon by all people of all cultures. The yearnings of mankind for "perfection" lead it to desire "something new," "something different." This very impulse, which stems from mankind's desire to find unification within itself, is the element that ensures continued revitalization of the arts. Just as no one hair on the head of any person is exactly the same, so also not a single work of art is exactly the same as another. For this reason, history will probably show the folly of fearing experimentation in reproductive/ multiple production of art, since it is in the nature of human beings to eventually utilize all things as but tools to create the unique, to express their own individuality.

The training of artists in the humanities at the university level will undoubtedly result in better educated artists, and it seems certain that the role of art in the life of the public-at-large will vastly increase. Yet we should not lose sight of the fact that the greatest landscapes of the past have been done by those not part of the land, and that the artists who seem to have had the most universal insight into human nature were those who sealed themselves away from the outside world and looked only into their own beings to find the key to life.

Mankind always seeks answers for the unanswerable. To seek to understand motivations is but part of man's humanness. To attempt to understand art which, in essence, does not lend itself to verbal explanation, is akin to impossible, yet it too is part of the human process; and as one ponders the wide choice and variety of movements in the art field today, one can find reflected in them the multiplicity of fears and aspirations that are the clues to mankind's greatness and endurance.

PART V

VALUES IN THE COMPUTER AGE

Throughout human history, the value system of society changed so slowly that the change in a lifetime was imperceptible. Alvin Toffler observed that the rate of change has increased in the past 300 years—to the point at which major shifts in a society's value system are observable *within* a lifetime.

Near the beginning of this century Max Weber asserted that values precede technology; Karl Marx claimed that technology comes first. The authors of the papers in this section skirt this chicken-egg problem, but provide four different perspectives from their various roles: a teaching minister, a specialist in mass communications, a campus director of religious life, and a philosopher. Actually each of the writers is a philosopher—and a special kind of philosopher. Each is a humanistic philosopher considering humankind's plight in the computer age.

In Chapter 13, Nolan Shepard suggests that the technological age may be viewed as the highest advance of the evolutionary process of humanity in which we achieve our greatest potential for creativity and development of the resources of the universe. He asserts, however, that such technological developments appear "Janus-faced" and bring threats of destruction as well as hopes for creativity. Shepard concludes that the question as to whether technology is the new messiah or a Frankenstein monster depends on the ethical and moral decisions we make.

Johnny Tolliver (Chapter 14) claims that the American value system is based primarily on the Protestant ethic—the principle

143

that man defines himself and manifests his unique and creative spirit through work, the labor of mind and body. Since the invention of the computer and the ogre of a technocracy that seems to threaten the very existence of American democracy and capitalism, man has become increasingly idle and psychologically troubled. Moreover, a large part of his life has been subjected to the control of computers. What will become of man's essential spirit, the Protestant ethic? asks Tolliver. He examines the extent to which man's life has come under computer control, assesses the effect of the computer on the essential spirit of man, and projects man's future in the age of the computer.

In Chapter 15 Polly Williams examines man's inner relationship to computer technology through insights from the psychological writings of Carl Jung. She draws from Erich Fromm's considerations of our technological society and its effects on us, and discusses his proposed corrective measures. Williams then explores the significant role of education from the prophetic view of Henry Adams and the present-day proposals of Nobel-prize winner, Gerald M. Edelman. She illustrates the ethical implications brought about through the computer's nearness to everyday living and uses the life and poetry of William Blake to reflect on the potential of the computer for good or evil as determined by the courage of each person to take responsibility for his or her actions.

In a fitting conclusion to both the section and the book, Wallace Murphree (Chapter 16) asserts that the prospects for the future of civilization look bright only on the condition that today's materialistic value system be replaced by humanism. His supporting argument is that our powerful contemporary techniques, developed out of the ancient ideal of gaining control over nature for the purpose of human welfare, have fallen into the hands of those who would risk human warfare in order to acquire material wealth. And since as these techniques become increasingly powerful the risk to civilization becomes correspondingly more universal, the only adequate safeguard against complete disaster is the return to the humanistic orientation.

13

Technology: Messiah or Monster?

NOLAN E. SHEPARD

> It was the best of times, it was the worst of times, it was
> the age of wisdom, it was the age of foolishness, . . . it was
> the season of light, it was the season of darkness, it was the
> spring of hope, it was the winter of despair, we had every-
> thing before us, we had nothing before us.
>
> Charles Dickens, *A Tale of Two Cities*

I. *Messianic Hopes*

Charles Dickens's opening lines of *A Tale of Two Cities* speak prophetically to contemporary culture. The modern age of technological advance offers messianic hope of the millenial utopia while struggling to maintain both meaning and existence. This is the age of "cybernation," the meshing of automation (the substitution of mechanical processes for human muscle and dexterity) and cybernetics (the substitution of electronic circuits for mental skills).[1] The resulting combination of automation and computer potentiality promises an epoch in which the drudgery of work will be eliminated, productivity will meet the total needs of man, and the enrichment of life can be pursued. Capek's play, *R. U. R.*, of 1923 in which the world is first served and then controlled by robots expresses this idealized hope: "Everything will be done by living machines. The Robots will clothe and feed us. The Robots will make bricks and build houses for us. The Robots will keep our accounts and sweep our stairs. There'll be no employment, but everybody will be free from worry, and liberated from the degradation of labour. Everybody will live only to perfect himself."[2]

145

The technocratic society promises a richness of information with immeasurable data resulting from the knowledge explosion stored in computers and instantly available. Increased leisure resulting from the productive capacity of the cybernation process will enable man to be more creative and arts to flourish. Individualized education will respond to the potential and uniqueness of each student.[3] Life expectancy will be increased and the suffering from poverty and disease diminished.[4] In the terms of the evolutionary development of humanity this may be seen to be a giant step forward in the growth of humanity toward maturity. Father Walter Ong has provided the classical text for this perspective: "Seen in larger historical, and prehistorical, perspectives, the age of technology is part of the great and mysterious evolution of the universe devised by God. It can be considered as an epoch in what we may call the 'hominization' of the world, that is, the taking over of our planet by mankind."[5]

II. *Monstrous Threats*

The response to the age of cybernation has not been wholly optimistic. People have often viewed the advances of technology with certain anxieties, and mechanization has often brought hostile reactions. A classical Chinese fable tells of Tzu-Gung's encounter with an elderly man who was irrigating his vegetable garden by the slow and toilsome efforts of descending into a well and carrying up a meager vessel of water to pour in the irrigation ditch. Tzu-Gung advised the ancient one of a means of using a lever to draw water from the well to simplify his task. The elderly peasant responded in the following manner: "Then anger rose up in the old man's face, and he said, 'I have heard my teacher say that whoever uses machines does all of his work like a machine. He who does his work like a machine grows a heart like a machine, and he who carries the heart of a machine in his breast loses his simplicity. He who has lost his simplicity becomes unsure in the strivings of his soul. Uncertainty in the strivings of the soul is something which does not agree with honest sense. It is not that I do not know of such things; I am ashamed to use them.' "[6]

In the history of the interaction of technology and philosophy much of the opposition rose from the struggle between a rational, mechanistic view of the universe and those of the vitalists and theologians. The invention of ingenious artificers and automata reflected a theory that the natural universe of physics and biology was susceptible to mechanistic explanations. During the Middle Ages Albertus Magnus worked thirteen years constructing a robot which advanced to the door when anyone knocked and opened it, only to have it broken to pieces by Thomas Aquinas. Pierre Droz devoted his life to the construction of clockwork automata still preserved in the museum at Neuchatel, Switzerland. Upon displaying these androids in Spain, however, he was thrown into the Dungeon of the Inquisition.[7] In more recent history religious sects such as Mennonites, Amish, and some Quakers have rejected the use of any form of mechanization for transportation, farming or other means of production as being unnatural for human beings and opposed to the natural law of God. The first manned flight to the moon was opposed by those who believed that such accomplishments were never intended by the Creator of the universe. Opposition to technological development based on religious beliefs which viewed the processes of automata as contrary to the will of God waged a fruitless battle, and eventually church and sect joined the stream of technological advance. Churches, like industries and education, now use computers to store data concerning their constituency. Theologians and biblical scholars have turned to the computer as a tool for research. Concordances of biblical vocabularies, research on authentic authorship, and evaluation of manuscripts for authenticity and originality are now accomplished by the computer without the laborious drudgery of individual readings of thousands of available texts. Studies have been made with the use of the computer concerning Pauline authorship, the Dead Sea Scrolls, John's Gospel, and both Greek and Latin New Testament texts.[8]

Not all opposition by theologians and philosophers to the development of mechanization has been based on theological attitudes. Much contemporary concern about the developments of the age of cybernation relates to social and ethical implications, human worth and dignity, and the preservation of values. Technology has been called "janus-faced" as it serves the constructive needs of humanity on the one hand and yet threatens to tear down and destroy civilization on the other. After the archeological discovery of a rather advanced invention of the ancient Egyptians called the "megamachine," Lewis Mumford writes: "The real gains in law, order and economic productivity the megamachine made possible need not be belittled. But unfortunately these gains were reduced, often entirely cancelled out, by the brutalizing institutions that the military megamachine brought into existence: organized war, slavery, class expropriation and exploitation, and extensive collective extermination. In terms of human development these evil institutions have no rational foundation."[9]

In looking beyond the undesirable effects of the efforts of mechanization of the Egyptians, Mumford speaks of the consequences of contemporary blind devotion to technologies' expansions and extensions: "Who can now remain blind to our polluted oceans and rivers; our smog choked air; our mountainous rubbish heaps; our sprawling automobile cemeteries; our sterilized and blasted landscapes, where the strip miner, the bulldozer, the pesticides, and the herbicides have all left their mark: the widening deserts of concrete, in motor roads and carparks, whose substitution of ceaseless locomotion for urban decentralization daily wastes countless man-years of life in needless transportation; not least our congested, dehumanized cities where health is vitiated and depleted by the sterile daily routine."[10]

The creation of the technological age has been compared to Mary Shelley's *Frankenstein or the Modern Prometheus*. Dr. Frankenstein intended to be the benefactor of humanity and sought altruistically the renewal of life. Instead, he created a monster of destruction that brought remorse and repentance to the inventor. Similarly, Capeck's robots were created to bring universal happiness, but first became the instruments of human evil, and finally subjected humanity to slavery and destruction. The creation turns against the creator, and the intended benefits are overwhelmed by the monstrous consequences which emerge. Anti-technologists point out the following ways in which cybernation threatens mankind: (1) Contemporary technological trends dehumanize people; they are made to be anonymous and lose significance and individuality. (2) Work loses dignity, creativity and meaning. (3) Cybernation encourages nonreflective conformity. (4) Materialism and technolatry replace traditional religious values. (5) Technique becomes autonomous and human beings its slaves.

(1) The first of these criticisms deals with the dehumanization and anonymity of people. Almost everyone in contemporary society knows something of the frustration of economic transactions through the use of computers. Names become numbers; complaints are answered by a mechanized process; and interpersonal services diminish. Ashley Montagu describes the individual of the technological age as an instrument or an object. He states, "In a technological age, it is people who are instruments or are the objects of technological instruments and it is people who are made into technological objects by other people."[11] A nine year old autistic child thought of himself as a machine and refused to eat, sleep, or walk about without batteries, wiring, and electrical devices being attached. The boy is something of a parable of modern society which has become so acutely interdependent with mechanization that the very life processes are dependent on a continued relationship to the mechanical sources of life. J.C.R. Licklider has borrowed the word *symbiosis* from the biological interdependence of two dissimilar organisms which require each other to maintain existence. He uses the phrase "man-computer symbiosis" to describe the status of a society in which human existence has become dependent on the cybernetic process.[12] Symbiosis is most effective when people conform and integrate their behavior to that of the machine. Thus people lose not only their individuality but something of their humanity as well.

(2) The second criticism of the technological age is the loss of dignity and creativity in work. Studs Terkel, in his monumental study of work in America writes: For the many there is hardly concealed discontent. . . . "I'm a machine," says the spot welder. "I'm caged," says the bank teller, and echoes the hotel clerk. "I'm

a mule,' says the steel worker. 'A monkey can do what I do,' says the receptionist. 'I'm less than a farm implement,' says the migrant worker. 'I'm an object,' says the high fashion model. Blue collar and white call upon the identical phrase: 'I'm a robot.'"[13]

The Protestant work ethic has always placed dignity and self-worth on the creative acts of fruitful labor. Even the inventors of the robots of *R.U.R.* admit, "There was something good in service and something great in humanity. . . . There was some kind of virtue in toil and weariness."[14] Work requires creativity, purposefulness, and accomplishment to preserve its dignity and meaningfulness. The assembly lines of automata and the push buttons of computers reduce men and women to a part of the machine and their work to meaningless routine. Quantity and speed become more significant than quality and personal creativity. The utopian hope of a laborless society threatens a loss of meaning of the use of one's hands.

(3) The critic also claims that cybernation encourages nonreflective conformity. In the story *The Spy Who Came in from the Cold*, Fiedler, the Marxist, questions Leamas, the Englishman representing Western values and technology, concerning his philosophy of life. Leamas responds that he is not Marxist, not really Christian, not really anything. He has no philosophy. Myron B. Bloy, Jr. comments: "Laemas, on the other hand, is a true representative of the technological spirit; his loyalty is simply to the job at hand, to good workmanship; he is non-reflective, his satisfactions being in the immediate experience and not in the vision of some grand design which is presumed to lie behind this facade of history."[15]

Gerald Sykes describes the new individual of the technological age as one who develops a "raincoat mind," one that has the capacity for abstractive, technical thought and can almost instantaneously shed any thought that is not profitable and does not apply to the job at hand. Sykes comments: "The technical mode of thought is necessary to survival, and it creates a mental vacuum. The technicized mind is drained of folklore, of human interest, of lazy give and take, of everything that does not contribute to doing the job and, more especially, since the job becomes more and more fool-proof, getting the most out of it."[16]

(4) The anti-technocrat sees materialism and technolatry replacing traditional religious values. The new religion asks "How?" and "How much?" but avoids the question "Why?" It espouses the accumulation of status symbols and values both individuals and their property in terms of monetary worth. Salvation is equated with this quantitative productivity; sin with any capacity for growing old, infirm, unphotogenic, or nonproductive; and God resides mysteriously in a box, the sovereign monarch of the cybernetic age. John Wilkinson has stated: "It might be maintained that the progressive assimilation to the machine of human values (and even of religion in the sense of a *deus in machina*) is a function of a decisive, unforeseen, and unforeseeable turn of Western culture in its successive passage through mercantilism, industrialism, automation, and cybernation, and as these mutations take place elsewhere in the world the same pathology of value is manifested."[17] Mumford defines technology as "the Pentagon of Power,"[18] and Sykes describes the "technolatry" of the cyberculture as "a New Salvation," "a New Supernatural," "a New Messiah."[19]

(5) The final criticism of technological advance is perhaps the most scathing. Mechanization is seen as an irreversible process in which human interdependence with machines becomes total dependence and finally enslavement. Ralph Waldo Emerson stated, "Things are in the saddle and ride mankind."[20] Jacques Ellul in his weighty work, *The Technological Society*, describes "technique" as that aspect of the development of the socialization process in which everything is adapted to efficiency. The machine "represents the ideal toward which technique strives." Ellul declares: . . . when technique enters into every area of life, including the human, it ceases to be external to man and becomes his very substance. It is integrated with him, and it progressively absorbs him. In this respect, technique is radically different from the machine. This transformation, so obvious in modern society, is the result of the fact that technique has become autonomous."[21]

Ellul goes on to say that technique judges itself in terms of practicality. It is beyond morality and spiritual values, beyond good and evil. In fact, technique has become the judge of what is moral and has created a new morality of efficiency. "Man is reduced to the level of a catalyst. Better still, he resembles a slug inserted into a slot machine: He starts the operation without participating in it. . . . It is commonplace to say that the machine replaces the human being. But it replaces him to a greater degree than has been believed."[22] Samuel Butler in "The Destruction of the Machines in Erewhon," 1872, describes the evolutionary development of the machine to the point of mechanized thought processes. The machines are already masters, and people spend most of their lifetime in service to them. Butler urges that the country "resolve upon putting an immediate stop to all further mechanical progress and upon destroying all improvements that have been made for the last 300 years."[23] The scientists of *R. U. R.* discover that the prayer book offers prayers against thunderstorms, illness, temptations, and floods but none against progress.[24]

III. *Challenge and Responsibility*

Kenneth E. Boulding relates a parable of a bird meticulously building her nest in a small hole in the end of the wing of a jet airplane, only to have her work scattered and the bird left behind. Mankind likewise builds hopes of security in a perilous setting on the wing of great sweeping progress. Boulding comments: "There were men in the cockpit, however, and we are men and not sparrows. We do have the gift of understanding, even of the systems that we create ourselves. It is not too much to hope, therefore, that man can learn to fly the great engine of change that he has made and that it may carry us not to destruction but to that great goal for which the world was made."[25] This view holds neither that this is the eve of the messianic utopia nor that doom and destruction are imminent. It holds, instead, that man is both the creator of the machine and responsible for its use. A popular song of several decades ago expresses this theme with its words, "It ain't what'cha got, but what'cha do with what'cha got." Ellul's position of the autonomy of technique is rejected by many. Bertrand de Jouvenel offers the following comment: "I deliberately refuse to think of technological progress as the *cause* of change in men's ways of life. I deliberately choose, rather, to think of it as the chief *means* of such change. The idea that man is being and will increasingly be driven along a determined path by the gathering forces of technology seems to me a nefarious idea, generating in the minority an impotent and paradoxical technophobia, and in the majority the same kind of blind ecstatic confidence in what shall come to pass that was characteristic of laissez-faire in the narrower field of economics."[26]

Frankenstein's creation becomes a monster only in reaction to the inhuman behavior of men and women, and Capek's play, *R. U. R.*, is an indictment of the materialism of humanity rather than technological development. It is people who wage war and cause the deterioration of the environment by spoilation of the countryside, air and water pollution, and the rot of our cities. Robert Boguslaw offers the following comments concerning the responsibilities of human beings in the age of cyberculture: (1) Our first concern should be about the impact of the social order on technology rather than the reverse. (2) Human beings are in control of their future. We should be asking which people and what set of values will control our destiny. (3) Should people be enslaved or destroyed, it will be by other people. There are no inanimate villains. (4) Technology is never neutral. It embodies a set of human values often latent, obscure, or deliberately disguised. "One of the tasks of well-motivated individuals is to expose the precise nature of value choices embodied in various forms of technology." (5) Technology cannot bring obsolescence to human values. "Humanistic values can be made obsolete only by anti-humanistic or non-humanistic values. " (6) Technology creates no new values. Old values may be strengthened or distorted. (7) Serious students of technological change must participate in value decisions. Boguslaw summarizes in the following statement: "This does not mean to engage in mindless activism. On the contrary it means to strip the gargoyles of ignorance from the outer surfaces of technology, and reveal the de facto value choices embodied in them for what they are. It involves using the intellect as a weapon in the battle against despotism disguised as technological progress. It also means organizing people to engage in the range of necessary activities to combat not technology per se but anti-humanistic technology."[27]

Ralph Wendell Burhoe has written two modern fables of Joseph and Jacob. In the first fable, Joseph dreams that he is offered a magic ring of scientific technology. Upon rubbing the ring three times Joseph and his children may have anything they desire. Poverty, suffering, and labor are replaced by abundance, pleasure, and leisure. Jacob, on the other hand, wrestles with the angel of technology concerning the kind of world the magic ring will bring. He is granted a book of the history of man and science which he must search until he discovers the human implications of the revelations and pen a new song for mankind.[28] Jacob's role is not only the responsibility of the humanist but of the technologist as well. In an age in which nations and peoples are interdependent, ethics take on international dimensions. Joseph Weizenbaum, in a chapter appropriately entitled "Against the Imperialism of Instrumental Reason," states: "Not only can modern man's actions affect the whole planet that is his habitat, but they can determine the future of the entire human species. It follows therefore that man, particularly man the scientist and engineer, has responsibilities that transcend his immediate situation, that in fact extend to future generations. These responsibilities are especially grave since future generations cannot advocate their own cause now. We are the trustees."[29]

The task of seeking value, dignity, and meaning in the cybernetic age is a religious task. Religious experience transcends culture. It goes beyond particular content and helps us to celebrate, to "glory in the fact that man can know, and value, and see, and find meaning in his experience."[30] Yet, it is never divorced from culture. Religion must deal with the concrete issues of life and struggle to both discover and preserve meaning and value within technology. Luther H. Harshbarger has listed the following humanistic imperatives for our age: (1) We must view the ends to which life can be directed and the principles by which life can be lived. (2) The dignity, worth, and individuality of men and women must be preserved. (3) Human beings must be viewed as both responsive and responsible within their culture. Dostoevski has stated, "The possibility of being able to place the question of right after the meaning of one's existence is the greatest and most ultimate freedom of man." (4) The greatness of humanity must be measured not in the dimensions of power or existence but in the sense of tragedy. It is in suffering and the awareness of the existential tragedy of human existence that one discovers redemption.[31] The humanist must then view the technological age as neither messianic with utopian dreams fulfilled nor monstrous with enslavement and destruction imminent but as an age of grave responsibility in which the preservation of those things which really matter depend on the moral and ethical decisions made by contemporary men and women.

1L

The Computer and the Protestant Ethic: A Conflict

JOHNNY E. TOLLIVER

Of all known living creatures man alone has the capacity to use his intelligence in order to learn about himself and his environment. The information explosion that has taken place during this century manifests man's almost infinite power to know—to know about life, about death, about his physical and social environment, about his complex psychology, and about his universe. More and more, man and woman are measuring up to the biblical edict that made them sovereign over the earth and all therein. Shakespeare's Hamlet, more eloquently than it has ever been expressed, exalts humanity to its supreme station among living things: "What a piece of work is a man, how noble in reason, how infinite in faculties, in form and moving how express and admirable, in action how like an angel, in apprehension how like a god: the beauty of the world, the paragon of animals! And yet to me what is this quintessence of dust?" (*Hamlet*, II. ii.300–305) In one of the most majestic literary passages in world literature, Hamlet praises man as a demigod, but he is perplexed over what he calls man's quintessence, that intangible, supernal quality that defines man as man, where he can be as celestial as the angels and yet be as mortal and frail as any living creature, as Rosencrantz and Guildenstern are evincing to Hamlet at this point in the drama.

Just as Hamlet is perplexed over the quintessence of mankind, so has man been perplexed about himself and his place in the order of

156

things. No other era in modern history shows man's ardent self-inquiry better than the Renaissance, for the period was not only one of a rebirth of man's interest in learning but one in which there was a rebirth of man himself as he began to recognize his own worth. Pico della Mirandola's *Oration on the Dignity of Man* is probably the most eloquent expression of this new-found self-esteem. Since the age of the Renaissance, man has striven to extend his mind to encompass all there is to know. And this extension of the mind to encompass all knowledge has created for modern man a paradox in existence—a paradox that he cannot resolve and which perplexes him and places him in a state of incessant anxiety.

The Industrial Revolution of the eighteenth and nineteenth centuries, with its deluge of machinery, whetted man's insatiable appetite for knowledge. He was fascinated by the dynamism of mechanical operations and sought to learn more and more about technology. Man began to improve upon this simple technology and to introduce new technology to such an extent that during the last thirty years or so (at least since the Sputnik phenomenon) technology has enabled man not only to gather masses of information but to store it and retrieve it at will. He has used his ingenuity to create machines that have replaced manual labor. The last thirty years have indeed produced the specter of automation that incites anxiety and dread in the minds of many individuals. The human capacity to know, therefore, has enabled our generation to create the means to facilitate the acquisition and uses of knowledge, but it has also deprived many people of work, a *sine qua non* for people's concept of self-worth.

The fear that society will become a technocracy pervades American society, and the facts of unemployment and increased time for leisure or idleness have stimulated some critics to examine this age of technology vis-à-vis the social and psychological problems that it seems to have produced. This is our self-created paradox. We have access to seemingly infinite stores of knowledge, and yet we are beset with social and psychological problems that have apparently sprung from these stores. More important, we do not seem to know how to use our knowledge to solve these problems.

What are we to do with our knowledge? How has this knowledge affected our self-esteem? How can we use such new and ever-changing technology to solve our social and psychological problems? Is science the bane of modern society? In this paper we will examine the conflict between the new technology (the computer) and man's essential spirit (the Protestant ethic), for this conflict is the veritable crux of our modern social and psychological problems.

Some Effects of the Computer on the Protestant Ethic

When one thinks of modern technology, the first thought that enters the mind is the computer. At the Data Processing Management Association Conference in 1969, J. R. Bradburn, Executive Vice President of RCA Information Systems Division, Camden, New Jersey, summarized the impact of the computer in our life: "The computer has been described as the dominant advance of the 20th century. Economists have predicted that by the end of the century more people will be employed in data processing and related industries than in any other single business.

"The statisticians tell us that one year ago, the world-wide total of U.S. computers numbered 57,000 systems, worth $17-billion. Today, the figure has reached 70,000 systems, valued at $24-billion. With the industry growth rate currently projected at between 15 and 18 percent a year, the cumulative value of just U.S.-produced computers by 1972 should exceed $40-billion." [1] This information about computers is very impressive, but what really staggers the imagination is the fact that 25 years ago there were only 10 computer systems in the United States and today there are 325,000 computers and 700,000 workers in the industry. [2] These latter figures far exceed Bradburn's prediction of a 15 to 18 percent growth rate in the computer industry. In consonance with this remarkable growth rate, it is predicted that by 1984 every secondary school in the country will have access to a computer for administrative or instructional use, or both. [3] Computers have thus become ubiquitous and are pervading every aspect of modern life.

In an article appearing in *The New York Times*, Evan Jenkins, an assistant news editor and former national education correspondent for that newspaper, looks at the revolutionary role of the computer in education and touches upon the two basic fears people have about the computer—fears that underscore this conflict between technology and the human spirit. He states, "Related to the fear of job losses is the fear that the computer will 'dehumanize' education."[4]

What, then, is the essential human spirit, that part of us that abhors anything that will "dehumanize" us? One critic, Robert H. Davis, calls it the Protestant ethic, the notion that labor is noble and idleness is immoral.[5] And it is our nobility of being that distinguishes us from other animals, besides our ability to reason. Davis goes on to cite some unsettling statistics about what automation is doing to the labor force, including the revelation that it is displacing 4,000 persons per week according to conservative estimates of the Department of Labor. Most of us are painfully aware of poverty and its attendant evil that afflicts our nation—crime. Poverty and crime are the cancerous malady that almost tears asunder the moral strength of our society, and unless something is done to resolve the almost irresolvable conflict between computer technology and our Protestant ethic, this malady will be exacerbated to the extent that our technology will become our doom.

How has automation (with the computer as its representative symbol) affected the human spirit? In the United States it has been detrimental to the American ethos of work. Davis states: "Underlying the relatively high value which we place on the machine is the notion that man really isn't a very efficient mechanism. Machines can do many things better than man, and some would assert that machines can do *most* things better than man. We are told that they are faster; that they are more accurate; that they are more dependable; and there are those who believe that computers rather than people should really make decisions.

" . . . *What really matters is the extent to which the average person is convinced that the machine will replace him because it is better than he is.* With the enormous prestige of science standing behind us, I submit that we have unwittingly convinced the average man (who may not in any case hold himself in very high esteem) that he is in fact not really worth very much."[6] This feeling of worth is the essence of the human spirit, a thought shared equally by people of the Renaissance and by people of modern America. Our worth in society is measured by our work, and if we *must* work and *cannot* work because of our displacement by the computer and other machines, then we cease to be human and become little more in worth than the animals over which we are supposed to have dominion.

Psychological Problems Caused by the Computer

In a society whose value system is predicated upon the work ethic, people must work for their own psychological well-being. Davis discusses the psychological problems that arise out of man's inability "to fulfill his potential as a unique and creative human being."[7] When we are threatened in this way we become uneasy. Some of the psychological mechanisms that we evoke in such a state are aggression, regression, and fixation. Furthermore, the conflict between computer technology and the Protestant ethic is more acute with minority groups, especially black people. Peter F. Drucker, a professor of management at New York University's Graduate School of Business, discusses how automation has affected American black people. His major premise, and one that we must accept as true if we are to accept his conclusion about black people, is that in the last twenty years the base of our economy has shifted from manual to knowledge work, that our society is basically a knowledge society, and that knowledge acquired in formal schooling is the foundation of skill and opportunity.[8] Because most black people are prepared only for manual labor, they are the group worst affected by this transition from a manual job society to a knowledge society. Drucker suggests that the black American's rebelliousness is attributable not to any impatience on his part, but to the *fear* that he will be deprived of the few gains he has made. This fear of being deprived of the opportunity to work lies at the heart of American racial and social strife. This fear, however, is not unique to American blacks; it affects everybody. The Protestant ethic, therefore, pervades every group in American society. In fact, it defines the American spirit; and unless we can resolve this conflict between this noble spirit and the computer and its associated technology, we will forever be plagued with severe social and racial problems.

A ramification of this paradox created by our quest for knowledge is the conflict between the computer and our ability to think. Our supreme essence is defined by our ability to think. The computer itself is a testament to our genius. But there are those who believe that the computer is a better thinker than we are, and such a notion is insidious and fallacious. The computer can never replace us as thinkers; it facilitates and speeds up the thinking process. Decisions in business, government, and education must not be made by the computer. Computers are aids in decisionmaking, and God forbid the day that we relinquish our thinking to a machine, notwithstanding the level of complexity, sophistication, and accuracy of the computer.

Resolution of Conflict Between Computer and Protestant Ethic

The problem, therefore, that faces contemporary America, is whether or not we are going to surrender the work ethic, which defines our self-worth, to the workings of a machine that is our creation. How then do we resolve this seemingly irresolvable conflict between the Protestant ethic and the computer, the heart of our modern technology? Davis has a fivefold solution:[9]

1. The computer scientist must become sensitive to the human and social costs of computer systems, which include the costs of retraining, of supporting the unemployed, of social dislocation, of the psychological misery of the displaced worker.

2. We must change the Protestant ethic. Modern man must learn to fulfill his potential not only through work but through the proper use of leisure.

3. We must re-examine the base of economy in our society. We must consider a guaranteed income for every individual so that he may "live his life in dignity."

4. We must educate every citizen to the limit of his abilities.

5. We need more information about the problems of the unemployed.

Davis is trying very realistically and practically to solve a very serious problem facing the American society. The indictment against the computer is that, with all its magnificent contributions to our improvement, it has created severe social and psychological problems. But Davis's solution also entails not only a reorientation in our thinking, but a considerable modification of our democratic principles. Parts 1 and 5 require information and consideration from leaders in government, business, and education. Parts 2-4, however, require a reorientation of our philosophical, economic, and educational systems.

We can agree with Davis that our worth is measured by our ability to work, to labor with body and mind. What he is suggesting is that we must seek to derive our worth from both work and leisure. The East Germans and the Russians are making leisure as much a part of their potential-fulfillment as work. Witness the emphasis placed on athletics by these countries in the 1976 Olympics in Montreal. In these countries people are required to participate in athletic programs from kindergarten throughout their adult lives. The best ones, in effect, become career athletes, appointed by their governments to become the best. Davis is not suggesting that we go to the extreme to which Russia and East Germany have gone, but he is asserting that Americans must learn how to derive as much a sense of worth out of leisure as they do out of work. It is an idea very much worth considering.

The suggestion of a guaranteed income invites the criticism of increased socialism, but it is Davis's proposed solution to the problem of increasing psychological misery in this computer age. The suggestion requiring education for all our citizens is the best and one that is more akin to our essential spirit.

We must accept the fact that the computer is going to be a part of our lives. We must also accept the proposition that the computer will do something *for* us. It will augment our existence.[10] It will help us to gather data about the world, restructure received data in order to arrive at new data, control complex and rapid processes, and reduce the tedium of information-handling. We must therefore educate every individual in the light of the computer. American education has recognized the utility of the computer in administration and instruction. Government has found the computer indispensable in administering its various responsibilities, and businesses use the computer in making decisions and projecting the future. The computer is the single most dominant machine in our life. We must learn to use it to our benefit, and we must learn to master it. Blanchard propounds four requirements to augment our cognitive processes by interaction with the computer:

1. Man must have a complete mastery of the language of his discipline *and of the computer.*[11]
2. He must know and be able to control and use all man or machine communication pathways.
3. His mastery of information, its source, location, and deficiencies must be complete.
4. His command of the computer system must be detailed, absolute, and comfortable. . . .[12]

The ultimate resolution to the conflict between the computer and the Protestant ethic is our recognition of ourselves as master of the computer. Each of us must recognize and accept the computer as a staple in his or her life. We must learn to understand it and learn how to use it. Since secondary education and higher education are using the computer to such a large extent, then we must ensure that our young people learn the operation and uses of the computer and its several languages. As more jobs are created in association with the computer and as more technology replaces manual tasks, we must ensure that our young people become technology-oriented and educated to assume these jobs. As a corollary to this technological orientation, we must also ensure that they be humanists. They must learn to appreciate humanness, and this means their study of various cultures, literatures, languages, and the human problems that consolidate all peoples as the human race. Scientists must be humanists, and humanists must be scientists in order to bring about the proper application of the computer and its technology to the benefit of mankind. If we do not diversify ourselves in this manner and render all our islands a part of the main, then society is condemned to a certain psychological death; and our lives will be controlled by the few who know and understand the computer but who do not know and understand the essential spirit of man—the Protestant ethic.

15

Reflection on Computers as Daughters of Memory

POLLY F. WILLIAMS

The Self, Consciousness and Carl Jung

How much does the average person know about computers? How many professional people have seriously considered the pervasive use of computers and their long-range implications on each of us? What is your conscious conception of your relationship to the technological age in which you live? The Swiss psychologist Carl Jung's writings have influenced many of the human sciences. I believe that his creative genius also gives fresh insight into each individual's relationship to computer technology. Jung states as follows: "Consciousness determines *Weltanschauung*. All conscious awareness of motives and intentions is a *Weltanschauung* in the bud; every increase in experience and knowledge is a step in the development of a *Weltanschauung*. And with the picture that the thinking man fashions of the world he also changes himself. The man whose sun still moves round the earth is essentially different from the man whose earth is a satellite of the sun."[1]

In light of Jung's idea that every increase in knowledge is a step in the development of *Weltanschauung*, the consumer as well as the designer of computer technology must ask if conscious awareness has been explored in terms of the psychological and ethical implications of computer technology. If, as users or inventors, we have not examined the value aspects of the Man-Computer Age, then we fit Jung's description of a person who is basically ignorant of

165

the universe. To be uninformed of the computer cosmos therefore brings about an essentially different person from a well-informed individual. The picture which our understanding creates of the world also creates us.

Jung further states: "A science can never be a *Weltanschauung* but merely the tool with which to make one. Whether we take this tool in hand or not depends on the sort of *Weltanschauung* we already have. For no one is without a *Weltanschauung* of some sort. Even in an extreme case, he will at least have the *Weltanschauung* that education and environment have forced on him."[2]

Accordingly whether or not each person will take the tool of computer science in hand and responsibly control it depends on what each individual person brings to the challenge. What each person brings is the total of what that person is. Each person therefore has to reestablish communication with the authentic self in order to have something to bring. Each individual needs to face the dilemma of knowing who he or she is, of accepting the courage to be one's self, of accepting the unacceptable feelings of alienation, of guilt, and of meaninglessness. To delve into one's motives and intentions helps in cutting through inauthenticity, in breaking the hold of comfortable conformity, in giving up simple, pat answers to unanswerable questions. A failure to take the journey to know both the conscious and the unconscious levels of one's self results in self-disintegration or a capitulation of freedom which accepts authoritarian religions and governments and the autonomy of an unexamined computerized program. The courage to assume full responsibility for one's life and actions surely includes in our age the courage to confront the computer! This confrontation is essential if humanity is to regain its freedom and if individuals are to engage in the individuation process.

Passivity and Erich Fromm's Humanized Technology

According to Erich Fromm's book, *The Revolution of Hope: Toward a Humanized Technology*, human beings are in danger of being dehumanized by a totally mechanized society directed by computers. The danger as Fromm sees it is that persons are allowing themselves to be transformed into a part of the total machine. He believes that the culprits of this process are passivity, a deadness of spirit, and a lack of feeling which results in a loss of individualism, privacy, and control over our own system. In this assumed passive role "we execute the decisions which our computer calculations make for us."[3] Fromm accuses individuals of aimlessness, of a lack of motivation to will anything beyond increased production and consumption and of failure to exercise responsibility as a decision-maker.

How did humanity come to be in this dilemma? Fromm suggests that human beings emphasized technical and material techniques to the extent that we lost touch with ourselves, with life, with religious faith, with humanistic values, and with the capacity for deep emotional experiences. The final indictment is that "the machine he built became so powerful that it developed its own program, which now determines man's own thinking."[4] Fromm asks if the situation is insoluble or if we can use our computers to serve the ends of humanity.

Although the answers differ, Fromm himself states that his position is in line with that of Jacques Ellul who has written that the technological society threatens the spiritual and personal lives of mankind and with Lewis Mumford who in *The Myth of the Machine* views technologies' unimpeded growth as a cancerlike growth threatening the individual and social life.[5]

Fromm, however, sees hope in a growing movement which he identifies with life as opposed to nonlife, a movement that advocates profound changes in our economic and social practice as well as in the spiritual approach to life. The specific aim is "the activation of the individual, the restoration of man's control over the social system, the humanization of technology."[6]

Fromm advocates the following changes which are necessary to "save it [society] from physical destruction, dehumanization and madness."[7] First, new patterns of production and consumption are recommended which are designed to enhance the maximum growth potential of each person as an alternative to the present alienating system in which individuals are secondary to technical effectiveness. Second, the transformation of individuals from a passive, easily manipulated human being, into an active, self-actualizing individual is recommended. Specifically, Fromm sees the need for "revitalizing the political bureaucracy by putting it under effective control of citizens, through the participation in decision-making of all who work in an enterprise. . . ."[8] Third, a cultural revolution is advocated which again aims at transforming the spirit of persons "whose goal in life is *being*, not *having* and *using*; one who aims at the full development of his powers of love and reason, and who achieves a new unity between thought and effect. . . ."[9] Fromm shifts the emphasis from a mechanized, dead, passive life to one that stresses values over things and actual concern and experience over rhetoric and theory. A new lifestyle is encouraged which minimizes consumption for the producer but makes it meaningful to life. The persons so motivated would "try to understand the forces within themselves which motivate them,"[10] relying on their own thinking and feeling and making their own judgments, in an effort to achieve freedom through openness and participation.

Education and Henry Adams Revisited

Both Carl Jung and Erich Fromm point to the significant role which education plays in influencing personal growth and in adapting to change. In the autobiographical *The Education of Henry Adams* Adams came to the conclusion that the education which he had been given was not adequate for the time in which he lived. As Adams observed the dynamo at the technological exposition in Paris in 1900, he recognized it as a symbol of force influencing his generation as the Virgin had been the symbolic force of the twelfth century.[11] As Adams considered his education inadequate I question whether or not our present educational system is adequate to prepare students to assess the implications of computer technology, particularly in evaluating and judging the complex value decisions implied in the ultimate effects on humanity and society. The force symbolized by the information available in giant computer networks has become the symbolic force of our era as the Virgin was for medieval times and the dynamo was for Adams's times. How will education adapt to this new symbol?

Adams observed the moral standards of his father's and grandfather's day deteriorating at every level of political life. Also in our day the erosion of moral standards is readily observable. Adams prophetically calculated that the rate of change due to mechanical forces was multiplying to such a degree that the generations to come would have to rely on impersonal forces.[12] Computer technology surely meets the description of that impersonal force. Adams's fear that the individual would be dwarfed to insignificance by the forces of technology have to a high degree been borne out by the use of computer technology if we listen to the voices of Ellul and Fromm.

However, in Adams's observation that his education had not prepared him for his time I disagree. I would say emphatically, "No, Henry Adams, there was something uniquely significant in your education which in fact did prepare you for the crisis of your age, for the explosion of technology. The essential element was the motivation and the capacity to adapt to change, to study and to understand the new developments in science, and further, to apply your new-found knowledge to the legislative process, to integrate the implications into the larger needs of life."

Values, Politics and Gerald Edelman

Dr. Gerald M. Edelman, a Nobel Prize winner in 1972 for his work in immunology, has also written on a method of educating leaders in our society for adapting to change. "We're inquiring into the deepest nature of our constitutions: how we inherit from each other. How we are changed. How our minds think. How our will is related to our thoughts. How our thoughts are related to our molecules. These questions are really upon us, and in the next 50 years, they'll be a central concern of humanity.

"There's no way this inquiry is going to be stopped, nor, in my opinion, should it be stopped. But it has to be associated with a set of values—okay?—that we cherish. It has to be built into our political life in a sense that is not sterile, or stupid, or automatic. And it has to be tested constantly by a legal process that is in the great American tradition."[13]

In order to bring technology, science, values and political action together Dr. Edelman proposes the idea of a retreat for the best of our scientists and members of Congress to live together, to become friends, to understand each other and what each is doing, not for the sake of science but for the sake of society. The very fact that "science is the most pervasive secular force in modern life"[14] suggests the need for training various groups of legislators, jurists, educators, theologians and philosophers to increase their mutual knowledge about computer technology and the humanistic disciplines. In addition to the ongoing seminar-retreat experience, I propose regular ethics or value courses and basic courses in computer technology at the secondary, undergraduate, graduate and professional schools. The courses should seek to integrate value decisions and scientific decisions through an interdisciplinary approach using a curriculum developed by humanists from various disciplines as well as outstanding computer analysts and scientists.

The Boy, the "Computer" and Ethics

To illustrate the nearness of the computer to each of us and the ethical questions which it raises in our lives, permit me to share a true personal story. Of all the wonderful gifts available in the world, what would you suppose a nine-year-old boy would most like to have for Christmas during the mid-1970s? Interestingly enough, my nine-year-old son's main request for Christmas was for a pocket-sized "computer." My initial reaction was one of pleasure that he showed an interest in calculators. My pleasure was furthered by the fact that a pocket-sized "computer" was readily available at Sears and Roebuck for only $8.95. My shopping was simplified, and my son's wishes were easily rewarded.

The reasons that a nine-year-old boy might want a "computer" for his personal use were only vaguely considered. My primary motivation was to fulfill his desires for a present, but I was also pleased that I could efficiently—in terms of quickly accomplishing the task—and economically—I would willingly have spent several times the cost of the calculator—do my shopping. In the back of my mind I may have rationalized that he was very bright to want a "computer," and I even envisioned higher mathematical computations and space probes being calculated—not unheard of for a twentieth-century "star trekkie."

To my surprise one January evening I discovered my son behind closed doors working his arithmetic problems with the help of his trusty calculator. Difficult equations? No, simple addition. Why the closed door? Although not admitted, I sensed an underlying intuition on his part that there was something not completely ethical in using the calculator for the purpose of arithmetic homework. If a true sense of ethics was not involved, at least he had the vague feeling that Mom or Dad might object to the use of the calculator for homework.

De-mythologizing the Computer

In this story some basic observations concerning the advent of the computer in our midst are notable. First is the attraction of the computer itself. It has become identified with the most sophisticated scientific technology. The attraction is especially strong for the lay-person who is not a scientist. There also exists the lure of the mystery of scientific technology, exemplified by efficiency, accuracy and economy which can be termed "the computer mystique." In order for the lay-person to deal with the computer in a rational objective manner the mystique of the computer will have to be de-mythologized. Translated into everyday practicality this requires basic information to be conveyed to the general public. A consciousness-raising attitude toward computer technology as it relates to every aspect of life is needed.

Second, the computer represents for a nine-year-old boy shortcuts in time and work. For society-at-large the computer stands for efficiency and economy. The underlying question is: What are we sacrificing for efficiency and economy? The third observation concerns the ethical implications. The increased power of the computer is a force which will have to be reckoned with in ways which we as the consumer have not fully considered. The highest level study and evaluation of the more subtle implications of computer technology are demanded for the decisions which are being made by Congress, by the courts, by educators and by legislators. On this evaluative and philosophical level an interdisciplinary task force is needed to set standards and guidelines. Decisionmaking on this level needs to take into consideration basic values, ethics and theology. The following questions are illustrative of the type to be considered:

1. Does computer technology give the individual more or less freedom?

2. Does computer technology contribute toward each individual's ability to be more fully human by developing his unique potentialities?

3. Does computer technology promote compulsive conformity?

4. What are the implications of the computer program's authoritarian role on school systems and businesses?

5. Does the computer tend to place an "other-directed" value system on individual lives?

6. Does the computer program allow the individual to be spontaneously creative?

William Blake and the Computer

If you were asked to select the person of English letters who best demonstrates the phenomenology of the computer, who would you choose? My choice would be William Blake. The enigmatic eighteenth century craftsman was an engraver with technical skills raised to the level of artistry. Yet Blake was also a visionary in Jung's sense of being in touch with the deepest archetypal images of his unconscious. His *Weltanschauung* provided the milieu for his poetical and mystical creativity. Blake labored at his trade daily, but he dreamed dreams and he saw visions. Within computer technology the same potential characteristics for greatness exist. The computer has the capabilities for storing the sacred wisdom of the ages, for continuous labor, for projecting in a visionary manner the solution to futuristic problems, and for raising the level of technology to poetic art.

Blake was emphatic in attributing his visions to the Daughters of Memory. According to Kenneth Clark's investigation it appears that the source of Blake's visions was an exceptional memory. From childhood on Blake was exposed to a great variety of visual images, especially prints.[15] Computer technology also partakes of the Daughters of Memory but with an incredible memory storage unequaled in human history. The heightened power given to the Daughters of Memory is frightening.

Although Blake's powers as an artist increased with the years, he could at anytime in his life "be incredibly bad when the subject failed to suck up from his subconscious one of his deeply buried images."[16] So also the long-range effects of the computer's program can be incredibly bad if the basic data and program designs are not built on positive value principles.

The liberated energy of computer technology becomes a lamb—the Christ figure, or a tiger—the anti-Christ figure, depending on its application. The frightening power of the computer is prophetically described in Blake's poem "The Tiger" with the substitution of the word *computer* for *tiger*.

> Computer! Computer! burning bright
> In the forests of the night,
> What immortal hand or eye
> Could frame thy fearful symmetry?
>
> In what distant deeps or skies
> Burnt the fire of thine eyes?
> On what wings dare he aspire?
> What the hand dare seize the fire?
>
> And what shoulder, and what art,
> Could twist the sinews of thy heart?
> And when thy heart began to beat,
> What dread hand and what dread feet?
>
> What the hammer? what the chain?
> In what furnace was thy brain?

What the anvil? what dread grasp
Dare its deadly terrors clasp?

When the stars threw down their spears,
And watered heaven with their tears,
Did He smile his work to see?
Did He who made the Lamb make thee?

Computer! Computer! burning bright
In the forests of the night,
What immortal hand or eye
Dare frame thy fearful symmetry?[17]

And the questions are only beginning to be asked. Individual humanists and scientists are asking the computer:

Are you alive?
Do you have a brain and does it think?
Do you have a heart and does it beat?
Can you be kind?
Can you show love?
Shall I listen to the computer prophets
of doom?
Or shall I listen to voices in praise of
computers?
I think I will listen for the voices of
honest men,
But if I do not know them when I hear
them,
Then I will listen to my own
For the problems and the answers abide
within.

16

The Necessity of Humanism in the Computer Age

WALLACE A. MURPHREE

In the history of civilization ours is a most awesome day. We—like kindergartners who incorporate live ammunition into their game of cops and robbers—hold at our greedy and immature fingertips the potential for worldwide devastation for the very first time ever. And daily the prospects for the future grow progressively grim. What is ironic is that the history of how we arrived at this brink of self-destruction is in many respects the legacy of how civilization tried to insure its survival.

The Problem in Historical Perspective

Nature appears never to have been a completely gracious hostess to the forms of life she entertains. One distinction between the subhuman and human forms is that the former react to nature's hostile forces as they occur with blind impulsiveness, whereas human beings have tried in advance to prepare ways of dealing with them. Although some have contended that the source of the problem lies in the essential unworthiness of the guest,[1] most have conceived it to lie in the capricious tyranny of the stepmotherly hostess. The history of the human race, in a very real sense, is the account of this struggle against those hostile elements in nature.[2]

The first instance of the struggle was religious. People attempted to invoke the powers they supposed to control the elements in order to be spared nature's wrath. They felt that if all such powers could become known and correctly named[3] there would be no reason that nature could not be coerced into becoming genuinely hospitable. However, the general lack of success in such tactics has long been well-known. Imagine a tribesman who, before his departure, takes every precaution for the safety of his family for the time he is away. He invokes the powers of all the gods—known and unknown—against every type of flood, fire, wind, ravenous beast, disease, etc., on his family's behalf. When he returns they are dead. The gods, he discovers, are every bit as capricious as the natural forces they had been invoked to control. He ponders: "If only I could understand the ways of nature then I would be able to struggle against them for myself."

Thus philosophy was born with the insight that knowledge (understanding) of nature, rather than knowledge (acquaintance) of persons transcending nature, is the more effective instrument in the struggle. Hence philosophers wondered, thought, imagined and speculated about first principles, final causes, primary substances, and utopias. But the various philosophical claims to knowledge of nature's ways proved to be incompatible with one another and equally impotent when applied in the war against her hostile forces. Nature would not disclose her ways to their speculative imaginations.[4] So the philosophers concluded that in order to discover them she must be continually watched and her behavior carefully examined. And to insure that she didn't somehow continue hiding her secrets she must be prodded—forced into releasing them.

Thus science was born. Armed with the methods of observation and experimentation, it was fully confident of its ability to understand, and hence control, the wanton forces. From the mechanical secrets nature disclosed, great machines were built up by which her power was harnessed under human control. The tyrannical hostess had finally been enslaved and forced into doing physical labor for the guests—marking the dawn of the industrial era. And from the electronic revelations she subsequently divulged, the computer was created, swiftly marking the beginning of yet another age: the present age in which nature has been coerced into performing intellectual functions for her inhabitants. And as her physical machines were superior to human labor so is her information machinery decidedly superior (in many respects) to human intellect. In fact, the computer, coupled with other electronic instruments, can collect data, store it, analyze it, assimilate it, draw logical inferences from it and then instruct labor machines on the basis of its inferences with staggering efficiency and rapidity. It may be a gross understatement to claim that the computers of the world amass and process more data daily than could have been handled by all the people who ever lived working all their lives all put together!

Could the tribesman who first realized that knowledge was the key to the control of nature ever have had a glimpse of the wealth of today's knowledge, surely he would have surmised that the struggle was finally being won and that the welfare of the human race was about to be insured. But in fact the very knowledge which was to have saved humanity has put us on a collision course with destiny. The utopian dream has turned into a doomsday nightmare. Something went wrong.

Description of the Problem

Perhaps it is inevitable that problems should be the by-product of change. Especially when one age gives way to another, the accompanying complications may be severe and require generations to be finally alleviated. Historically there has always been sufficient time for the wounds to heal. Today, however, the situation is different. Being in the immediate wake of the Industrial Revolution we find our air unsafe to breathe, our streams unsafe to drink, our foods unsafe to eat and our beaches unsafe for swimming. Our cities have been replaced by slums, our meadows by junkyards and our lakes by cesspools, etc. Time is needed to deal with these problems; but there is no time, because the technology which spawned them is still in a period of accelerated growth. Hence the problems continue to accumulate exponentially while the solutions seem to advance at best at a constant rate. Consequently not only are the solutions lagging behind but they are lagging increasingly far behind with there being no apparent way to make up any lost ground. The result is that our civilized ideal of handling problems deliberately and rationally is inapplicable, and we are forced to deal with them as best we can on the run. All this, however, is the less ominous part of our present difficulty.

Today we find ourselves in the midst of still another revolution—the computer revolution. Although everyone has been hearing of computers for the past decade or so, only few have been aware that a full-blown revolution was underway. But quietly, overnight, our society became saturated with computer technology, and it is only today that the average person feels the first problematic shock waves of its impact. Although the computer age was born out of the Industrial Revolution it is not a mere extension of it; rather, technologically a quantum leap has occurred over the entire distance between the physical and the information sciences. Hence the resultant problems are of a type-level difference from the ones mentioned earlier. Already our property rights have become threatened from a heretofore unconceived direction, which, nevertheless, can be exploited by the common criminal[5] as well as by computer experts.[6] Our right to privacy has already been so violated that our lives have become open books for anyone from political surveillance organizations to unscrupulous lending agencies.[7] We find that we have been robbed of our names and issued numbers instead (and woe unto him whose number is misrecorded in the computer's book of life). Etc. More importantly we hear that the warmongers have their computers programmed to release enough thermonuclear warheads to destroy the earth as many times over as they deem appropriate—and the computer age is barely in its infancy. And there appears to be no good reason to believe that the age will not provide the potential for universal catastrophe in an indefinite number of ways, and available to an indefinite number of people, in the course of its development.

It would be vain to speculate as to what the nature of potentials for universal destruction will be. Like the tribesman who could not in his wildest fantasies envision today's world, our imaginative capacities are limited with respect to the future of this age. But all that needs to be noted is that prior to this generation every scientific discovery, every invention and every technological innovation that has reshaped history down paths inconceivable to earlier generations were made on the basis of extremely meager information compared to what the average American graduate student has at hand daily.

Furthermore since it is impossible to foresee what the nature of the possible future destructive capabilities will be it is likewise impossible to provide any safeguards in advance. Hence each new capacity for such destruction will exist prior to the installment of safeguards to deal with it, if indeed safeguards can be installed at all.

Finally the fact is that the susceptibility to disaster is often not treated seriously until after there has actually been a victim. After the fatality at the intersection the traffic light is installed; after the airplane crash the runway is lengthened. Etc. Civilization has survived such tragedies because they have been of local scope. But today the problem is of universal scope so that any one tragedy will be of ultimate gravity. We can hope, of course, that those who acquire such capacities will behave judiciously. But given the character of our society the reliance on such a hope, as the capacities and persons who have them multiply, is most unreasonable.

Analysis of the Problem

Hence the precarious status of civilization is not the result of advanced technology alone; rather it is the result of such technology *in conjunction with* our social character, viz. materialism, in the sense explained below.

In a narrow sense materialism is the view that that which is worthwhile in and of itself is the possession of material goods. Obviously this is not our system of values because we aren't a society of misers, which would be the case if it were practiced. Rather we are misers in our businesses, but when we leave the office we become gluttonous consumers at home. It is in a broader sense that today's society is materialistic. In this sense, materialism is the belief that the only thing worthwhile in and of itself is the possession of material goods and those immaterial things for which the material goods may be exchanged. This view is coupled with the further contention that material goods may be exchanged for pleasure, personal power, political power, prestige and a satisfactory life in general. Perhaps this could be restated as the view that the possession of material wealth is the only way to store up pleasure, power, etc., and that having it so stored up is alone intrinsically valuable.

The consequence of this orientation is that the materialist would risk anything to acquire or to retain wealth. The forty-niners risked their existence for the chance of getting gold, and rightly so from a materialist's point of view, because a life of poverty was not fit to be lived. The industrialist risks the destruction of the environment; airlines risk the safety of their passengers; mining companies risk the lives of the miners; food refineries risk the health of the consumers—to say nothing of tobacco manufacturers, etc. Of course, the materialists do not intend to destroy the environment or endanger lives. Their intention is the acquisition of wealth; risking lives (even their own) simply happens to be the most expedient means to this goal on some occasions.

Now the essence of electronic technology's threat to civilization is that it undoubtedly holds within its scope many potential ways of increasing wealth (or power) which at the same time would risk widespread—even universal—catastrophe. And as such techniques become available materialists will naturally take the chance and employ them—until The Inevitable Accident happens. In short, it is materialism as the end, together with an ever advancing technology as the means, that spells almost certain disaster for the future.

The Rejection of Materialism

In order to avoid this crisis at least one of these elements must be abandoned. The proposal here advanced is that materialism should be rejected while technology is retained. There are several reasons to support this proposal.

First of all, to reject technology is to abandon the tribesman's dream. It seems unduly tragic that individuals should forever be sacrificed to the whimsicality of nature in order to allow civilization a longer life expectancy.

In the second place it seems completely unnecessary that this should be done because, as mentioned above, it is not technology *per se* but technology in the hands of materialists that creates the crisis. Mere technology, although it may give rise to temporary dislocations and/or nostalgia, creates no widespread problems. Rather it normally simply reflects the preexisting heinous elements in society straightforwardly. That is, the computer didn't create the computer criminal; the criminal was already there. It didn't create alienation in business transactions; it simply forced us to acknowledge the preexisting fact that most entrepreneurs are interested in us only as possible sources of material gain to them. (Here it might be added that it also provides an easy scapegoat for those of us who have difficulty being authentic). Technology has not ruined our environment; rather materialists have ruined it by applying this power over nature for the purpose of robbing her of her graciousnesses instead of controlling her excesses. The fact is that technology is valuatively neutral: it offers its awesome services impartially to any end whatever.

In the third place, it seems to be physically impossible to discontinue, or even to impede, technological advance while materialism is retained as the value system, because advanced computer technology is expedient to the goal of increased acquisition of wealth. Hence, for example, if all computers were declared illegal and destroyed, computer engineers would simply rebuild and bootleg them. And the government agency assigned to catch the bootleggers would have to have computers in order to do their job effectively. Etc.

Looking now to materialism, there seems—quite apart from the crisis stated above—to be something inherently inadequate with this value orientation. For one thing, it is an ideal which in principle can never be universally realized. If material wealth is intrinsically good, then nothing short of total ownership can constitute the *summum bonum*. And at the logical best only one person could achieve this at a time, leaving everyone else, therefore, in absolute poverty. But not only is materialism unrealizable; it appears also to be a goal which, to the extent that it is realized, is finally unsatisfying. Of course this is not easily detected by the materialist, because the basic assumption is that wealth is that in virtue of which life can be satisfactory. Hence when the accumulation of a measure of wealth is followed by the discovery that life is no richer than it was before, the materialist concludes that the amount is simply not yet sufficient. And so on perpetually. Many nevertheless have become disillusioned with the system, having experienced that it never pays what it promises. By and large it has been the affluent—not the poor—who have made the discovery. They have "dropped out" to become occultists, mystics, thrill seekers, dopers, homesteaders, etc. This leads to one final point about materialism: viz. it can be dethroned if a viable alternative is available.

Perhaps it is immodest to sit back and speak airily about changing society's values. But in the history of Western civilization the values have been changed—from those of the Graeco-Roman world to those of the middle ages, to those of the Renaissance, to those of modern materialism—and they can be changed again. The "drop outs" just mentioned of the past decade show that materialism's firm grasp on society is already being weakened, and no doubt its attrition rate would be greater if there were a general awareness of a positive alternative value system.

The Necessity of Humanism

The one and only alternative system which in principle seems compatible with both technology and the future of civilization is humanism. Humanism, as here intended, is the view that each actual human existence is intrinsically valuable and that, in the natural world, only actual human existences are intrinsically valuable.

It will be noticed that this definition, although somewhat awkward, has been framed with sufficient generality to include theists as well as atheists. Unfortunately it appeals to the vague term of "actual human existence," which prevents the specification of some of its ethical implications. For example, although this definition of humanism implies that one ought not destroy a human existent, it does not directly address the questions of abortion and euthanasia, because where human existence begins and ends has not been defined. Perhaps it does address the question of capital punishment. The phrase "actual human existence" has been used in the definition instead of mere "human existence," in order to prevent its being interpreted as implying that birth control should not be practiced. That is, from the statement, "Human existence is intrinsically valuable," one might conclude that therefore everyone ought to have as many babies as possible. Unlike materialism, however, the value system here being proposed is not a matter of quantity. What it says, rather, is that at any given time—whether the earth is underpopulated or overpopulated—all and only human existences at that time on earth are intrinsically valuable.

The real difference between this view and all other value systems, including materialism, is that it assumes the locus of intrinsic value to be in human existence itself, rather than in some state of human existence; it is the "is-ness," not the "what-ness," that is inherently good. Hence for the humanist it doesn't take money or happiness to make life worth living; life is worth living simply because it *is* that which is intrinsically worthwhile. Money and happiness well may have value, but only instrumentally—as means; never as ends in themselves.

This, then, is a sketch of the value system which offers the brightest prospects for the future of the human race when coupled with computer age technology. The reason for this is that it is the only value orientation which in principle could never allow risking human existence. For example, the materialist would sacrifice the lives of others and risk his own to acquire wealth if the "stakes were high enough." But the humanist would risk all the wealth of the world to insure human life. Furthermore, the same reasoning holds for any value system whose cornerstone is some state of human existence, instead of existence itself, like the view that knowledge is that which is intrinsically good. Although it would be refreshing to see people participate in the search for truth as avidly as they now do in the search for wealth, the position still holds the same liability. Certainly human existence could be risked for the sake of learning as easily as it could for the sake of acquiring wealth. The same would hold for the ideal of universal happiness, for if the odds were good enough the utilitarian would wager any-thing—including civilization—on the hopes of achieving the ideal. It is only humanism, as defined above, that cannot in princple take such a chance.

Hence, if humanism were as universally internalized as materi-alism has been, the nightmare character of the future could once again become a vision of hope, notwithstanding the earlier claim that the capacity for universal disaster will precede its safeguards. For when in a technological project a hazard develops—whether of local or universal scope—the humanist will proceed no further un-til it is securely safeguarded. The humanist will not take a chance with human lives. Furthermore, with the thrust of electronic tech-nology directed to humanistic ends there would be nothing in principle preventing the progressive realization of the tribesman's ancient ideal. Of course humanism cannot guarantee the realiza-tion of this ideal; in fact it cannot guarantee the continued existence of civilization for an hour. What it offers us, rather, is the best pos-sible chance because—in the final analysis—it is our only chance.

Notes

Notes to **Computers and the Idea of Progress**

[1] The standard work is J. B. Bury, *The Idea of Progress: An Inquiry into Its Origin and Growth* (New York: The Macmillan Co., 1932).

[2] E. P. Thompson, *The Making of the English Working Class* (New York: Vintage Books, 1963), pp. 547–602.

[3] Asa Briggs, *Victorian People: A Reassessment of Persons and Themes, 1851–67* (New York: Harper and Row, 1955), pp. 19–20, 49–51.

[4] A useful introduction to the problem of Progress in the 20th century is Sidney Pollard, *The Idea of Progress: History and Society* (Baltimore: Penguin Books, 1968).

[5] John H. Douglas, "Brave New Components," *Science News*, 108 (September 13, 1975), 170.

[6] Typical of prevailing attitudes is the news article which devotes 80% of its space to positive aspects of computers and 20% to negative aspects. "Coming, Another Revolution in Computers," *U.S. News and World Report*, 81 (July 19, 1976), 54–57.

[7] "Get Ready for Cashless, Checkless Living," *Changing Times*, 29 (October, 1975), 6–8.

[8] Asa Briggs, *The Making of Modern England, 1783–1867* (New York: Harper and Row, 1959), pp. 296–99.

[9] Charlotte Erickson, "Quantitative History: A Review Article," *American Historical Review*, 80 (April, 1975), 351–65.

[10] Ruth Davis, "Impermanent Balance between Man and Computer," *Science*, 186 (October 11, 1974), 99.

[11] Franklin Tugwell, ed., *Search for Alternatives: Public Policy and the Study of the Future* (Cambridge, Mass.: Winthrop Publishers, Inc., 1973), p. viii.

[12] Alvin Toffler, *Future Shock* (New York: Random House, 1970), p. 429.

[13] Ibid., p. 425.

[14] Tugwell, *Search for Alternatives*, p. xiv.

Notes to **A Historian Looks at the Computer's Impact on Society**

[1] The word does not appear in the *Oxford English Dictionary* (Supplement, 1972) or in *Webster's New Collegiate Dictionary* (1976).

[2] Robert P. Swierenga, "Computers and American History," *Journal of American History*, 60 (1974), 1067.

[3] Vol. 80, no. 2 (April, 1975).

[4] Ibid., pp. 329–50.

[5] Ibid., pp. 365, 363.

[6] New York: Charles Scribner's Sons, 1966.

[7] New York: World University Library, McGraw-Hill, 1969.

[8] Boston: Little, Brown and Company, 1974.

[9] See for example the essays by Kenneth Stampp, Eugene Genovese et al. in *Irony and Perspectives in American Slavery*, ed. H. P. Owens (Jackson: University Press of Mississippi, 1976).

[10] New York: Norton, 1975 (first published in 1971).

[11] Ibid., p. 9.

[12] Ibid., p. 8.

[13] Charles Tilly, quoted by Shorter, p. 21.

[14] Charles Hirschfeld, ed., *Classics of Western Thought*, 3, *The Modern World* (New York: Harcourt, Brace and World, 1968), p. 436.

[15] *Time on the Cross*, pp. 109–11.

[16] "Sketch for a Historical Picture of the Progress of the Human Mind," Hirschfeld, p. 224.

[17] For a discussion of these aspects of the computer's role in the modern world see James Martin and A. R. D. Norman, *The Computerized Society* (Englewood Cliffs, N. J.: Prentice-Hall, Inc., 1975), chaps. 14–21.

[18] Numbers, I:2–3.

[19] J. A. Giles, ed., *The Anglo-Saxon Chronicle* (London: G. Bell and Sons, Ltd., 1914), pp. 156–57.

[20] "Dooms of Canute (1020–1034)" in *Sources of English Constitutional History*, ed. C. Stephenson and F. G. Marcham (New York: Harper and Brothers, 1937), p. 23.

[21] Toffler suggests (pp. 210–11) the possibility of sophisticated computers in the future that could function in most ways just like men. But it seems unlikely that, as bureaucrats sometimes can be, they could be moved by the power of sex-appeal or by threats of physical violence. A human machine is surely, by definition, an impossibility.

[22] Martin and Norman, *Computerized Society*, pp. 409–12.

[23] Lydel Sims, "When Computer Goes Mad Only Its Victims Foam," *The Commercial Appeal* (Memphis), July 28, 1976, p. 1, cols. 2–6.

Notes to **Computers and Society: Today and Tomorrow**

[1] John H. Douglas, "Beyond the Industrial Revolution," *Science News*, 108 (October 4, 1975), 220.

[2] Amitai Etzioni, "Effects of Small Computers on Scientists," *Science*, 189 (July 11, 1975), 93.

[3] Douglas, "From Number Crunchers to Pocket Genies," *Science News*, 108 (September 6, 1975), 154–157.

[4] "Computer Slashes Electric Bill," *Factory*, 7 (September, 1974), 21.

[5] *New York Times*, October 2, 1975, p. 26, col. 1.

[6] Douglas, October 4, 1975, p. 221.

[7] Herman Kahn, "Impact of the Friendly Computer," in Dennie Van Tassel, ed., *The Compleat Computer* (Palo Alto, Calif., Science Research Associates, 1976), p. 204.

[8] Douglas, October 4, 1975, p. 221.

[9] Kahn, p. 204.

[10] Donald Michael, "Decisions and Public Opinion" in Dennie Van Tassel, ed., *The Compleat Computer* (Palo Alto, Calif.; Science Research Associates, 1976), pp. 154–55.

[11] Fred Gruenberger, *Computers and the Social Environment* (Los Angeles: Melville, 1975), p. 149.

[12] *IEEE Spectrum*, April, 1975.

[13] Douglas, October 4, 1975, p. 221.

[14] Ibid., p. 222.

[15] Richard A. Weiss, *A View of the Future* (Poughkeepsie, N.Y.: International Business Machines, 1975) p. 10.

[16] Kahn, pp. 205–206.

[17] See, for example, the discussion in the first edition of Stanley Rothman and Charles Mosmann, *Computers and Society* (Palo Alto, Calif.: Science Research Associates, 1972).

[18] "Machines Smarter Than Men? An Interview with Norbert Wiener," *U. S. News and World Report* (February 24, 1964), pp. 84–86.

[19] Michael, p. 153.

[20] Hank E. Koehn, "Privacy, Our Problem for Tomorrow," *Journal of Systems Management*, 24 (July, 1973), 8–10.

[21] Joseph R. Weizenbaum, "On the Impact of the Computer on Society," *Science*, 176 (May 12, 1972), p. 609–614.

[22] Ibid.

[23] Kahn, pp. 204–205.

[24] "Machines Smarter than Men?" p. 84.

Notes to **Computers—For Better and For Worse**

[1] Grahame Clark, *World Prehistory: A New Outline*, 2nd ed. (Cambridge: Cambridge Univ. Press), 1969, p. 24.

[2] "The Computer Bandits," *Newsweek*, August 9, 1976, p. 58.

[3] Ibid.

[4] "Systems Installed to Deter $250 Million in Stolen Books," *The Commercial Appeal* (Memphis), July 20, 1976, p. 18, cols. 1–2. The newspaper story quotes "Graham Gurr . . . manager of the Library Systems branch of the 3M Company."

[5] "The Computer Bandits."

[6] Robert W. Fogel and Stanley L. Engerman, *Time on the Cross: The Economics of American Negro Slavery* (Boston: Little, Brown, 1974).

[7] For a review of the controversy concerning the validity of the figures in *Time on the Cross*, see Douglas W. Steeples, "*Time on the Cross*, Cliometrics, Clio and the American Crisis," *The Key Reporter*, 41, (Spring, 1976), pp. 2–4.

[8] Robert C. Hall, who signs himself as chairman and president, Securities Industry Automation Corp., "Letters to the Editor," *New York Times*, August 14, 1976, p. 20, cols. 1–2.

[9] The "neonatal behavior scale" of Dr. T. Berry Brazelton of Harvard University is described by Margen Penick in "Kid Stuff," *House and Garden*, June, 1976, pp. 26 and 56. The work of Dr. Brazelton, as well as that of Colwyn Trevarthen and Martin Richards, is discussed by Patrick Young in " 'Babies Can Communicate at Birth,' " *The National Observer*, July 24, 1976, 105.

[10] For a discussion of current efforts to ensure the safety of computer messages, see "A Cryptic Warning to Academe," *The Chronicle of Higher Education*, November 21, 1977, p. 1.

Notes to **Computers and Persons**

[1] John G. Kemeny, *Man and the Computer* (New York: Charles Scribner's Sons, 1972), pp. 3–20.

[2] Paul Armer, "Attitudes Toward Intelligent Machines," in *Computers and Thought*, ed. Edward A. Feigenbaum and Julian Feldman (New York: McGraw-Hill Book Company, Inc., 1963), pp. 389–405.

[3] Marvin Minsky, "Steps Toward Artificial Intelligence," in *Computers and Thought*, ed. Edward A. Feigenbaum and Julian Feldman (New York: McGraw-Hill Book Company, Inc., 1963), pp. 406–450.

[4] Alvin Toffler, *Future Shock* (New York: Bantam Books, 1970).

[5] Philip Slater, *Earthwalk* (New York: Bantam Books, 1974), p. 23.

[6] Jeremy Bernstein, "When the Computer Procreates," *New York Times Magazine* (February 15, 1976), pp. 9+.

[7] Jeremy Bernstein is a professor of physics at Stevens Institute of Technology and a staff writer for *The New Yorker*. His latest book is entitled *Einstein* (*New York Times Magazine*, February 15, 1976, p. 9).

[8] Bernstein, Ibid., p. 38.

[9] Ibid.

[10] Joseph Weizenbaum, "Letter to the Editor," *New York Times Magazine* (March 21, 1976), p. 82.

[11] Ibid.

[12] Ibid.

[13] Fred Hapgood, "Computers Aren't So Smart After All," *Atlantic*, 234 (August, 1974), 39.

[14] Mortimer Taube, *Computers and Common Sense* (New York: Columbia University Press, 1961).

[15] Joseph Weizenbaum, "On the Impact of the Computer on Society," *Science*, 176 (May 12, 1972), 614.

[16] May Brodbeck, "Mind: From Within and From Without," *Proceedings of the American Philosophical Association*, 45 (1971–72), 54–55.

[17] John Dewey, *Reconstruction in Philosophy* (Boston: Beacon Press, 1948), p. 186.

Notes to **Printout Appeal**

[1] Frederick P. Brooks, Jr., *The Mythical Man-Month: Essays on Software Engineering* (Reading, Mass.: Addison-Wesley, 1975), p. 7.

[2] James Martin, *Design of Man-Computer Dialogues* (Englewood Cliffs, N.J.: Prentice-Hall, 1973), p. 203.

[3] Leo P. Kadnoff, "From Simulation Model to Public Policy: An Examination of Forrester's 'Urban Dynamics' " in *The Best Computer Papers of 1971*, ed. Orlando R. Petrocelli (Princeton: Auerbach Publishers, 1972), 221.

[4] Kadnoff, p. 220.

[5] "Wurmzauberspruch" in *Schriftwerke deutscher Sprache*, ed. Werner Burkhard, I (Aarau: H. R. Sauerlaender, 1961), 10.

[6] See K. D. Eason, "Understanding the Naive Computer User," *The Computer Journal*, 19 (1976), 3–7.

[7] The conventions are implicit in Robert S. Kuehne, Herbert W. Lindberg, William F. Baron, *Manual of Computer Documentation Standards* (Englewoods Cliffs, N.J.: Prentice-Hall: 1973), p. vii.

[8] See Uri Margolin, "The Demarcation of Literature and the Reader," *Orbis Litterarum*, 31 (1976), 1–29, especially 15.

[9] Brooks, pp. 54–58.

Notes to **Sex Shock: The Humanistic Woman in the Super-Industrial Society**

[1] José Luis Aranguren, *Human Communication* (New York: World University Library, McGraw-Hill, 1967), p. 209.

[2] Kenneth Clark, *Civilisation* (New York: Harper and Row, 1969), p. 346.

[3] Gilbert Highet, *Man's Unconquerable Mind* (New York: Columbia University Press, 1954; rpt. *Reader's Digest*, February, 1972), p. 281.

[4] Alvin Toffler, *Future Shock* (New York: Bantam Books, 1970), p. 466.

[5] Aranguren, p. 209.

[6] Daniel Bell, "Douze Modes de Prévision en science sociale," *Futuribles*, September 20, 1963, cited in Aranguren, p. 212.

[7] Aranguren, p. 209.

[8] Ibid., p. 143.

[9] Daniel Bell, "The Coming of the Post-Industrial Society," *The Educational Forum*, 40 (May, 1976), p. 576.

[10] Ibid., p. 577.

[11] Toffler, p. 466.

[12] James L. Jarrett, *The Humanities and Humanistic Education* (Reading, Mass.: Addison-Wesley Publishing Company, 1973), p. 93.

[13] Ibid., p. 90.

[14] E. Adamson Hoebel, "The Nature of Culture," in *Man, Culture and Society*, ed. H. L. Shapiro (New York: Oxford University Press, 1956), p. 168.

[15] Ruth Benedict, *Patterns of Culture* (New York: Penguin, 1946), p. 4.

[16] Ibid., p. 3.

[17] Ibid.

[18] Hoebel, p. 175.

[19] Ibid., p. 176.

[20] Caroline Bradford, "The Need for Anthropology in the Social Studies," master's thesis, The Ohio State University, 1969.

[21] Raymond J. Endres, "Humanities, Social Studies and Values," *Social Education* (May, 1970), p. 544.

[22] Toffler, p. 466.

[23] Bell, p. 577.

[24] Toffler, p. 219.

[25] Bell, p. 577.

[26] Aranguren, p. 227.

[27] Toffler, p. 219.

[28] G.L. Shackle, *Decision, Order and Time in Human Affairs*, 1961, in Aranguren, p. 214.

[29] Aranguren, pp. 214, 215.

[30] Ibid., p. 215.

[31] Bell, p. 578.

[32] Toffler, p. 219.

[33] Report to the United Nations, 1968: "The Status of Women in Sweden," in *Voices of the New Feminism*, ed. Mary Lou Thompson (Boston: Beacon Press, 1970), pp. 155–178.

[34] N.V. Scarfe, "Education for Values Judgement," *Education Canada*, June, 1970 pp. 12–14.

[35] Ibid.

[36] Aranguren, p. 233.

[37] Toffler, p. 433.

[38] McGeorge Bundy, "Justice as Fairness Between Men and Women," in *Women in Higher Education*, ed. W. Todd Furniss and Patricia Albjerg Graham (Washington, D. C.: American Council on Education, 1974).

[39] John Rawls, *A Theory of Justice* (Cambridge, Mass.: Harvard University Press, 1971), p. 302.

[40] Shirley Chisholm, "Women Must Rebel," in *Voices of the New Feminism* (Boston: Beacon Press, 1970), pp. 210, 216.

[41] Mary Lou Thompson, "Forecast for Feminism" in *Voices of the New Feminism* (Boston: Beacon Press, 1970), p. 206.

[42] Betty Friedan, "Our Revolution Is Unique" in *Voices of the New Feminism* (Boston: Beacon Press, 1970), p. 35.

43 Ibid., p. 37.

44 Roxanne Dunbar, "Female Liberation as the Basis for Social Revolution" in *Voices of the New Feminism* (Boston: Beacon Press, 1970), p. 46.

45 Alice Rossi, "Sex Equality: The Beginnings of Ideology" in *Voices of the New Feminism* (Boston: Beacon Press, 1970), p. 74.

46 Ibid., p. 72.

47 Bell, p. 578.

48 Clare Booth Luce, "The 21st Century Woman—Free At Last?" *Saturday Review World*, August 24, 1974, pp. 58–62.

49 George E. Berkley, *The Administration Revolution* (Englewood Cliffs, N.J.: Prentice-Hall, 1971), p. 24.

50 Luce, pp. 58–62.

51 Ibid.

52 Aranguren, p. 218.

53 Clark, p. 346.

54 Toffler, p. 227.

55 Kurt Waldheim, "Toward Global Interdependence," *Saturday Review World*, August 24, 1974, pp. 63–64, 122.

56 Toffler, p. 343.

57 Viktor Frankl, *Man's Search For Meaning, An Introduction to Logotherapy*, (New York: Washington Square Press, 1968).

58 Highet, p. 287.

Notes to **Computer Technology and the Mass Media**

1 Paul R. Ehrlich and John P. Holdren, "Technology for the Poor," *Saturday Review*, July 3, 1971, p. 46.

2 Raymond Williams, *Television: Technology and Cultural Form* (New York: Schocken Books, 1974), pp. 129–131; see also Alvin Toffler, *Future Shock* (New York: Random House, 1970), pp. 368–369; Lewis Mumford, *The Myth of the Machine: The Pentagon of Power* (New York: Harcourt Brace Jovanovich, Inc., 1964), p. 329; and Joseph P. Martino, "The Role of Forecasting in Technology Assessment," *The Futurist*, 6 (October, 1972), 210.

3 Neil Postman, "Keynote Address," in Robert C. Jeffrey and William Work, eds., *Proceedings of Summer Conference IX: Long Range Goals and Priorities in Speech Communication* (New York: Speech Communication Association, 1973), p. 4.

4 Ibid.

5 Postman, p. 7.

6 Toffler, p. 26.

7 Joan Sweeney, "Radio Stations Dial 'A' for Automation," *Issues in Broadcasting*, eds., Ted C. Smythe and George A. Mastroianni (Palo Alto, California: Mayfield Publishing Company, 1975), p. 394.

8 Sweeney, p. 394.

9 Marshall McLuhan, *Understanding Media: The Extensions of Man* (New York: McGraw-Hill Book Company, 1964), p. 346.

[10] "Radio Automation Gives Extra Working Arms to Talented People," *BME*, July, 1976, p. 50.

[11] Sweeney, p. 398.

[12] "Keeping Automated Tabs on Broadcast Ads," *Business Week*, August 25, 1975, p. 68.

[13] Ibid., p. 69.

[14] Kenneth H. Wright, "Computer Helps Operators Promote On-Time Payments," *TV Communications*, March, 1975, p. 52.

[15] Williams, p. 142.

[16] Nathaniel E. Feldman, *Interconnecting Cable TV Systems by Satellite—An Introduction to the Issues* (Santa Monica, California: The Rand Corporation, T-5035, June, 1973), p. 8.

[17] Ibid.

[18] "NHK Installs Computer Broadcast Programming," *Broadcasting*, September 16, 1968, p. 71.

[19] "Man Bites Computer," *Newsweek*, April 18, 1976, p. 88.

[20] Ibid.

[21] Ibid.

[22] Joel E. Rubin, "Computerized Lighting Control," reprinted from *Theatre Crafts*, May-June, 1975, p. 1.

[23] "A Satellite Network that Bypasses AT&T," *Business Week*, January 12, 1976, p. 26.

[24] Louis Calta, "Telestat Buys Teleprompter Unit to Bring TV to Remote Quebec," *New York Times*, September 25, 1974, p. 79.

[25] Pool, "The Rise of Communication Policy Research," *Journal of Communication*, 24 (1974), 31–42, cited by W. Phillips Davison et al., *Mass Media Systems and Effects* (New York: Praeger Publishers, 1976), p. 208.

[26] Toffler, p. 121.

[27] McLuhan, pp. 328–337.

[28] Jacques Ellul, *The Technological Society* (New York: Vintage Books, 1964), p. 380.

[29] R. Buckminster Fuller, "Now and When," *Harper's*, April, 1972, pp. 58, 61.

[30] Mumford, p. 61.

[31] Alvin Toffler, "Coping With Future Shock," *Playboy*, March, 1970, p. 175.

[32] Toffler, *Future Shock*, pp. 343–345.

[33] McLuhan, p. 24.

[34] Ellul, p. 380.

[35] Melvin L. DeFleur and Sandra Ball-Rokeach, *Theories of Mass Communication* (New York: David McKay Company, Inc., 1975), p. 258.

[36] DeFleur and Ball-Rokeach, pp. 258–259.

[37] Williams, p. 133.

[38] Martino, p. 210.

[39] Williams, p. 134.

[40] Pool, cited by Davison, p. 208.

[41] Ellul, p. 431.

[42] Martino, p. 210.

[43] Toffler, *Future Shock*, p. 409.

Notes to **Computer Impact and the Social Welfare Sector**

[1] Paul Abels, "Terra Incognita: The Future of the Profession," *Public Welfare*, 31, 4 (Fall, 1973), p. 25.

[2] *The Oxford* [Mississippi] *Eagle*, August 4, 1976, p. 4.

[3] Murray Gruber, "Total Administration," *Social Work*, 19, 5 (September, 1974), p. 625.

[4] William J. Reid, "Developments in the Use of Organized Data," *Social Work*, 19, 5 (September, 1974), p. 586.

[5] Gruber, p. 626.

[6] Carol H. Weiss, "Alternative Models of Program Evaluation," *Social Work*, 19, 6 (November, 1974), p. 680.

[7] Verne R. Kelley and Hanna B. Weston, "Computers, Costs, and Civil Liberties," *Social Work*, 20, 1 (January, 1975), p. 15.

[8] Gruber, p. 625.

[9] Edith Fein, "A Data System for an Agency," *Social Work*, 20, 1 (January, 1975), p. 21.

[10] Edward A. Suchman, *Evaluative Research*, (New York: Russell Sage Foundation, 1969), pp. 4–5.

[11] Reid, "Developments in the Use of Organized Data," *Social Work*, 19, 5 (September, 1974), p. 586.

[12] George Hoshino and Thomas P. McDonald, "Agencies in the Computer Age," *Social Work*, 20, 1 (January, 1975), p. 11.

[13] Ibid.

[14] Ibid., p. 10.

[15] Weiss, p. 679.

[16] Claire M. Anderson, "Information Systems for Social Welfare: Educational Imperatives," *Journal of Education for Social Work*, 11, 3 (Fall, 1975), p. 16.

[17] Reid, p. 588.

[18] Hoshino and McDonald, p. 14.

[19] Joe R. Hoffer, "Social Work in the 70's—A Management Partner in the Resolution of Social Issues and Problems," *Social Work Papers*, The Ohio State University, 1973, p. 22.

[20] Victor A. Thompson, "How Scientific Management Thwarts Innovation," *Trans-Action*, 5, 7 (June, 1968), p. 53.

[21] Ibid.

[22] Norman L. Bonney and Laurence H. Streicher, "Time Cost Data in Agency Administration: Efficiency Controls in Family and Children's Services," *Social Work*, 15, 4 (October, 1970), p. 25.

[23] Reid, p. 588.

[24] Theo Haimann and William G. Scott, *Management in the Modern Organization* (Boston: Houghton Mifflin Company, 1974), p. 213.

[25] Paul Abels, "The Managers are Coming! The Managers are Coming!" *Public Welfare*, 31, 4 (Fall, 1973), p. 14.

[26] Gruber, p. 636.

[27] Fein, p. 23.

[28] Reid, p. 588.

[29] Marvin L. Rosenberg and Ralph Brody, "The Threat or Challenge of Accountability," *Social Work*, 19, 3 (May, 1974), p. 344.

[30] Abels, "The Managers are Coming," p. 15.

[31] Fred W. Vondracek, Hugh B. Urban, and William H. Parsonage, "Feasibility of an Automated Intake Procedure for Human Services Workers," *Social Service Review*, 48, 2 (June, 1974), p. 277.

[32] Anderson, p. 17.

[33] Hoshino and McDonald, p. 14.

[34] Reid, p. 592–593.

Notes to **Computer Impact on Society: A Personal View from the World of Art**

[1] An analysis of how much technology has changed man is found in Victor C. Ferkiss, *Technological Man: The Myth and the Reality* (New York: George Braziller, 1969). See also, J. Weizenbaum, "On the Impact of the Computer on Society," *Science*, 176 (May 12, 1972), 609–614 for a discussion of the side-effects of technology.

[2] Perhaps the best publicized instance of defining "proper" painting occurred during the libel suit filed by the American artist, James Whistler, against the art critic, John Ruskin. See James Abbott McNeil Whistler, *The Gentle Art of Making Enemies*, (New York: Putnam, 1953). For a survey of recent attempts to define art, see Harold Rosenberg, *The De-definition of Art: Action Art to Pop to Earthworks* (New York: Horizon Press, 1972).

[3] Harold Taylor points out how " . . . this move toward a new and attractive side of the masses is an inevitable development from roots in technology—the speed and comparative ease of comparatively inexpensive transport, the speed and comparative ease of temporary and permanent building construction, etc.—and the breakdown of the idea that only the wealthy and the educated can understand art and life, that only the permanent is worth having." *Art and the Future* (New York: Art Education, Inc., 1969), 17.

[4] For a brief history and analysis of the chemical interactions and major characteristics of artists' materials, see Ralph Mayer, *The Artist's Handbook of Materials and Techniques*, 3d ed. (New York: Viking Press, 1970). See also Lawrence W. Jensen, *Synthetic Painting Media* (Englewood Cliffs, N.J.: Prentice-Hall, 1964).

[5] An extensive coverage of these new movements is found in Frank Popper, *Origins and Development of Kinetic Art* (New York: New York Graphic Society 1968).

[6] An excellent, concise summary of these events can be found in H.H. Arnason, *History of Modern Art* (New York: Prentice-Hall, Abrams 1976). It might be noted that the Constructivists in Russia were among the first to emphasize a need for "Utilitarian" qualities in art. See George Rickey, *Constructivism: Origins and Evolution* (New York: G. Braziller, 1967).

[7] These attitudes are apparent in the earth works of contemporary artists, the more recent trends in conceptual art and in some of the kinetic art produced by people holding the view of Jean Tinguely who creates self-destructive art. See Gregory Battcock, *Idea Art: A Critical Anthology* (New York: Dutton, 1973); Ur-

sula Meyer, *Conceptual Art* (New York: Dutton, 1972); Popper, *Origins and Development of Kinetic Art*.

[8] Vasarely is one of the primary leaders of this movement. See Victory Vasarely, *Vasarely* (Neuchatel, Switzerland: Editions du Griffon Neuchatel, 1965) and *Vasarely II* (Neuchatel, Switzerland: Editions du Griffon Neuchatel, 1971).

[9] Many sculptors, such as Donald Judd and Robert Morris, rely on technicians to turn their prepared design specifications into art works. While this has precedent in the tradition of European sculpture, it is unique today in that the technicians need not have artistic training. These artists seem to have none of the fears expressed by William Morris at the turn of the century: "I beg you to consider these two ideas of production, and you will then see how wide apart they are from one another. To the commercial producer the actual wares are nothing; their adventures in the market are everything. To the artist the wares are everything; his market he need not trouble himself about; for he is asked by other artists to do what he does do, what his capacity urges him to do." *Art and Its Producers, and the Arts and Crafts of Today: Two Addresses Delivered Before the National Association for the Advancement of Art* (London: Longmans and Co., 1901), p. 38.

[10] Marcel Duchamp and the rest of the "Dada" artists originated this idea which, while primarily "anti-art" in concept, eventually became a part of art production itself. See W. Rubin, *Dada, Surrealism and their Heritage* (New York: Museum of Modern Art, 1968).

[11] The process known as Kamagraphy is patented by Lichine and Co., in Paris. Artists commissioned to use this process, which can make up to 250 perfect copies of a painting, destroying the original in the process, include Max Ernst, Magritte, and Pignon.

[12] In holography, patterns of the complex wave fronts of light reflected from a laser-illuminated object are recorded on a special high-resolution photographic emulsion, usually on a glass plate. When the hologram is developed, much as a film is developed, there is no image of the object visible. Instead, the hologram presents a smoky, gray appearance, with perhaps a few swirls or wavy lines detectable to the naked eye. However, when the hologram is illuminated by laser light—or "reconstructed"—a precise, realistic, three-dimensional image of the object is visible. Through proper projection techniques, "life-size" measurements can be made. J. Benthall claims that "Holography will over the years influence our art, our everyday perception, our language, reality itself—perhaps no less than did the discovery of the lens and optical perspective." See "Laser Holography and Interference Patterning" *Science and Technology in Art Today* (London: Thames and Hudson, 1972), p. 98; see also "Holos! Holos! Velazque,! Gabor! S. Dali," *Art News*, 71 (April, 1972), 45 ff.; "Laser Light Looks at Art," *American Artist*, 36 (June, 1972), 36 ff.

[13] A woodcut done in 1517 by Albrecht Durer, *Draftsman Drawing a Portrait*, shows the artist behind a table looking through an eyepiece that gives him a fixed viewpoint of the seated model who is behind a pane of glass. The artist then painted on the glass exactly what he saw. It would appear that many Renaissance artists utilized convex and concave mirrors to reflect the desired subject matter onto their drawing surface in proper proportion.

[14] It might be noted that this process occurred at the same time that the middle or merchant class began to have greater importance.

[15] See Jack Morrison, *The Rise of the Arts on the American Campus* (New York: McGraw-Hill, 1973); Morris Risenhoover and Robert T. Blackburn, *Artists as Professors* (Urbana: University of Illinois Press, 1976).

[16] In the 1960s, many new organizations were founded to foster cooperation between artists and engineers in industrial companies. It should be noted, however, that recent concerns with environmental factors and the popularity of conceptual art theories has lessened many artists' interests in collaboration with industry. See Maurice Tuchman, *A Report on the Art and Technology Program of the Los Angeles County Museum of Art 1967–1971* (New York: Viking Press, 1971) for a summary of the international developments in art that provided for some contemporary artists to work with sophisticated technological personnel and resources. Some of the works which artists produced in this manner were exhibited at the 1970 Expo.

[17] An example of this type of "public art" would include the cybernetic tower at Liège, Belgium, by Nicholas Schoffer which has thirty-seven elements turning on their axes at different speeds of rotation as well as individual elements made up of sixty-four sheets and blades of polished aluminum which reflect light. Regulated by an electronic brain, which is sensitive to sound, temperature, and humidity, it produces an appropriate kind of music based on street sounds and recorded bird-song. See Popper, p. 135; see also Jewish Theological Seminary of America, *Two Kinetic Sculptors: Nicolas Schoffer and Jean Tinguely*, Catalogue with introductory essays (New York: Jewish Museum, 1965). Nicolas Schoffer also projects a tower for Rond-Point de la Defense in Paris. Based on the same techniques as a skyscraper frame, it would be 307 meters tall, and affected by sound, temperature, traffic flow, and humidity, so that it could serve as a barometer and announcer of weather forecasts by lights. See Jasia Reichardt, ed., *Cybernetic Serendipity*, Studio International Special Issue (New York: Frederick A. Praeger, 1969), p. 44.

[18] As pointed out by Lewis Mumford, "the very expansion of the machine during the last few centuries has taught mankind a lesson that was otherwise, perhaps, too obvious to be learned: the value of the singular, the unique, the precious, the deeply personal." *Art and Technics* (New York: Columbia University Press, 1952), p. 109.

[19] This is reflected in the formation of the Business Committee for the Arts. Since 1967, it has served as an intermediary to help art groups approach corporations and inform corporate executives of the advantages of arts support. For performing and visual arts, the funding grew from $110 million in 1970 to $144 million in 1973. The funding takes varied forms: some businesses underwrite major museum exhibitions, some purchase their own collections or commission art for offices and public spaces, some run their own galleries at corporate headquarters. *Art Letter*, 5 (February, 1976), 1. See also, Arnold Gingrich, *Business and the Arts: An Answer to Tomorrow* (New York: Paul S. Ericksson, 1969).

[20] For a discussion of possible implications, see R. Sandek, "Visual Arts in the Age of Mass Communications," *Arts in Society* (USA), 9 (Summer-Fall, 1972), 258–62.

[21] René Dubois has pointed out that "The demon to be exorcised is not in tech-

nology, but in those men—the immense majority of us—who are more interested in things than in conditions suitable for the development of human potentialities." "Despairing Optimist," *American Scholar*, 40 (Summer, 1971), 392.

Notes to **Technology: Messiah or Monster?**

[1] Myron B. Bloy, Jr., "The Christian Norm," *Technology and Human Values* (New York: The Fund for the Republic Inc., 1966), p. 18.

[2] Karel Capek, *R. U. R.* (London: Oxford University Press, 1961), p. 24.

[3] Charles R. Dechert, "Symposium on Technology and Humanism," *Studies in Social and Economic Process* (Lexington, Massachusetts: D. C. Heath and Company, 1972), pp. 132–136.

[4] Bertrand de Jouvenel, "Some Musings," *Technology and Human Values* (New York: The Fund for the Republic Inc., 1966), p. 33.

[5] Bloy, p. 20.

[6] Werner Heisenberg, "The Physicists' Conception of Nature," *Perspectives on the Computer Revolution* (Englewood Cliffs, N.J.: Prentice-Hall, Inc., 1970), p. 157.

[7] Zenon W. Pylyshyn, "Man-Machine Confrontation" *Perspectives on the Computer Revolution* (Englewood Cliffs, N.J.: Prentice-Hall, Inc., 1970), p. 158.

[8] G. Rattray Taylor, "The Age of the Androids," *Perspectives on the Computer Revolution* (Englewood Cliffs, N.J.: Prentice-Hall, Inc., 1970), p. 170.

[9] Lewis Mumford, "Two Views on Technology and Man," *Studies in Social and Economic Process* (Lexington, Massachusetts: D.C. Heath and Company, 1972), p. 9.

[10] Mumford, p. 12.

[11] Ashley Montagu, "Symposium on Technology and Humanism," *Studies in Social and Economic Process* (Lexington, Massachusetts: D.C. Heath and Company, 1972), p. 137.

[12] J.C.R. Licklider, "Man-Computer Symbiosis," *Perspectives on the Computer Revolution* (Englewood Cliffs, N.J.: Prentice-Hall, Inc., 1970), p. 306.

[13] Quoted in Joseph Weizenbaum, *Computer Power and Human Reason* (San Francisco: W.H. Freeman and Company, 1976), pp. 258, 259.

[14] Capek, p. 26.

[15] Bloy, p. 19.

[16] Gerald Sykes, "A New Salvation, A New Supernatural," *Technology and Human Values* (New York: The Fund for the Republic Inc., 1966), p. 10.

[17] John Wilkinson, *Technology and Human Values* (New York: The Fund for the Republic Inc., 1966), p. 3.

[18] Mumford, p. 4.

[19] Sykes, p. 6.

[20] Melvin Kranzberg, "Symposium on Technology and Humanism," *Studies in Social and Economic Process* (Lexington, Massachusetts: D.C. Heath and Company, 1972), p. 117.

[21] Jacques Ellul, "The Technological Society," *Perspectives on the Computer Revolution* (Englewood Cliffs, N.J.: Prentice-Hall, Inc., 1970), p. 444.

[22] Ellul, pp. 445, 446.

[23] Samuel Butler, "The Destruction of Machines in Erewhon," *Perspectives on the Computer Revolution* (Englewood Cliffs, N.J.: Prentice-Hall, Inc., 1970), p. 167.

[24] Capek, p. 42.

[25] Kenneth C. Boulding, "Conflict and Defense," *Perspectives on the Computer Revolution* (Englewood Cliffs, N.J.: Prentice-Hall, Inc., 1970), p. 402.

[26] de Jouvenel, "Some Musings," p. 330.

[27] Robert Boguslaw, "Symposium on Technology and Humanism," *Studies in Social and Economic Process* (Lexington, Massachusetts: D.C. Heath and Company, 1972), p. 109.

[28] Ralph Wendell Burhoe, "The Impact of Technology and the Sciences on Human Values," *Automation, Education, and Human Values* (New York: School and Society Books, 1966), pp. 125–129.

[29] Weizenbaum, p. 262.

[30] Emmanuel G. Mesthene, "Technology and Humanistic Values," *Computers and the Humanities* (Flushing, New York: Queens College of the City University of New York, 1969–70), p. 7.

[31] Luther H. Harshbarger, "Technological Change, Humanistic Imperatives, and the Tragic Sense," *Automation, Education, and Human Values* (New York: School and Society Books, 1966), pp. 118–123.

Notes to **The Computer and the Protestant Ethic**

[1] J. R. Bradburn, "Where Is the Computer Industry Heading?," *Perspectives on Electronic Data Processing*, ed. James D.J. Holmes and Elias M. Awad (Englewood Cliffs, New Jersey: Prentice-Hall, 1972), p. 235.

[2] "The Ubiquitous Computers," *The New York Times*, Section E., 13 June 1976, p. 8, cols. 3–4.

[3] Evan Jenkins, "Classroom Revolution: Computer Interaction," *The New York Times*, Section E, 13 June 1976, p. 9, cols. 1–4.

[4] Jenkins, p. 9, col. 2.

[5] Robert H. Davis, "The Computer Revolution and the Spirit of Man," *Perspectives on Electronic Data Processing*, ed. Holmes and Awad, p. 180.

[6] Davis, pp. 182–183.

[7] Davis, p. 181.

[8] See Professor Drucker's discussion of the worker, particularly the American black, in the knowledge society in the chapter entitled "Work and Worker in the Knowledge Society," from his book *The Age of Discontinuity* (New York: Harper and Row, 1968), pp. 287–310.

[9] Davis, "The Computer Revolution," pp. 185–186.

[10] The term *augment* is taken from a discussion of augmented man by Hawley A. Blanchard, "Some Social and Individual Implications of Augmented Man," *Computers in the Service of Society*, ed. Robert Lee Chartrand (New York: Pergamon Press, 1972), pp. 73–79.

[11] Italics are mine.

[12] Blanchard, p. 75.

Notes to **Reflection on Computers as Daughters of Memory**

[1] C. G. Jung, *Psychological Reflections: A New Anthology of His Writings, 1905–1961*, edited by Jolande Jacobi in collaboration with R. F. C. Hull (Bollingen Series XXXI, Princeton: Princeton University Press, 1970 revised edition), p. 275.

[2] Ibid.

[3] Erich Fromm, *The Revolution of Hope: Toward a Humanized Technology* (New York: Harper & Row, 1968), p. 1.

[4] Ibid., p. 2.

[5] Ibid., p. 3.

[6] Ibid., p. 5.

[7] Ibid., p. 155.

[8] Ibid., p. 156.

[9] Ibid.

[10] Ibid., p. 158.

[11] William Rose Benét and Norman Holmes Pearson (eds.), *The Oxford Anthology of American Literature* (New York: Oxford University Press, 1952), Vol. II, pp. 1037–1042.

[12] Ibid., p. 1037.

[13] Gerald M. Edelman, "Our American—The Nobel Scientist," *Newsweek*, Vol. 88, July 4, 1976. p. 21.

[14] Ibid., p. 22.

[15] Kenneth Clark, *The Romantic Rebellion: Romantic versus Classic Art* (New York: Harper & Row, 1973), pp. 150–151.

[16] Ibid.

[17] Paul Robert Lieder, Robert Morss Lovett, and Robert Kilburn Root (eds.), *British Poetry and Prose*, shorter edition; (Boston: Houghton Mifflin Co., 1951), p. 614.

Notes to **The Necessity of Humanism in the Computer Age**

[1] E.g. cf. Genesis 3:9–24.

[2] A similar account is given by Emmanuel G. Mesthene, in "Technology and Wisdom," *Philosophy and Contemporary Issues*, eds. John R. Burr and Milton Goldinger (New York: Macmillan Co., 1972), pp. 385–394 *passim*, where he describes the struggle against the "tyranny of matter."

[3] Hence Exodus 20:7, for to "take the Lord's name in vain" is to invoke supernatural power for unworthy purposes.

[4] This, of course, is not an attempt to discredit the value of what religion and/or speculative philosophy are in themselves.

[5] James Martin and Adrian R. D. Norman, *The Computerized Society* (Englewood Cliffs, N.J.: Prentice-Hall, 1970), pp. 380–82.

[6] Cf. Robert S. Strother, "Crime by Computer," *Reader's Digest*, April, 1976, pp. 143–48, for an explanation of computer theft to the lay person.

[7] Martin and Norman, pp. 303–37. For an insight into the difficulty of securing privacy rights see Harold Borks, "Information Sciences," *1976 Yearbook of Sciences and the Future, Encyclopedia Britannica*, pp. 318–320.

BIBLIOGRAPHY

LAURENZO

Briggs, Asa. *The Making of Modern England, 1763–1867*. New York: Harper and Row, 1959.

———. *Victorian People: A Reassessment of Persons and Thengs, 1851–67*. New York: Harper and Row, 1955.

Bury, J. B. *The Idea of Progress: An Inquiry into its Origins and Growth*. New York: The Macmillan Co., 1932.

* "Coming, Another Revolution in Computers." *U.S. News and World Report*, 81 (July 19, 1976), 54–57.

* Davis, Ruth. "Impermanent Balance between Man and Computer." *Science*, 186 (October 11, 1974), 99.

Douglas, John H. "Brave New Components." *Science News*, 108 (September 13, 1975), 170–72.

Erickson, Charlotte. "Quantitative History: A Review Article." *American Historical Review*, 80 (April, 1975), 351–65.

* "Get Ready for Cashless, Checkless Living." *Changing Times*, 29 (October, 1975), 6–8.

Pollard, Sidney. *The Idea of Progress: History and Society*. Baltimore: Penguin Books, 1968.

Thompson, E. P. *The Making of the English Working Class*. New York: Vintage Books, 1963.

Toffler, Alvin. *Future Shock*. New York: Random House, 1970.

Tugwell, Franklin, ed. *Search for Alternatives: Public Policy and the Study of the Future*. Cambridge, Mass.: Winthrop Publishers, Inc., 1973.

LANDON

The Anglo-Saxon Chronicle. Ed. J. A. Giles. London: G. Bell and Sons, Ltd., 1914.

Erickson, Charlotte. "Quantitative History." *American Historical Review*, 80, no. 2 (April, 1975), 351–65.

Fogel, Robert W. "The Limits of Quantitative Methods in History." *American Historical Review*, 80, no. 2 (April, 1975), 329–50.

Hirschfeld, Charles. *Classics of Western Thought*. Vol. 3. *The Modern World*. New York: Harcourt, Brace and World, Inc., 1968.

Irony and Perspectives in American Slavery. Ed. H. P. Owens. Jackson: University Press of Mississippi, 1976.

Laslett, Peter. *The World We Have Lost*. New York: Charles Scribner's Sons, 1966.

Martin, James and Norman, Adrian R. I. *The Computerized Society*. Englewood Cliffs, N.J.: Prentice-Hall, Inc., 1970.

Shorter, Edward. *The Historian and the Computer*. New York: W. W. Norton and Company, Inc., 1975.

Sims, Lydel, "When Computer Goes Mad Only Its Victims Foam." *Commercial Appeal* (Memphis), July 28, 1976, p. 1, cols. 2–6.

Stephenson, Carl and Marcham, F. G. *Sources of English Constitutional History*. New York: Harper and Brothers, 1937.

Swierenga, Robert P. "Computers and American History: The Impact of the 'New' Generation." *Journal of American History*. 60 (1974), 1045–70.

Toffler, Alvin. *Future Shock*. New York: Bantam Books, 1974.

Wrigley, E. A. *Population and History*, New York: World University Library, McGraw-Hill Book Company, 1969.

HALLBLADE/MATHEWS

"Computer Slashes Electric Bill," *Factory*, 7 (September, 1974), p. 21.

Douglas, John H. "Beyond the Industrial Revolution," *Science News*, 108 (October 4, 1975), pp. 220–221.

————. "From Number Crunchers to Pocket Genies," *Science News*, 108 (September 6, 1975), pp. 154–157.

Etzioni, Amitai. "Effects of Small Computers on Scientists," *Science*, 189 (July 11, 1975), p. 93.

Gruenberger, Fred. *Computers and the Social Environment*. Los Angeles: Melville, 1975.

IEEE Spectrum, April 1975.

Kahn, Herman. "Impact of the Friendly Computer," in Dennie Van Tassel, ed., *The Compleat Computer*. Palo Alto, Calif.: Science Research Associates, 1976.

Koehn, Hank E. "Privacy, Our Problem for Tomorrow," *Journal of Systems Management*, 24 (July, 1973), pp. 8–10.

"Machines Smarter Than Men? An Interview with Norbert Wiener," *U.S. News and World Report*, (February 24, 1964), pp. 84–86.

Michael, Donald. "Decisions and Public Opinion," in Dennie Van Tassel, ed., *The Compleat Computer*. Palo Alto, Calif.: Science Research Associates, 1976.

New York Times, October 2, 1975, p. 26, col. 1.

Rothman, Stanley, and Charles Mosmann. *Computers and Society*. Palo Alto, Calif.: Science Research Associates, 1972.

Weiss, Richard A. *A View of the Future*. Poughkeepsie, N.Y.: International Business Machines, 1975.

Weizenbaum, Joseph R. "On the Impact of the Computer on Society," *Science*, 176 (May 12, 1972), pp. 609–614.

BERGMARK

Anderson, Alan Ross, ed. *Minds and Machines*. Englewood Cliffs, New Jersey: Prentice-Hall, Inc., 1964.

Bernstein, Jeremy. "When the Computer Procreates." *New York Times Magazine*, February 15, 1976, p. 9+.

Bowles, Edmund A., ed. *Computers in Humanistic Research*. Englewood Cliffs, New Jersey: Prentice-Hall, Inc., 1967.

Brodbeck, May. "Mind: From Within and From Without." *Proceedings and Addresses of the American Philosophical Association*, 45 (1971–72), 42–55.

Dechert, Charles R. *The Social Impact of Cybernetics*. Notre Dame, Indiana: University of Notre Dame Press, 1966.

Feigenbaum, Edward A. and Julian Feldman, eds. *Computers and Thought*. New York: McGraw-Hill Book Company, Inc., 1963.

Hapgood, Fred. "Computers Aren't So Smart After All." *Atlantic*, 234 (August, 1974), 37–45.

Hatt, Harold E. *Cybernetics and the Image of Man*. Nashville, Tennessee: Abingdon Press, 1968.

Kemeny, John G. *Man and the Computer*. New York: Charles Scribner's Sons. 1972.

Nikolaieff, George A. *Computers and Society*. New York: The H. W. Wilson Company, 1970.

Spencer, Donald D. *Computers in Society*. Rochelle Park, New Jersey: Hayden Book Company, Inc., 1974.

Slater, Philip. *Earthwalk*. New York: Bantam Books, 1974.

Taube, Mortimer. *Computers and Common Sense*. New York: Columbia University Press, 1961.

Weizenbaum, Joseph. "On the Impact of the Computer On Society." *Science*, 176 (May 12, 1972), 609–614.

Wiener, Norbert. *The Human Use of Human Beings*. Garden City, New York: Doubleday and Company, Inc., 1956.

KIBLER

Bell, C. Gordon and Allen Newell. *Computer Structures: Readings and Examples*. New York: McGraw-Hill, 1971.

"Effects of Machinery: A Review of the Working Man's Companion, No 1," *Changing Attitudes Toward America's Technology*. Edited by Thomas Parke Hughes. New York, Harper-Row 1975. 120–135.

Forrester, Jay W. "Overlooked Reasons for Our Social Troubles." *Fortune*, 80 (December, 1969), p. 191.

Knuth, Donald E. "Von Neumann's First Computer Program." *Computing Surveys*, 2 (December, 1970), pp. 247–260.

JOHNSON

Brooks, Frederick P. Jr. *The Mythical Man-Month: Essays on Software Engineering*. Reading, Mass.: Addison-Wesley, 1975.

Eason, K. D. "Understanding the Naive Computer User." *The Computer Journal*, 19, no. 1 (1976), 3–7.

Kadnoff, Leo P. "From Simulation Model to Public Policy: An Examination of Forrester's 'Urban Dynamics.'" *The Best Computer Papers of 1971*, ed. Orlando R. Petrocelli. Princeton: Auerbach Publishers, 1972.

Kuehne, Robert S., Herbert W. Lindberg, and William F. Baron. *Manual of Computer Documentation Standards*. Englewood Cliffs, N.J.: Prentice-Hall, 1973.

Margolin, Uri. "The Demarcation of Literature and the Reader." *Orbis Litterarum*, 31, no. 1 (1976), 1–29.

Martin, James. *Design of Man-Computer Dialogues*. Englewood Cliffs, N.J.: Prentice-Hall, 1973.

"Wurmzauberspruch," *Schriftwerke deutscher Sprache*. Ed. Werner Burkhard. Aarau: H. R. Sauerlaender, 1961.

SCHRADE

Aranguren, José Luis. *Human Communication*. New York: McGraw-Hill, 1967.

Bell, Daniel. "The Coming of the Post-Industrial Society," *The Educational Forum*, 40, no. 4, May, 1976.

Benedict, Ruth. *Patterns of Culture*. New York: Penquin Society, 1946.

Berkley, George E. *The Administration Revolution*. Englewood Cliffs, N.J.: Prentice-Hall, 1971.

Bradford, Caroline. "The Need for Anthropology in the Social Studies," master's thesis, The Ohio State University, 1969.

Bundy, McGeorge. "Justice as Fairness Between Man and Woman," *Women in Higher Education*, eds. W. Todd Furniss and Patricia Albjerg Graham, Washington, D.C.: American Council on Education, 1974.

Clark, Kenneth. *Civilization*. New York: Harper and Row, 1969.

Endres, Raymond J. "Humanities, Social Studies and Values." *Social Education*, May, 1970.

Frankl, Viktor. *Man's Search for Meaning, An Introduction to Logotherapy*. New York: Washington Square Press, 1968.

Highet, Gilbert. *Man's Unconquerable Mind*. New York: Columbia University Press, 1954.

Hoebel, E. Adamson, "The Nature of Culture," in *Man, Culture and Society*, ed. H. L. Shapiro, New York: Oxford University Press, 1956.

Jarrett, James L. *The Humanities and Humanistic Education*. Reading, MA: Addison-Wesley, 1973.

Luce, Clare Booth, "The 21st Century Woman-Free at Last?" *Saturday Review World*, August 24, 1974.

Rawls, John. *A Theory of Justice*. Cambridge, MA: Harvard University Press, 1971.

Scarfe, N.V. "Education for Values Judgement." *Education Canada*, June, 1970.

Thompson, Mary Lou, ed. *Voices of The New Feminism*, Boston, MA: Beacon Press, 1970.

Toffler, Alvin. *Future Shock*, New York: Bantam Books, 1970.

Waldheim, Kurt. "Toward Global Interdependence." *Saturday Review World*, August 24, 1974.

CAMPBELL

Allen, John R., "The Cybernetic Curtain: Advances in Computer-Assisted Instruction." *Computers and the Humanities*, 7 (September-November, 1973), 373–387.

Atkinson, R. C. and H. A. Wilson, "Computer-Assisted Instruction" in *Computer-Assisted Instruction: A Book of Readings.* R. C. Atkinson and H. A. Wilson, eds. New York: Academic Press, 1969.

Berry, D. P. and S. S. Richards, "CLASSIC: Classroom Interactive Computer Focal Point for New Teaching and Learning Horizons." *THE Journal*, (January, 1975), 6–10.

"Computers: A New Wave," *Newsweek*, February 23, 1976, p. 73.

Gardner, Olcott, "What is CAI?" Jamesville, New York: Jamesville-Dewitt Public Schools, 1972.

Hansen, D. N., Walter Dick and Henry T. Lipput, "Research and Implementation of Collegiate Instruction of Physics Via Computer-Assisted Instruction." Final Report Project No. 7–0071, November 15, 1968.

Jamison, Dean, Patrick Suppes and Stuart Wells, "The Effectiveness of Alternative Instructional Media: A Survey." *Review of Educational Research*, 44. (Winter, 1974), pp. 1–69.

Kibler, Tom R. and Patricia B. Campbell, "A Semantic-based CAI System," unpublished paper, 1975.

Kibler, Tom R. and Patricia B. Campbell, "Readin', Writin' and Computin': Skills of the Future." *Educational Technology*, 16 (September, 1976), pp. 44–46.

Lindsay, R.E., "CAI Physics Experiments." IBM Research, RC2490, May 29, 1969.

Lindsay, R.E., "IBM CAI Electronics at the Naval Personnel and Training Research Laboratory, San Diego, California." IBM Research, RC2780, January 30, 1970.

Magarrell, Jack, "Computerized Education: Time to Sink or Swim." *The Chronicle of Higher Education*, 12 (April 26, 1976), p. 5+.

"News from Industry." *IEEE Spectrum*, 13, (July, 1976), 115.

Odeh, A. and L. Cook, "Computer-Assisted Instruction: Example of a Complete Guide for Users." IBM Research, RC2339, January 19, 1969.

Saretsky, Gary, Personal communication with the author, November, 1974.

Solomon, Cynthia J., "Leading a Child to a Computer Culture." *Computer Science and Education*. Ron Colman and Paul Lorton, eds. (New York: ACM, 1976), pp. 24–28.

Stolurow, L. M., "The Harvard University Computer-Assisted Instruction Laboratory." U.S. Department of Commerce, AD 658873, May, 1967.

Suppes, Patrick, "Computer Technology and the Future of Education" in *Computer-Assisted Instruction: A Book of Readings*. R. C. Atkinson and H. A. Wilson, eds. New York: Academic Press, 1969.

Suppes, P. and M. Morningstar, *Computer-Assisted Instruction at Stanford, 1966–68: Data, Models and Evaluation of the Arithmetic Programs*. New York: Academic Press, 1972.

"Teachers Should Be Dedicated: Not Computers." *THE Journal*, (January, 1975), inside front cover.

Wells, S., B. Whelchel and D. Jamison, "The Impact of Varying Levels of Computer-Assisted Instruction on the Academic Performance of Disadvantaged Students." Princeton, N.J.: ETS, 1974.

GUERRA

Calta, Louis. "Telestat Buys Teleprompter Unit to Bring TV to Remote Quebec." *New York Times*, September 25, 1974.

Davison, W. Phillips, James Boylan and Frederick T. C. Yu. *Mass Media Systems and Effects*. New York: Praeger, 1976.

DeFleur, Melvin L. and Sandra Ball-Rokeach. *Theories of Mass Communication*. New York: David McKay, 1975.

Ehrlich, Paul R., and John P. Holdren. "Technology for the Poor." *Saturday Review*, July 3, 1971, p. 46.

Ellul, Jacques. *The Technological Society*. New York: Vintage, 1964.

Feldman, Nathaniel E. *Interconnecting Cable TV Systems by Satellite—An Introduction to the Issues*. Santa Monica, California: Rand Corporation, T-5035, June, 1973.

Fuller, R. Buckminster. "Now and When," *Harper's*, April, 1972.

"Keeping Automated Tabs on Broadcast Ads," *Business Week*, August 25, 1975, pp. 68–69.

"Man Bites Computer," *Newsweek*, April 18, 1976, p. 88.

Martino, Joseph P. "The Role of Forecasting in Technological Assessment." *The Futurist*, 6 (October, 1972), 210–211.

McLuhan, Marshall. *Understanding Media: The Extensions of Man.* New York: McGraw-Hill, 1964.

Mumford, Lewis. *The Myth of the Machine: The Pentagon of Power.* New York: Harcourt Brace Jovanovich, 1964.

"NHK Installs Computer Broadcast Programming," *Broadcasting*, September 16, 1968, p. 71.

Postman, Neil. "Keynote Address," in Robert C. Jeffrey and William Work, eds. *Proceedings of Summer Conference IX: Long Range Goals and Priorities in Speech Communication.* New York: Speech Communication Association, 1973, p. 4.

"Radio Automation Gives Extra Working Arms to Talented People," *BME*, July, 1976, pp. 40–52.

Rubin, Joe E. "Computerized Lighting Control." Reprinted from *Theatre Crafts*, May–June, 1975, pp. 1–40.

"A Satellite Network that Bypasses AT&T," *Business Week*, January 12, 1976, p. 26.

Smythe, Ted C. and George A. Mastroianni, eds. *Issues in Broadcasting.* Palo Alto, California: Mayfield, 1975.

Toffler, Alvin. "Coping With Future Shock." *Playboy.* March 1970, pp. 89–90, 96, 174–175.

———. *Future Shock.* New York: Random House, 1970.

Williams, Raymond. *Television: Technology and Cultural Form.* New York: Schocken, 1970.

Wright, Kenneth H. "Computer Helps Operators Promote On-Time Payments." *TV Communications*, March, 1975, pp. 50, 52.

MOOERS

Abels, Paul. "The Managers are Coming! The Managers are Coming!" *Public Welfare*, 31, 4 (Fall, 1973), pp. 13–15.

———. "Terra Incognita: The Future of the Profession." *Social Work*, 20, 1 (January, 1975), pp. 25–28.

Anderson, Claire M. "Information Systems for Social Welfare: Educational Imperatives." *Journal of Education for Social Work*, 11, 3 (Fall, 1975), pp. 16–21.

Booney, Norman L. and Laurence H. Streicher. "Time-Cost Data in

Agency Administration: Efficiency Controls in Family and Children's Services." *Social Work*, 15, 4 (October, 1970), pp. 23–31.

Briar, Scott. "The Future of Social Work: An Introduction." *Social Work*, 19, 5 (September, 1974), pp. 514–518.

Cruthirds, C. Thomas. "Management Should Be Accountable Too." *Social Work*, 21, 3 (May, 1976), pp. 179–180.

Fein, Edith. "A Data System for an Agency." *Social Work*, 20, 1 (January, 1975), pp. 21–24.

Goldstein, Harris K. and Rachel Dedmon. "A Computer-Assisted Analysis of Input, Process, and Output of a Social Work Educational Program." *Journal of Education for Social Work*, 12, 2 (Spring, 1976), pp. 17–20.

Greenhouse, Samuel M. "The Planning-Programming Budgeting System: Rationale, Language, and Idea-Relationships." *Social Work Administration: A Resource Book*. New York: Council on Social Work Education, 1970.

Gruber, Murray. "Total Administration." *Social Work*, 19, 5 (September, 1974), pp. 625–636.

Haimann, Theo and William G. Scott. *Management in the Modern Organization*. Boston: Houghton Mifflin Company, 1974.

Hoffer, Joe R. "Social Work in the 70's—A Management Partner in the Resolution of Social Issues and Problems." *Social Work Papers*, The Ohio State University, 1973.

Hoshino, George and Thomas P. McDonald. "Agencies in the Computer Age." *Social Work*, 20, 1 (January, 1975), pp. 10–14.

Kahn, Alfred J. *Social Policy and Social Services*. New York: Random House, 1973.

Kelly, Verne R. and Hanna B. Weston. "Computers, Costs, and Civil Liberties." *Social Work*, 20, 1 (January, 1975), pp. 15–19.

The Oxford [Mississippi] *Eagle*, August 2, 1976.

Reid, William J. "Developments in the Use of Organized Data." *Social Work*, 19, 5 (September, 1974), pp. 585–593.

Rosenberg, Marvin L. and Ralph Brody. "The Threat or Challenge of Accountability." *Social Work*, 19, 3 (May, 1974), pp. 344–350.

Simon, Herbert A. "New Techniques for Programmed Decision Making." *Social Work Administration: A Resource Book*. New York: Council on Social Work Education, 1970.

Smith, Russell E. and John N. Hester. "Social Services in a Technological Society." *Journal of Education for Social Work*, 12, 2 (Spring, 1976), pp. 17–20.

Spindler, Arthur. "Systems Analysis in Public Welfare." *Social Work Administration: A Resource Book*. New York: Council on Social Work Education, 1970.

Suchman, Edward A. *Evaluative Research*. New York: Russell Sage Foundation, 1967.

Thomas, Edwin J., Claude L. Walker, and Kevin O'Flaherty, "Computer-Assisted Assessment and Modification: Possibilities and Illustrative Data." *Social Service Review*, 48, 2 (June, 1974), pp. 170–183.

Thompson, James D. "Pittsburgh Committee Report on Common and Uncommon Elements in Administration." *Social Work Administration: A Resource Book*. New York: Council on Social Work Education, 1970.

Thompson, Victor A. "How Scientific Management Thwarts Innovation." *Trans-Action*, 5, 7 (June, 1968), pp. 51–55.

Toffler, Alvin. *Future Shock*. New York: Random House, 1970.

Vondracek, Fred W., Hugh B. Urban, and William H. Parsonage, "Feasibility of an Automated Intake Procedure for Human Services Workers." *Social Service Review*, 48, 2 (June, 1974), pp. 271–278.

Weiss, Carol H. "Alternative Models of Program Evaluation." *Social Work*, 19, 6 (November, 1974), pp. 675–681.

GOROVE

Books

Arnason, H. H. *History of Modern Art*. New York: Prentice-Hall, Abrams, 1976.

Battcock, Gregory. *Idea Art: A Critical Anthology*. New York: Dutton, 1973.

Benthall, J. *Science and Technology in Art Today*. London: Thames and Hudson, 1972.

Davis, Douglas. *Art and the Future*. New York: Praeger, 1973.

Ferkiss, Victor C. *Technological Man: The Myth and the Reality*. New York: George Braziller, Inc., 1969.

Gingrich, Arnold. *Business and the Arts: An Answer to Tomorrow*. New York: Paul S. Ericksson, 1969.

Jensen, Lawrence W. *Synthetic Painting Media*. Englewood Cliffs, N. J.: Prentice-Hall, 1964.

Kranz, Stewart. *Science and Technology in the Arts*. New York: Van Nostrand Reinhold Co., 1974.

Mayer, Ralph. *The Artist's Handbook of Materials and Techniques*. 3d ed. New York: Viking Press, 1970.

Meyer, Ursula. *Conceptual Art*. New York: Dutton, 1972.

Morris, William. *Art and Its Producers, and the Arts and Crafts of Today: Two Addresses Delivered Before the National Association for the Advancement of Art*. London: Longmans and Co., 1901.

Mumford, Lewis. *Art and Technics*. New York: Columbia University Press, 1952.

Popper, Frank. *Origins and Development of Kinetic Art*. New York: New York Graphic Society, 1968.

Reichardt, Jasia, ed. *Cybernetic Serendipity*. New York: Frederick A. Praeger, 1969.

Rickey, George. *Constructivism: Origins and Evolution*. New York: G. Braziller, 1967.

Rubin, W. *Dada, Surrealism and their Heritage*. New York: Museum of Modern Art, 1968.

Taylor, Harold. *Art and the Future*. New York: Art Education, Inc., 1969.

Whistler, James A. M. *The Gentle Art of Making Enemies*. New York: Putnam, 1953.

Articles

Bell, D. "Technology, Nature and Society." *American Scholar*, 42 (Summer, 1973), 385–404.

Cohen, H. "On Purpose: An Inquiry into the Possible Roles of the Computer in Art." *Studio International*, 187 (January, 1974), 9–16.

Davis, R. "Technology as a Deterrent to Dehumanization." *Science*, 185 (August 30, 1974), 737.

Dubois, René. "The Despairing Optimist." *American Scholar*, 40 (Summer, 1971), 389–92.

Goldin, A. "Art and Technology in a Social Vacuum." *Art in America*, 50 (March, 1972), 46–51.

Goldsmith, M. "Crisis in Aspen: Report on Conference on Technology, Man and Culture." *Bulletin of Atomic Science*, 26 (November, 1970), 28–30.

———. "Holos! Holos! Velazquez! Gabor! S. Dali." *Art News*, 71 (April, 1972), 45 ff.

Herrmann, R. P. "Art, Technology and Nietzsche." *Aesthetics*, 32 (Fall, 1973), 95–102.

————. "Laser Light Looks at Art." *American Artist*, 36 (June, 1972), 36 ff.

Sandek, R. "Visual Arts in the Age of Mass Communications." *Arts in Society* (USA), (Summer–Fall, 1972), 258–62.

Temko, A. "Which Guide to the Promised Land: Fuller or Mumford?" *Horizon*, 10 (Summer, 1968), 24–31.

Weizenbaum, J. "On the Impact of the Computer on Society." *Science*, 176 (May 12, 1972), 609–614.

SHEPARD

Bloy, Myron B. "The Christian Norm," *Technology and Human Values*. New York: The Fund for the Republic Inc., 1966.

Boguslaw, Robert. "Symposium on Technology and Humanism," *Studies in Social and Economic Process*. Lexington, Massachusetts: D.C. Heath and Company, 1972.

Boulding, Kenneth C. "Conflict and Defense," *Perspectives on the Computer Revolution*. Englewood Cliffs, N.J.: Prentice-Hall, Inc., 1970.

Burhoe, Ralph Wendell. "The Impact of Technology and the Sciences on Human Values," *Automation, Education, and Human Values*. New York: School and Society Books, 1966.

Butler, Samuel. "The Destruction of Machines in Erewhon," *Perspectives on the Computer Revolution*. Englewood Cliffs, N.J.: Prentice-Hall, Inc., 1970.

Capek, Karel. *R. U. R.* London: Oxford University Press, 1961.

de Jouvenel, Bertrand. "Some Musings," *Technology and Human Values*. New York: The Fund for the Republic Inc., 1966.

Dechert, Charles R. "Symposium on Technology and Humanism," *Studies in Social and Economic Process*. Lexington, Massachusetts: D.C. Heath and Company, 1972.

Ellul, Jacques. "The Technological Society," *Perspectives on the Computer Revolution*. Englewood Cliffs, N.J.: Prentice-Hall, Inc., 1970.

Harshbarger, Luther H. "Technological Change, Humanistic Imperatives, and the Tragic Sense," *Automation, Education, and Human Values*. New York: School and Society Books. 1966.

Heisenberg, Werner. "The Physicists' Conception of Nature," *Perspectives on the Computer Revolution.* Englewood Cliffs, N.J.: Prentice-Hall, Inc., 1970.

Kranzberg, Melvin. "Symposium on Technology and Humanism," *Studies in Social and Economic Process.* Lexington, Massachusetts: D.C. Heath and Company, 1972.

Licklider, J. C. R. "Man Computer Symbiosis," *Perspectives on the Computer Revolution.* Englewood Cliffs, N.J.: Prentice-Hall, Inc., 1970.

Mesthene, Emmanuel G. "Technology and Humanistic Values," *Computers and the Humanities.* Flushing, New York: Queens College of the City University of New York, 1969–70.

Montagu, Ashley. "Symposium on Technology and Humanism," *Studies in Social and Economic Process.* Lexington, Massachusetts: D.C. Heath and Company, 1972.

Mumford, Lewis. "Two Views on Technology and Man," *Studies in Social and Economic Process.* Lexington, Massachusetts: D.C. Heath and Company, 1972.

Pylyshyn, Zenon W. *Perspectives on the Computer Revolution.* Englewood Cliffs, N.J.: Prentice-Hall, Inc., 1970.

Sykes, Gerald. "A New Salvation, A New Supernatural," *Technology and Human Values.* New York: The Fund for the Republic Inc., 1966.

Taylor, G. Rattray. "The Age of the Androids," *Perspectives on the Computer Revolution.* Englewood Cliffs, N.J.: Prentice-Hall. Inc., 1970.

Weizenbaum, Joseph. *Computer Power and Human Reason.* San Francisco: W. H. Freeman and Company, 1976.

Wilkinson, John. ed. *Technology and Human Values.* New York: The Fund for the Republic Inc., 1966.

TOLLIVER

Blanchard, Hawley A. "Some Social and Individual Implications of Augmented Man." *Computers in the Service of Society.* Ed. Robert Lee Chartrand. (New York: Pergamon Press, 1972), pp. 73–79.

Bradburn, J. R. "Where Is the Computer Industry Heading?" *Perspectives on Electronic Data Processing: A Book of Readings.* Ed. James D. J. Holmes and Elias M. Awad. (Englewood Cliffs, New Jersey: Prentice-Hall, 1972), pp. 235–241.

Davis, Robert H. "The Computer Revolution and the Spirit of Man." *Perspectives on Electronic Data Processing: A Book of Readings.* Ed. James

D. J. Holmes and Elias M. Awad. (Englewood Cliffs, New Jersey: Prentice-Hall, 1972), pp. 180–186.

Drucker, Peter F. *The Age of Discontinuity.* New York: Harper and Row, 1968.

Jenkins, Evan. "Classroom Revolution: Computer Interaction." *The New York Times,* Section E, 13 June 1976, p. 9.

"The Ubiquitous Computers." *The New York Times,* Section E, 13 June 1976, p. 8.

MURPHREE

Borko, Harold. "Information Sciences," *1976 Yearbook of Science and the Future, Encyclopedia Britannica.*

Burr, John R., and Goldinger, Milton, eds., *Philosophy and Contemporary Issues.* New York: Macmillan Co., 1972.

Diebold, John. *Man and the Computer.* New York: Fredrick A. Praeger, 1969.

Fisch, Max H., ed., *Classic American Philosophers.* New York: Appleton-Century-Crofts, 1951.

Fromm, Erich. *The Revelation of Hope.* New York: Harper & Row, 1968.

Martin, James. and Norman, Adrian R. D. *The Computerized Society.* Englewood Cliffs, N.J.: Prentice-Hall, 1970.

Montagu, Ashley, and Snyder, Samuel S. *Man and the Computer.* Philadelphia: Auerbach, 1972.

Schumacher, E. F. *Small is Beautiful.* New York: Harper & Row, 1973.

Strother, Robert S. "Crime by Computer," *Reader's Digest,* April, 1976, pp. 143–48.

Toffler, Alvin. *Future Shock.* New York: Random House, 1970.

WILLIAMS

Benét, William Rose and Pearson, Norman Holmes (eds.). *The Oxford Anthology of American Literature.* Vol. II. New York: Oxford University Press, 1952.

Clark, Kenneth. *The Romantic Rebellion: Romantic versus Classic Art.* New York: Harper & Row, 1973.

Edelman, Gerald M. "Our America-The Nobel Scientist," *Newsweek,* Vol. 88 July 1976. pp. 20–22.

Fabun, Don. *The Dynamics of Change*. Englewood Cliffs, N.J.: Prentice-Hall, Inc., 1967.

Fromm, Erich. *The Revolution of Hope: Toward a Humanized Technology*. New York: Harper & Row, 1968.

Jung, C. G. *Psychological Reflections: A New Anthology of His Writings*, 1905 –1961. Edited by Jolande Jacobi in collaboration with R. F. C. Hull. 2d ed. revised. (Bollingen Series XXXI) Princeton: Princeton University Press, 1970.

Lieder, Paul, Lovett, Robert, and Root, Robert (eds.). *British Poetry and Prose*. Shorter ed. Boston: Houghton Mifflin Co., 1951.

CONTRIBUTORS

ROBERT E. BERGMARK received the B.A. Degree from Emory University in 1943, and the S.T.M. and Ph.D. degrees from Boston University in 1946 and 1961 respectively. The field of speciality for all degree work was philosophy. He is currently serving as J. Reese Linn Professor of Philosophy at Millsaps College in Jackson, Mississippi, and as chairman of the Department of Philosophy there, having served as a member of that department since 1953.

PATRICIA B. CAMPBELL is currently director of Grants, Research and Academic Development at William Patterson College in Wayne, N.J. Formerly an associate professor at Georgia State University, she received a Ph.D. in teacher education from Syracuse University in 1973. Her current research interests center on improving techniques for teaching research, dialogue CAI systems and sex-role stereotyping. Campbell also wrote CAI programs for IBM Research for two years.

EDWIN DOLIN received the B.A. and Ph.D. degrees from Harvard University. His academic specialties are classical philology and literary criticism. Dolin has taught at Amherst College, University of California (Berkeley), and University of California (San Diego). He came to the University of Mississippi in 1972, and currently serves as a professor of Greek and Latin and chairman of the Classics Department.

MARGARET J. GOROVE is Chairman of the Department of Art and Associate Professor of Art at the University of Mississippi. Recipient of the Master of Fine Arts degree, her studies in Europe and at the Art Students League, as well as her years as free-lance Research Editor for the Grolier Corporation in New York have provided background for her interest in the relationships between art and science. Professor Gorove, who exhibits paintings and drawings in many national and regional galleries, is American co-ordinator for humanities sessions of the International Astronautical Federation and co-chaired the 1979 Munich session on "The Influence of Space Technology on the Humanities."

DAVID M. GUERRA received his bachelor's degree in radio-TV-film from the University of Miami, his master's degree in broadcasting from Brooklyn College and his doctorate in media ecology from New York University. He has been in radio and television work for fifteen years, serving as producer, director, production manager and news director. He is currently an associate professor and chairman of the Department of Radio, Television and Film at the University of Arkansas at Little Rock.

SHIRLEY HALLBLADE received the B.A. degree in education from Roosevelt University and the M.A. in library science from Northern Illinois University. Her Ph.D. was earned at the University of Iowa in educational administration. From 1975 to 1978 she was on the faculty of the University of Mississippi where she taught graduate courses in information science, library management, and use of computers in libraries. Hallblade is currently employed at the Mississippi Research and Development Center, Information Services Division.

Following an undergraduate education in German and mathematics, ROGER JOHNSON, JR. received the Ph.D. from the University of Illinois in 1968 in the field of comparative literature. He specialized in German, British and French literature of the nineteenth century. He is a professor of foreign languages and director of comparative literature at the University of Southern Mississippi. He is coeditor of *Molière and the Commonwealth of Letters: Patrimony and Posterity* (1975), as well as the author of several articles and papers on literature and on language pedagogy.

TOM R. KIBLER is currently a principal member of the research staff of Perkin Elmer Data Systems in Tinton Falls, New Jersey. He received a B.A. in philosophy from San Francisco State University in 1967. His research interests include computer applications in the social sciences and dialogue CAI. He spent several years developing CAI operating systems for IBM research.

MICHAEL de L. LANDON was educated in England at Eastbourne College and Worcester College, Oxford, where he took an M.A. in modern history. After three years of schoolmastering in England, Scotland and Canada he began graduate work at the University of Wisconsin (Madison) and received a Ph.D. in British history there in 1966. A specialist in the Tudor-Stuart period and English legal and constitutional history, he is the author of two books and some dozen articles in various scholarly journals. He is a Fellow of the Royal Historical Society of Great Britain, and has been on the faculty of the History Department of the University of Mississippi since 1964, now holding the rank of professor.

FREDERICK E. LAURENZO was awarded the Bachelor of Arts degree, *Magna Cum Laude*, in 1961 from Houghton College. His graduate work in British history was completed at the University of Illinois, Urbana, which awarded him the Master of Arts degree in 1963 and the Doctor of Philosophy degree in 1969. At present, Dr. Laurenzo is associate professor of history at the University of Mississippi and acting chairman of the Department of History.

WALTER M. MATHEWS received a bachelor's degree in physics and mathematics, and then taught mathematics and computer science in the Philadelphia Public Schools. After a master's degree in mathematics education he was a USOE Fellow at the University of Wisconsin (Madison) where he earned his Ph.D. in educational administration and research in 1971. Twice he was a Fulbright Scholar spending a year in Turkey and in Sri Lanka. Dr. Mathews has over two dozen publications and has presented more than forty papers at professional meetings. He has previously published a series of three books on grantwriting, one of which has been translated into Spanish. Currently, Dr. Mathews is an associate professor of educational administration at the University of Mississippi.

GARY R. MOOERS received his B.S. from Brigham Young University, and his master's degree in social work from Florida State University. The University of Pittsburgh awarded him a Master's of Science in Public Health and a Ph.D. in Social Work. Mooers is an associate professor and the director of the Social Work Program at the University of Mississippi. He has taught at Weber State College, the University of Pittsburgh and Auburn University. He has held various positions with the Utah Department of Family Services. His areas of specialization are child welfare, juvenile corrections, social policy and aging.

WALLACE A. MURPHREE received his Ph.D. degree from Vanderbilt University in 1972, specializing in process philosophy and philosophy of mind. Since 1967 he has been on the faculty in the Department of Philosophy and Religion at Mississippi State University, where he currently holds the rank of associate professor.

ARLENE SCHRADE received her B.A. degree from Beloit College in English, theatre and Spanish, her M.A. degree in education from Northwestern University, her Master's Certification in Teaching English to Speakers of Other Languages and her Ph.D. in foreign language education from Ohio State University. Fields of specialization are linguistics, Spanish literature, and anthropology. She has also studied at the University of Costa Rica, the University of Madrid, and in Morelia, Mexico. Schrade is currently an associate professor of curriculum and instruction in the School of Education at the University of Mississippi.

NOLAN E. SHEPARD studied history at Wayne State University and Murray State College. He holds master's degrees from Southern Baptist Theological Seminary (in theology) and the University of Mississippi (in speech and philosophy). His Ph.D. is in student personnel and was earned at the University of Mississippi. In addition he has studied oriental philosophy at the University of Wisconsin. Shepard is an associate professor of religions and is the Foreign Student Advisor at the University of Mississippi.

JOHNNY E. TOLLIVER received his B.A. degree in English from Jackson State University, Jackson, Mississippi in 1966. In 1974 he earned his Ph.D. degree in English and American language and literature from Harvard University, with a specialty in the English Renaissance. He has taught at Harvard University, Cameron State College (Lawton, Oklahoma), and the United States Military Academy at West Point. Since 1973 he has been at Jackson State University and is an associate professor of English and head of the Department of Mass Communications.

POLLY FRANKLIN WILLIAMS is the Director of Religious Life at the University of Mississippi where she received her doctorate in higher education and student personnel in 1972. A former high school and college English teacher, she served as director for

Project Upswing, a national HEW program which developed a model for tutoring first grade children who were experiencing learning difficulties. She is the author of *A Philosophical Approach for Volunteers* and *Some Lessons Learned: Volunteers in Education*. Her special interests include literature and theology.